Praise for
I Could Sing Your Love Forever

I Could Sing of Your Love Forever provides great insight into the inspiration behind these great worship songs. The stories are heartfelt and awe-inspiring. Once you start reading, you'll be so fascinated you won't be able to put it down!

> — RICKEY MINOR,
> *Music Director of TV Show,*
> *American Idol*

I love how great songs tell our story. The songs represented in this book have been tried and found worthy to be there. They have stood the test of time, and represent what our hearts have been longing to say.

> — MARK LOWRY

Reading these inspiring stories behind the songs had a profound effect on me. This is a book for anyone who has ever been touched by the right song at the right time.

> — DON MOEN,
> *Songwriter / President of*
> *Integrity Music*

God has often used personal experiences to help gifted songwriters create music that will inspire and bless others. This book helps us understand the mountain tops and valleys that produce even deeper praise to God.

> — CAROL CYMBALA,
> *Director, Brooklyn*
> *Tabernacle Choir*

A great favor was done for us by Lindsay Terry in his researching and reporting the striking and substance-filled experiences that provided the climate for the appearance of many songs born in the last 30 years—songs that, given time, will become the "old hymns" of generations to come.

— JACK W. HAYFORD,
*Author / Chancellor, The
King's Seminary*

Lindsay has done a good work for the churches of America and other parts of the world by helping us to better understand how God gave these worship songs. It gives us a glimpse into the lives of those who would seek to make our worship more intense and sincere.

— ANDRAE CROUCH,
Songwriter / Pastor

Lindsay Terry is a dear friend from my Florida days, who has, in this book, given the body of Christ-rich stories of beloved, worshipful, new songs of the spirit which lift us up as we preach Jesus to the world.

— ANITA BRYANT

These songs have been passed on to the people of God to be used in their praise and worship. I recommend you read the stories and let them make the wonderful songs come alive to you.

— DARLENE ZSCHECH,
*Worship Leader / Songwriter /
Author*

I Could Sing of
Your Love Forever

I COULD SING OF YOUR LOVE FOREVER

Lindsay Terry

THOMAS NELSON
Since 1798

NASHVILLE DALLAS MEXICO CITY RIO DE JANEIRO BEIJING

In searching for Matt Redman's story, the author was led by Ellie Redman, in Matt's office in England, to his Web site, heartofworship.com, where the story first appeared. The story also appears in chapter 8 of The Unquenchable Worshipper by Matt Redman, published by Regal Books, 2001, a division of Gospel Light in Ventura, CA. © 2001 by Matt Redman.

Published in Nashville, Tennessee, by Thomas Nelson. Thomas Nelson is a trademark of Thomas Nelson, Inc.

Thomas Nelson, Inc., titles may be purchased in bulk for educational, business, fund-raising, or sales promotional use. For information, please e-mail SpecialMarkets@ThomasNelson.com.

Unless otherwise noted, Scripture quotations are taken from the King James Version of the Bible.

Scripture quotations marked NIV are from HOLY BIBLE: NEW INTERNATIONAL VERSION®. © 1973, 1978, 1984 by International Bible Society. Used by permission of Zondervan. All rights reserved.

Library of Congress Cataloging-in-Publication Data

Terry, Lindsay.
    I could sing of your love forever : stories behind 100 of the world's most popular worship songs / by Lindsay Terry.
        p. cm.
    ISBN 978-1-4185-1969-8 (pbk.)
    1. Church music. I. Title.
    ML3000.T47 2008
    264'.23—dc22   2008027180

Printed in Canada

08 09 10 11 12 TCP 5 4 3 2 1

To our three children, Rex, Lance, and Amy.

They have been supportive in this and all projects
that their mother, Marilyn, and I have undertaken.
Each of them has a special appreciation for the
worship songs represented in this volume.

CONTENTS

FOREWORD

M usic is one of the great gifts God has extended to his children. It not only brings joy to our lives, but it allows us a wonderful avenue of expression as we bring our praise and adoration to our Savior.

The sort of worship represented in these worship songs will continue to play a large part in the future effectiveness of our churches. God has much to say about music in his Word. He says in Ephesians 5:18 that we are to sing and make melody in our hearts to the Lord. He also says in Psalm 150 that everything that has breath should praise the Lord. We can perhaps do that best in the songs that he has provided for us through dedicated songwriters.

Lindsay Terry has been interviewing songwriters for many years. The stories behind the songs that he has received from them he has compiled into books that enrich our lives. As we learn how God gave the writers these powerful worship songs, it brings more meaning into the lyrics. It gives us a glimpse into the lives of those who would seek to make our worship more intense and sincere.

The messages of the songs written about in this book were taken directly out of the Scriptures. It is my prayer that you will read these stories and allow them to speak to your heart. Those of you who are music directors and worship leaders will find this volume helpful as you share the background of the songs with your audiences.

Lindsay has done a good work for the churches of America and other parts of the world by helping us to better understand how God gave us these worship songs.

ANDRAE CROUCH
San Fernando, California

xiii

INTRODUCTION

W hy worship? Have you ever asked yourself that question? Why do we worship the way we do? Why do we spend so much time perfecting the art? Is this what is really required? What is valuable in heaven?

Worship, or *worthship* (as I love to refer to it) is so very important because it is one of the few things we are involved with on earth that holds immense value throughout all of eternity. And whether we are musically skilled or not, every one of us is designed to adore and connect with our magnificent Savior, to bring our worshipful lives as a daily offering. The only thing that we need to have to qualify us as sincere worshipers is a willing and thankful heart.

Our need to worship is inbuilt—part of our DNA—and as I was recently reminded, worship of God provides the ultimate union with him that our existence craves.

There are many scriptures about music and song that relate to majestic celebration and the freedom we have in Christ, as well as many scriptures bidding us to lift our voices; to make a decision of the will; to lift our hands, open our hearts, and bring songs of worship and praise, thanksgiving and adoration.

But there are also countless scriptures on worship that require so much more than a beautiful song of the heart. When King David, the ultimate psalmist—a man after the heart of God who was an imperfect and sometimes very vulnerable leader—spoke in 2 Samuel 24:24 on the value of a worship offering, he so beautifully declared that he would not bring before his God that which cost him nothing.

Choose to be a worshiper when it's hard and when it's easy—wholeheartedly, sacrificially, and deliberately, with devotion, passion, conviction, and reverence, in quietness and trust, with revealed understanding. Worship as one who knows God and knows how to stand, as one who is familiar with the secret place, as one who has given his or her life away as a living sacrifice—for *this* is our spiritual act of worship.

Lindsay Terry has brought together in this volume the stories behind one hundred songs of worship and praise. The songs written about in this volume came to the writers in myriad personal circumstances in their lives. Out of darkened days came a song to God's servant. Out of the study of his Word came a vehicle of our praise. Out of trials, seemingly beyond endurance, came an expression of worship into the heart of a yielded, obedient child of God. These songs have been passed on to the people of God to be used in their praise and worship. I recommend that you read the stories and let them make these wonderful songs come alive to you.

DARLENE ZSCHECH
Sydney, Australia

PREFACE

For many years I have delighted in writing the stories behind the famous Christian songs that have impacted the lives of God's people. At times I have been amazed at how the songs were given, and to whom. God is truly no respecter of worldly boundaries. Some of the most popular songs, especially worship songs, were given to Christians with little or no formal music training—ordinary people living ordinary lives but with an extraordinary love for the Savior.

On the other hand, many highly trained and dedicated musicians have been singularly honored by our heavenly Father in that he also gave to them songs that would bless the hearts of millions of people around the world. In the process, they went through the same emotions and experiences as did those of lesser musical ability.

In this volume I have, for the most part, let the authors tell their own stories. In reading about their adventures in songwriting, you are allowed to "see" the hearts of these composers.

Through the years I have come to realize that many of the great, classic hymns came as a result of human suffering. And the same has been true with a host of worship songs. Out of a dark period in the life of a Christian, like a ray of heavenly sunlight, came a wonderful song from the Lord—an instrument of blessing to the writer and then later to the multitudes who would sing it.

This volume is a great ministry source for worship leaders, ministers of music, pastors, evangelists, and Bible study teachers. As I have led congregations in worship,

I have on countless occasions seen audiences sit motionless as I told them the "story behind the song." They always sang more heartily and joyfully after hearing of the birth of the song. Those occasions gave rise to the books of song stories I have written.

Some of these stories are humorous, some are filled with joy, some are sad, but all are true—true stories of God's interaction with his children. Read them, enjoy them, and then share them with a friend.

LINDSAY TERRY
St. Augustine, Florida

I Could Sing of
Your Love Forever

ABOVE ALL

VERSE 1

Above all powers, above all kings,
Above all nature and all created things,
Above all wisdom and all the ways of man,
You were here before the world began.

CHORUS

Crucified, laid behind the stone,
You lived to die rejected and alone,
Like a rose trampled on the ground,
You took the fall and thought of me,
Above all.

VERSE 2

Above all kingdoms, above all thrones,
Above all wonders the world has ever known,
Above all wealth and treasures of the earth,
There's no way to measure,
What You're worth.

The Contrast of Our Savior

*Surely he hath borne our griefs, and carried our sorrows: yet we did esteem him stricken,
smitten of God, and afflicted. But he was wounded for our transgressions, he was bruised for
our iniquities: the chastisement of our peace was upon him; and with his stripes we are healed.*

ISAIAH 53:4–5

Above All" is one of the most moving and thought-provoking worship songs of all time. It has not only touched the lives of Christians around the globe, but its message has been heard by some of the most powerful people in the world today. It was cowritten by two very talented worship leaders, Lenny LeBlanc and Paul Baloche.

Lenny and Paul were professional singers and musicians before coming to

2

Christ. Lenny, a pop singer, confessed, "My career was my 'god,' and I began to worship the gift God had given me, even to the point of leaving my family behind." Thankfully, God had other plans for him. Over a period of weeks, the Lord began to reveal himself to the singer. Lenny said, "I started to realize how shallow and selfish my life was, and there in my home I cried out to Jesus for mercy and forgiveness. I could have continued in the field of pop music, but I sensed that God had something different for me."

For Paul Baloche, who was caught up in the rock music scene, an unexpected altar call brought him into the presence of Christ. "I asked the Lord to come into my life," Paul said, "and he totally changed me. I started going to an Assembly of God church and became part of the music ministry."

By 1991, Paul and Lenny had become well-known songwriters and worship leaders. Lenny invited Paul to come to his home in Muscle Shoals, Alabama, to do some cowriting for a music project. While sharing ideas for songs, Paul sang the verse of an unfinished song he had been working on for a while. He had tried several choruses, but none of them had really felt right.

Lenny liked Paul's verse and set out to write a chorus for it. "Early the next morning, while Paul was still sleeping in his room," he said, "I slipped out to my studio and God gave me the lyric and the melody for finishing the song.

"After lunch I shared my ideas for the chorus with Paul. He almost fell out of his chair because it was so different from what he thought it would be. When you hear the verse, it would seem that a writer would expound on Christ's majesty, might, and power. Yet I decided to go immediately into his crucifixion.

"Paul's verse," Lenny said, "and the chorus I had written seemed to fit perfectly. Each time we sang the chorus, Paul and I began to weep. It was difficult to get through it even once. I said to Paul, 'This is going to be a huge song for the church.' I knew it in my heart."

In addition to becoming a part of the worship of millions of Christians, "Above All" was introduced to President Bush, his cabinet, and other government officials at the Inaugural Prayer Service at the National Cathedral the day following the swearing-in ceremony. It was sung by Michael W. Smith.

Lenny and Paul continue to write and record songs, teach worship seminars, and lead great crowds in praise to the Lord around the world. Yet the ministry that seems to be very near and dear to each of their hearts is that of being the worship leader in a local church—Paul in Lindale, Texas, and Lenny in Florence, Alabama.

Only when we get to heaven will we be able to understand the suffering of our Lord when he paid, on our behalf, a debt he did not owe because we owed a debt we could not pay. What a wonderful Savior!

VERSE 1

Worship the Lord in the beauty of holiness;
Bow down before Him, His glory proclaim.
With gold of obedience and incense of lowliness
Kneel and adore Him; the Lord is His name.

VERSE 2

Fear not to enter His presence in poverty,
Bearing no gifts to present as your own;
Bring truth in its beauty and love in its purity,
These are the off'rings to lay at His throne.

(ENDING)

We worship You, Lord,
Amen.

It Was Too Long and Too Archaic

O worship the LORD in the beauty of holiness.

PSALM 96:9

The song "Adoration" is perhaps the most complete worship song ever written. I agree with Tom Fettke, who wrote the musical setting, that in the singing of the song we not only are adoring Christ but are bringing everything we have to him—even our very lives. The writing of this song was the effort of three unique and talented men: John Monsell, Tom Fettke, and Ken Bible.

Monsell was born in Londonderry, Ireland. After attending Trinity College in Dublin, he was ordained in 1834. He was a gifted Anglican clergyman who could hold a congregation spellbound. He advocated more "fervent and joyful singing" in his church. "We sing, but not as we should, to him who is the Chief among ten thousand, the altogether lovely." In his lifetime he wrote the lyrics to almost three hundred hymns and was the author of a number of books.

Tom Fettke was born to Gus and Irene Fettke in Bronx, New York, in 1941.

He told me, "They started voice lessons for me at age seven, but singing has not been my first love—it is choral directing." He has arranged fifty-five choral collections and more than four hundred anthems over the past thirty years. On top of that he has produced more than 250 choral projects. Probably more choir members sing his arrangements in churches across the United States than those of any other arranger. He has been the senior editor for two major hymnals and has been involved in every aspect of church music.

Ken Bible is a Cincinnati, Ohio, native, born there in 1950. His parents, Ralph and Virginia, also provided music for him early in life. He started playing clarinet as a youngster. He became interested in songwriting in high school and has since written approximately three hundred songs. He is the editor of a major hymnal and has been connected with the Nazarene Publishing House in various positions for many years. He has authored fifteen books, and his songs appear in nine hymnals.

In 1985, Tom was arranging a choral collection called *Star Carols* about the birth of Christ and needed something for the coming of the wise men bearing their gifts and bowing before him. Tom said, "The only song I could think of was 'We Three Kings.' I wanted something different.

"I found an archaic text written by John Monsell in a 1956 Presbyterian hymnal. It was in the Adoration section of the hymnal and began, 'Worship the Lord in the beauty of holiness,' but from that point on, it needed to be rewritten and brought into a language that could be more easily understood.

"I sent the original text to Ken Bible, asking him to rewrite it and bring it down from its five or six stanzas to only two stanzas. He did so, and I wrote an original melody for it."

Then Tom added, "God gave me that song. God gave me the ability to write songs, but this specific one was God-given and anointed by him. Every time I play it, I am moved by it. There is the sense that you are not only adoring the Christ child, but you are at the same time committing everything you have to him. We bring ourselves to him."

Tom and his wife, Jan, are members of the Brentwood Baptist Church in Brentwood, Tennessee. Ken sings in the choir at Kansas City First Church of the Nazarene, and he and his wife, Gloria, work very closely with the shut-in ministry of the church.

Every person reading this volume should read, or sing, very carefully and thoughtfully the lyrics of this song. You, too, will find yourself questioning if you have really and truly brought your "gift" to him—yourself.

All hail King Jesus,
All hail Emmanuel,
King of kings,
Lord of lords,
Bright Morning Star.
And throughout all eternity,
I'm going to praise Him,
And forevermore
I will reign with Him.

Surprised by a Song

*Which in his times he shall shew, who is the blessed and only Potentate, the King of kings, and
Lord of lords; Who only hath immortality, dwelling in the light which no man can approach
unto; whom no man hath seen, nor can see: to whom be honour and power everlasting.*

1 TIMOTHY 6:15–16

You and I would be thrilled to have millions of people around the world sing our songs. But what about our first published song? How exciting is that? That is exactly what Dave Moody experienced after the publishing of his "All Hail King Jesus."

During a trip to India and Japan in 1987, only ten years after writing the song, he experienced that joy firsthand while visiting churches in those countries. He said, "I had no idea that people over there even knew the song, so to have heard it sung in those nations, not expecting anything of that nature, was probably the most significant feeling I've ever experienced regarding my song."

Through his teen years, Dave worked hard toward a goal of being a piano teacher. He later graduated from the Royal Conservatory of Music in Toronto in 1970 with a piano teaching degree and then taught piano for fourteen years.

Dave shared with me the following story behind his famous song "All Hail King Jesus":

"I was at home one Wednesday afternoon in 1977, preparing to teach some piano classes. The youngsters were to come for their lessons after school, beginning at about 3:30 p.m. On that particular afternoon I had some time before they arrived, so I sat down at the piano and began worshiping the Lord.

"The furthest thing from my mind was the writing of a song. My only purpose was to spend time with the Lord. Quite suddenly, I began to develop a melody that was coming to me—something I had never played before. And just as quickly came some words that I began to sing, using the melody the Lord was giving. When I finished, I realized that the Lord had given me a song. I played it over several times and put it on paper so I wouldn't forget it. During the next couple of days, I played it for a couple of friends, just to see their response, which was very favorable.

"The following Sunday I was eager to share 'All Hail King Jesus' with the congregation. From my position at the Hammond organ, I sang the song a couple of times, allowing the congregation to learn it. I then asked them to sing it through with me. They did so and afterward sat with very passive and stoic expressions. I thought the song had flopped. I was puzzled. I remember that I also thought, *Well, maybe it's just that they don't know it well enough.* So I sang it through again with them. As we were finishing the song, the associate pastor, Lou Peterson, who was leading the service in the absence of the pastor, stepped over to me and asked that I sing it with them again. I did so, and as we were nearing the end of the song, I opened my eyes, and to my surprise I saw the congregation of more than eight hundred people on their knees, with their hands raised toward heaven, singing my song."

As Dave's song is sung by people everywhere, and as the different names given to the Lord Jesus, such as "Morning Star," "King of kings," and "Lord of lords," flow from the congregation, it creates a wonderful spirit of joy and worship.

The song has been placed in a number of hymnals and has been arranged into choral settings, greatly helping it to be sung and heard by believers around the world. It has also been recorded by scores of recording artists and choral groups.

There is something about the names of Jesus that evoke a spirit of worship in all of us who know him as personal Savior and Lord.

All Hail the Power of Jesus' Name

VERSE

All hail the pow'r of Jesus' name,
Let angels prostrate fall.
Bring forth the royal diadem
And crown Him, crown Him, crown Him,
Crown Him Lord of all.

VERSE

Let ev'ry kindred ev'ry tribe
On this terrestrial ball,
To Him all majesty ascribe
And crown Him, crown Him, crown Him,
Crown Him Lord of all.

VERSE

O that with yonder sacred throng
We at His feet may fall.
We'll join the everlasting song
And crown Him, crown Him, crown Him,
Crown Him Lord of all.

Our Most Renowned Worship Song

Wherefore God also hath highly exalted him, and given him a name which is above every name.

PHILIPPIANS 2:9

I would rank "All Hail the Power of Jesus' Name" as the most popular song of worship and praise in the English language. Edward Perronet, the writer of the verses, was born in Sundridge, England, in 1726. He was educated for the ministry in the Church of England, following the examples of his father and grandfather. In modern terms, he was a PK, a preacher's kid.

Perronet objected to many of the practices of the church, leaning strongly to the doctrines of John and Charles Wesley. He would listen as his dad, an older preacher, would counsel with the Wesleys. Although his admiration for them ran very deep, his association with them was not without persecution.

John Wesley wrote in his diary, "He [Perronet] was thrown down and rolled in mud and mire. Stones were hurled and windows broken." Still Edward stuck by his friends, attending most all of the services where John Wesley was the speaker.

Perronet was a strong, impulsive, self-willed individual, so he started an independent church in Canterbury, England. In 1780, shortly after he established his church, one of his poems was published in the *Gospel Magazine*, edited by Augustus Toplady, author of the famous song "Rock of Ages."

A few years later those same verses appeared in a book of poems by an anonymous author. One of the poems was written as an acrostic, the letters of which spelled Edward Perronet. Most of his work was done under an assumed name, or he used no name at all.

The tune "Coronation," which is almost as popular as the verses, was written by one of America's most noted hymn tune writers, Oliver Holden. He composed it during a time of great rejoicing. It is reported that the four-and-a-half-octave organ on which he composed the tune is still displayed in the Old State House in Boston.

Holden was a carpenter by trade and a self-taught musician who would take time out from his work on many occasions, play a melody or two, and then return to the task at hand. One day he failed to show up for work, and his friends went to his home to check on him. They found him perfecting a musical composition that he had written in celebration of the birth of his daughter. That wonderful occasion put a song in his heart.

Just short of his thirtieth birthday, Holden put his carpentry tools aside and began to deal in real estate. He also served for a time in the legislature, and he built a Baptist church with his own money. Using the wealth he made from other enterprises, Holden published a hymnal, which he titled *American Harmony*. While searching for music for his book of hymns, he came across Perronet's poem in the *Gospel Magazine*. Holden had no knowledge of Perronet's background; he only knew that the poem would fit his music written in celebration of his daughter's birth. The phrase "crown Him Lord of all" in Perronet's verses gave Holden the idea of calling his tune "Coronation."

In churches today, the words are sung to three tunes—"Coronation," "Miles Lane," or "Diadem." "Coronation" is, by far, the most popular.

England and America came together in the persons of Edward Perronet and Oliver Holden, who gave to the world this wonderful song of worship and praise to the King of kings and Lord of lords.

Christ left his majestic position and condescended to provide salvation for lowly human beings. May he enjoy an exalted position in our hearts today. He and only he is worthy of our worship.

ALL RISE

VERSE

There was a holy hush all over
As I walked into the room,
And as I stood before Him face to face
I was gloriously made new.
There was a great and awesome presence
And the light bright as the day,
And as I bowed to kneel with the angels
I heard the Spirit say:

CHORUS

All rise, all rise,
To stand before the throne
In the presence of the Holy One.
All rise, all rise,
As we worship the Messiah, all rise.

VERSE

Then I looked at those around me
With their hands uplifted high,
Then the Spirit laid His hands on me
And I uplifted mine.
And we were singing hallelujahs
And praises to His name,
And as I bowed to kneel with the angels
I heard the Spirit say:

God Used a Defeat

For we shall all stand before the judgment seat of Christ.

Romans 14:10

I don't remember a time in my life when I wasn't interested in music," Babbie Mason told me in a 2001 interview. She was born into a pastor's home, that of Reverend Willie George Wade, in 1955, in Jackson, Michigan. Her dad and her mother, Georgie, saw to it that she had everything she needed to help her with her music. She remembers some good times as she and friends and neighbors gathered around the piano, which was kept, at that time, in the garage.

At age nine, Babbie became the regular pianist of the Lily Missionary Baptist Church, founded by her dad. She later graduated from Spring Arbor College in Spring Arbor, Michigan. After graduation she began to teach music and English in a middle school in a small town in Michigan.

In 1980, Babbie and her husband, Charles, moved to Atlanta, Georgia. They did everything they could possibly do to promote her singing ministry. She said, "I sang anywhere I could—in churches, Bible studies, senior citizen centers, women's conferences, and youth gatherings. I made five recordings on my own and sold the albums out of the trunk of my car. Charles took my albums to radio stations and asked them to play my songs."

Babbie and Charles lived very near a large church in the Atlanta area. After a series of events, she finally made her way into the music program of that church, particularly the choir ministry.

She said, "In 1984, Charles and I drove to Estes Park, Colorado, and the famed Christian Artist Seminar, where I entered the songwriting and vocal contests." Babbie lost the songwriters' contest and came in third as a vocalist. "I thought I had failed. The devil told me that I was 'only the best of the worst and the worst of the best.'

"Three weeks later I was walking through my home, still reflecting on the Estes Park experience, when God gave me a thought: *one day we will all stand before the Supreme Judge, the Head Adjudicator of all of our hearts.* Right then and there the Lord gave me a song. I called it 'All Rise.' That would be the song that would basically propel my ministry.

"The following year I returned to the Christian Artist Seminar, and my song won the songwriting contest. And I won the vocal contest. That was the beginning of getting my feet wet as a songwriter. I then went to Billy Jack Green, one of the leaders of the seminar, and asked him to do a choral arrangement of 'All Rise.' He did so, and I took it back to our choir at home, and we began singing it.

"Sometime later the choir was invited to sing at an evangelism conference near Atlanta, headed by Dr. Bailey Smith, a former president of the Southern Baptist Convention. We sang 'All Rise' on Tuesday night of the meetings to a standing ovation. We were asked to repeat the song, and we did. They asked us to sing it again. After the third time, and with a most unusual response, they went on with the service, but only with a promise that we would sing the song again at the close of the service.

"A videotape was made of the service, and it began to be circulated across the country in Southern Baptist churches. The phone began to ring. People wanted me to come to their churches to sing 'All Rise.'" Thus began the worldwide ministry that God has given to Babbie. Her award-winning song was the song most recorded by other artists in 1987.

She and Charles have now started the Babbie Mason Music Conference International to help aspiring singers, songwriters, worship leaders, and Christian musicians.

God turned seeming defeat into glorious victory for Babbie. He will do the same for us as we surrender, completely, to his will and follow him through the direction given in his Word.

True worship gives an overwhelming consciousness of the greatness of our salvation.

LEE ROBERSON

ANCIENT OF DAYS

Blessing and honor, glory and power,
Be unto the Ancient of Days.
From ev'ry nation all of creation
Bow before the Ancient of Days.

CHORUS

Ev'ry tongue in heaven and earth
Shall declare Your glory,
Ev'ry knee shall bow
At Your throne in worship.
You will be exalted O God,
And Your kingdom shall not pass away,
O Ancient of Days.

VERSE

Your kingdom shall reign
Over all the earth,
Sing unto the Ancient of Days.
For none can compare
To Your matchless worth,
Sing unto the Ancient of Days.

In a Rented House in Mobile

*For it is written, As I live, saith the LORD, every knee shall bow to me,
and every tongue shall confess to God.*

ROMANS 14:11

Jamie Harvill and Gary Sadler consider their song "Ancient of Days" to be a gift from God.

Gary Sadler was born in 1954, in Farmville, Virginia. He was classically trained in piano and grew up in a home where the rules for practice were strictly enforced, sometimes to Gary's annoyance. But when he was fifteen, his parents gave him a guitar. "That," he said, "opened up a whole new world for me. I fell in love with music, including the piano again."

Gary was raised in a Christian home but admits he did not fully understand that there was a lifestyle attached to it. "I was twenty-two years old," he said, "before I really became a Christian."

Jamie Harvill, born in 1960, in Fullerton, California, became a Christian when he was fourteen at a New Life Youth Crusade Bible study. "I saw the reality of God," he said, "and was introduced to praise and worship that same night." Jamie is a graduate of the University of Mobile in Mobile, Alabama.

Jamie recalls meeting Gary for the first time in North Carolina while visiting his parents. "I met him at a church just down the street from my dad's house," he said. "I had already heard that he was very talented. The next time I returned, I invited him and his family to come to Mobile for a visit so we could try writing some songs together."

A few months later, Gary's family made the trip down to the Harvill's small, rented home in Mobile. Conditions were crowded in the little dwelling, but Gary and Jamie's cowriting venture began that first night with "Ancient of Days." The song was born out of an idea given in Daniel 7:22: "Until the Ancient of days came, and judgment was given to the saints of the most High . . ."

Gary recalls the writing process. "We got a start on some lyrics that night but didn't finish them. I continued playing keyboard and found a Caribbean rhythm that gave me an idea for the song.

"The next morning I showed Jamie my idea, and we both felt that there was merit in it for this song. We finished 'Ancient of Days' in about an hour and then made a demonstration tape of it in my home studio.

"The next Sunday, I was scheduled to sing at the church where Jamie was attending. Gerrit Gustafson, the music director of the church, was also employed in the creative department of Integrity Music, headquartered in Mobile. Gerrit

> *Praise ye the* LORD. *Praise ye the name of the* LORD; *praise* *Him, O ye servants of the* LORD. *Ye that stand in the house of the* LORD, *in the courts of the house of our God.*
>
> PS. 135:1−2

15

wanted to hear what I was planning to sing, so I sang and played the songs for him, and he loved them.

"On the way out, Jamie said to me, 'Since Gerrit loves your songs, why don't you let him hear "Ancient of Days"? Maybe we could get some feedback from him.' So I played it for him, and he said, 'This is just the kind of song we're looking for at Integrity! We need a song for Ron Kenoly. He's recording a new album, and this would be great for him. May I take it to the creative meeting?'"

Gary and Jamie found out in just a few days that Integrity had decided to use "Ancient of Days." In a short time, Kenoly's album *Lift Him Up* had successfully helped to launch this wonderful worship song. Gary gives God the credit not only for the song but also for the perfect timing surrounding the presentation of it to Integrity Music and the changes it made in his life. "I had never in fourteen years of writing sent a tape to a publisher," he said, "but because of this song, Integrity signed me as a writer the following year." Jamie has also enjoyed a good relationship with the company, and he and Gary have gotten together many times to write since that evening in the little rented house in Mobile.

You and I can only be strong in the Lord as we surrender our all to the Ancient of Days, the one to whom every knee will bow and every tongue will confess that he is Lord.

And what greater calamity can fall upon a nation than the loss of worship?

RALPH WALDO EMERSON

As the Deer

VERSE

As the deer panteth for the water,
So my soul longeth after Thee.
You alone are my heart's desire,
And I long to worship Thee.

CHORUS

You alone are my strength, my shield.
To You alone may my spirit yield.
You alone are my heart's desire,
And I long to worship Thee.

VERSE

You're my friend and You are my brother,
Even though You are a King.
I love You more than any other,
So much more than anything.

Writing a Song during a Fast

As the hart panteth after the water brooks, so panteth my soul after thee, O God.

PSALM 42:1

In Seoul Stadium, one hundred thousand Koreans gathered in 1991 for a great worship conference. As Marty Nystrom entered the arena, he heard the mammoth throng open the conference by singing "As the Deer." He was moved very deeply in his heart to think that God had used him to provide that scriptural song, not only for the people of Korea, but for Christians around the world.

Nystrom said, "I seem to write songs best when I am not purposefully trying to write one." A good example of that would be the writing of "As the Deer." Following is that story as Marty told it to me:

"I was a schoolteacher here in Seattle, and since I had the summer off, I decided to go back to Bible college, but only for the summer term. I headed for

Dallas and Christ for the Nations Institute. Little did I know what was about to happen to me, especially with all that I would be exposed to and all of the worship emphasis at the school.

"It was a spiritual renewal time for me. I had graduated from Oral Roberts University, and frankly I was a little overwhelmed in ministry. I had been involved in so many things at the school, not the least of which was the television ministry. All of my studies, mixed with the many other activities, caused the stress of it all to take its toll on my spiritual life.

"The summer was a time for me to restore my passion for Jesus, who had saved me years earlier. I didn't need man's approval or other motivations; it was just time for me to get back to my relationship with Jesus. I was not messed up horribly, but I knew that Jesus was not number one in my life at the time.

"I had a roommate at CFNI who was a very vibrant Christian. He challenged me to go on a fast, thinking it would help me to recover my joy. I took up the challenge, and on the nineteenth day of the fast, I found myself sitting at a piano in a room of the school, trying to write a song. I was simply playing chord progressions when I noticed a Bible on the music stand of the piano, and it was open to Psalm 42. My eyes fell on the first verse of that chapter. After reading the verse, I began to sing its message right off the page. I wrote the first verse and the chorus of a song pretty much straight through. The whole of the adventure was completed in a matter of minutes. I then repeated the song I had just written, just to seal it in my mind.

"I had no intention of showing it to anyone. It was to be for my own worship time with the Lord. However, before leaving the school to go back to Seattle, I did share it with one person, Dave Butterbaugh. He in turn introduced it to the kids of the school, and it became a favorite.

"As was their custom, the school recorded the song and put it into one of their cassette projects and mailed it out across the country, and apparently to other nations. The next thing I knew, 'As the Deer' was being sung everywhere. It has been translated into several different languages. Orchestras have used it. It has been sung in unusually different styles."

Marty travels the world teaching in worship conferences, spending a considerable amount of time in Asia. He speaks for numerous church retreats, for choirs, and for worship teams here in the United States. Marty shares his joy of worship through his many popular albums and CDs.

Fortunate is the soul who, when thirsty for God, can determine how to remedy the problem, just as Marty did. It can only be done as we find fellowship with the Lord in his Word. Then we rest in him and praise him for his goodness.

Awesome God

CHORUS

Our God is an awesome God!
He reigns from heaven above
With wisdom pow'r and love.
Our God is an awesome God!

VERSE

When the sky was starless
In the void of the night,
Our God is an awesome God!
He spoke into the darkness
And created the light,
Our God is an awesome God!
Judgment and wrath
He poured out on Sodom,
Mercy and grace
He gave us at the cross.
I hope that we have not
Too quickly forgotten
That our God is an awesome God!

Rich Mullins © 1988 BMG Songs, Inc. (ASCAP)
(Administered by Brentwood-Benson Music Publishing, Inc.)

Rich and the Indian Children

Let all the earth fear the LORD: let all the inhabitants of the world stand in awe of him.
PSALM 33:8

Michael W. Smith had this to say about his friend: "Rich Mullins's life and music have impacted me more than anyone I know. . . . Nobody on this planet wrote songs like he did, and I feel we've lost one of the only true poets in our industry. I love Rich Mullins. No one will ever know how much I'll miss him."

Would you like to have known the spirit and humility of Rich Mullins? It was manifested one evening in 1995 in the Ryman Auditorium in Nashville, Tennessee. A great crowd had gathered for the opening of the Gospel Music Association's annual convention. Excitement mounted as the attendees awaited many of the recognizable names in contemporary music. The performers were dressed in their best, and this was to be an evening of worship.

Each person on the program presented his or her musical offering accompanied by beautiful lighting and unusual special effects. After several performances a man walked onto the stage and took his place at the piano. A choir was behind him. As the lights were going up, Rich Mullins began to play, some thought somewhat prematurely. He was dressed in scruffy jeans and a flannel shirt and was unshaven. He scarcely looked up from the piano. He was presenting his signature song, "Awesome God." The music ceased, the lights went down, and Rich Mullins slipped away—out of sight. Such was this man.

Before I go any further with this story, I readily admit that I do not have the facts surrounding the writing of Rich Mullins's song "Awesome God." Rich went home to be with the Lord on September 19, 1997, before I could get his story. He died in a tragic automobile accident. But my brief summary of Mullins's life is the story behind his song.

Rich was born Richard Wayne Mullins in 1955, in a small community near Richmond, Indiana, into a Quaker home. The people in his community called him Wayne as he grew up, for fear of confusing him with his uncle Richard Mullins, who loaned him the money to make his first album. His parents, John and Neva Mullins, recognized that he showed a tremendous music ability early in life.

> *. . . come before*
> *his presence with*
> *singing.*
>
> Ps. 100:2

Rich's mother said that one day when Rich was about five years of age, he was in the room listening to his older sister, Debbie, practice her piano lesson. She became very frustrated after trying several times to play a song without making mistakes. In desperation she left the room. Rich climbed onto the piano bench and played the song perfectly. Mrs. Mullins, from another room, complimented Debbie on finally getting it right.

As a youngster attending the Quaker church, Rich's opinion of some of the music of the church was less than complimentary. He thought the poetry and the musical settings were poor. It was not until he saw the effects the music had on people he respected that he changed his mind.

He attended Cincinnati Bible College and while there formed a band called Zion, which played local engagements. Of course, he later became a major recording artist and formed a band to tour with him, which he called the Ragamuffin Band.

Rich loved poor children and spent his money for causes that benefited them.

He lived the last two years of his life on the Navajo Indian Reservation near the Arizona–New Mexico border, working with poor Native Americans. He believed that music was the language of the soul and wanted to give this gift to the children.

I also learned from Rich's uncle Dick, as Rich called him, that during the last years of his life, although Rich could have lived sumptuously, he only allowed himself a yearly wage of twenty-seven thousand dollars, the average wage for a man in the United States. Mullins was never married, so his mother is making sure that the money he left goes to the causes he loved so dearly—which include helping children.

"Awesome God" was voted one of the top three songs of the 1990s by the Christian Research Report.

May you and I recognize that in everything, our heavenly Father is omnipotent, omniscient, and omnipresent. His majesty, power, and might are far beyond our ability to comprehend. Yet this great God invites you and me to fellowship with him, offering us eternal life in his presence.

Worship is an act of obedience of the heart. It is a response that requires the very core of who you are, to love the Lord for who He is, not just for what He does.

DARLENE ZSCHECH

BE EXALTED, O GOD

VERSE

I will give thanks to Thee,
O Lord, among the people.
I will sing praises to Thee
Among the nations.
For Thy steadfast love is great,
Is great to the heavens,
And Thy faithfulness,
Thy faithfulness to the clouds.

CHORUS

Be exalted, O God, above the heavens,
Let Thy glory be over all the earth.
Be exalted, O God, above the heavens,
Let Thy glory be over all the earth.

While Skipping Classes

Be thou exalted, O God, above the heavens; let thy glory be above all the earth.

PSALM 57:5

The following is the testimony of Brent Chambers in 2001, as he sat in his home in New Zealand, and I in Tucson, Arizona.

He began, "I was in a church in Singapore in 1987, when a missionary approached me who had served in Japan for twenty years. She gave me a copy of 'Be Exalted, O God' in Japanese, and it was extremely meaningful to me. I have now heard my song in approximately sixteen languages."

Brent Chambers was born in 1948, in the beautiful coastal town of Napier, in Hawke's Bay, on the island nation New Zealand. His parents, Dinty and Joyce Chambers, saw to it that their son had voice lessons from age five to age nine. A few years later, when the Beatles came along, this "southpaw" was so intent on playing the guitar that he learned to play left-handed with the instrument upside down.

Brent continued, "In 1966, a teenager invited me to a Youth for Christ meeting.

I didn't have a great deal of interest in the meeting but decided to go along. The Lord spoke to me during that service, and I became a Christian that very night. A couple of years later, I realized that I was not at all including Jesus into my life's activities. I somehow knew that I could not be an effective Christian unless he had my whole life. Consequently, I surrendered everything to Christ, and from that time, even as a new Christian, songs began to pour out of me."

The story behind "Be Exalted, O God" is repeated here as Brent shared it with me during our phone interview:

"The day that I wrote 'Be Exalted, O God,' I was actually skipping classes from Auckland University, where I was working on a bachelor's degree in the classics. I had finished three years in the Bible College of New Zealand, and not wanting time to get by me, I quickly entered the university.

"During the course of my studies, I got behind in some of my assignments and decided to take a few hours off. During the middle of the afternoon, sitting in our one-bedroom flat, with an ancient tape recorder going and a cockatiel making noises in the background, I was reading the Bible. I came across Psalm 57, and the verses seemed so meaningful.

"I thought, *Wow! I'd love to be able to put some music to those words; they really stand out to me.* So I picked up my guitar and began to play a tune that the Lord gave me for that scripture.

"That evening David and Dale Garrett, founders of the Scripture in Song music publishing company, attended a study group held in our home, and during the course of the evening, I sang my song for them. David had me repeat it some five times. During the following years, Scripture in Song published about twenty of my compositions, of course including 'Be Exalted, O God.'

"After hearing my song, David asked me, 'Brent, do you think maybe God is speaking to you through these words?' Up until that moment it was just another song that I had written, but when he said those words, my song became the Word of God to me, and my life's call—my heart's desire. I suddenly wanted to give thanks among the people and to sing praises among the nations. By the grace of God, we've done just that in many places, singing 'Be Exalted, O God' and other songs."

The fundamental reasons for the success and greatness of this song, as mentioned earlier, are that, first, it is God's Word set to music, and second, God gave the melody.

In addition to reading the Scriptures daily, you and I would do well to recite the lyrics of this song. It encompasses our thanksgiving and praise to God, as well as our recognition of his love and faithfulness to his children.

Because He Lives

God sent His Son, they called Him Jesus.
He came to love heal and forgive.
He bled and died to buy my pardon.
An empty grave is there to prove
My Savior lives.

CHORUS

And because He lives, I can face tomorrow.
Because He lives, all fear is gone.
Because I know He holds the future,
And life is worth the living
Just because He lives.

VERSE

How sweet to hold our newborn baby,
And feel the pride and joy he gives.
But greater still the calm assurance
This child can face uncertain days,
Because Christ lives.

From the Darkness, a Sunbeam

Yet a little while, and the world seeth me no more; but ye see me: because I live, ye shall live also.

JOHN 14:19

When Bill and Gloria Gaither were teachers in the same high school, they met and began to share ideas about songs. Gloria, an English major in college, would become in later years the predominant author of the lyrics in their songs, while Bill's forte was the musical setting. Bill had also earned a master's degree that allowed him to become the head of the English department of their high school. The joint efforts that had their beginning in that school blossomed into the most prolific husband-and-wife songwriting team of modern times.

One of the most admirable characteristic of the Gaithers is their desire to be of assistance to other songwriters and musicians, especially young people. I have been interviewing songwriters for more than forty years, and on several occasions young people have recounted to me their experiences with Bill and Gloria. At least one teenager, who is a famous songwriter and musician today, showed up unannounced at their home one afternoon in Alexandria. He was invited to come in and stay for supper. During the course of the evening, he was greatly encouraged.

Of late, many of the older singers and songwriters who had all but gone into retirement are now back out on the road singing from one church to another and from one homecoming concert to the next—thanks to Bill and Gloria and their Homecoming series of videos, concerts, and music recordings. The Gaithers have cowritten with scores of songwriters in their home, in their studio in their Indiana town, or in some other location. It is an honor for any songwriter to have his or her name appear at the top of a music selection as a cowriter with Bill and Gloria.

Now for the story behind "Because He Lives." In the late 1960s, while expecting their third child, the Gaithers were going through a rather traumatic time in their lives. Bill was recovering from a bout with mononucleosis. They and other members in their church family were the objects of false accusations and belittlement. It was a time of fear for Gloria. The thought of bringing another child into this world with all of its craziness was taking its toll on her.

She remembered that on New Year's Eve she was sitting in their living room, overwhelmed by agony and fear. The educational system was being infiltrated with the "God is dead" idea, while drug abuse and racial tension were increasing. Then suddenly and quite unexpectedly, she was filled with a sweet, calming peace. It was as if her heavenly Father, like an attentive mother bending over her baby, saw his Gloria and came to her rescue. The panic gave way to a calmness and an assurance that only the Lord can give. She was assured that the future would be just fine, left in God's hands.

Both Bill and Gloria remembered that the power of the blessed Holy Spirit seemed to come to their aid. Christ's resurrection, in all of its power, was reaffirmed in their lives and their thinking. To Gloria it was life conquering death in their daily lives. Joy once again dominated the fearful circumstances of the day.

All of this gave rise to one of the most famous worship songs of our time, "Because He Lives." We can face tomorrow, with all of the uncertainty that it brings, as we realize that God holds the future and makes life worth living for all who trust in him.

As we remember Christ's resurrection, we gain assurance and strength to overcome the frightening obstacles of life. It is also very meaningful and empowering to realize that Jesus lives, every day, in our hearts.

BLESSED BE THE LORD GOD ALMIGHTY

VERSE

Father in heaven, how we love You.
We lift Your name in all the earth.
May Your kingdom be established in our praises,
As Your people declare Your mighty works.

CHORUS

Blessed be the Lord God Almighty,
Who was and is and is to come.
Blessed be the Lord God Almighty,
Who reigns forevermore.

Bob Fitts © 1984 Scripture in Song/Maranatha Music/ASCAP
(All rights administered by Music Services)

How Could I Forget My Song?

Blessed be the God and Father of our Lord Jesus Christ, who hath blessed us
with all spiritual blessings in heavenly places in Christ.

EPHESIANS 1:3

During Bob Fitts's early childhood years, his father, Bob Sr., was a Southern Baptist minister in Cleburne, Texas. In his later teen years, the family moved to California, where he was greatly influenced by a contemporary Christian music group called the 2nd Chapter of Acts.

Bob received a bachelor of arts degree in Christian ministry from the Melodyland School of Theology in Anaheim, California. In 1982, he, his wife, Kathy, and their first child, Andy, about eighteen months old at the time, moved to Hawaii, where they became involved with an organization called Youth With A Mission (YWAM). During their twenty years in that island state, God has given them three more children and has given Bob many wonderful songs.

During my long-distance interview with Bob, he told me the unusual story behind his very popular song "Blessed Be the Lord God Almighty."

"My family and I had just moved from California to Hawaii. Although I was under the umbrella of YWAM and had agreed to teach in their Discipleship Training School, my initial reason for coming here was to write Christian songs.

After a short time, I found myself getting involved in so many other activities that my songwriting was being pushed further and further into the background.

"I became somewhat disenchanted. The living conditions that our family was struggling with were adding to the displeasure. The only housing available to us was an old, run-down building, now owned by YWAM, that had formerly been a shelter for coffee bean pickers. It was a mess and greatly contributed to the discouragement I was feeling at that time in my life.

"One night I began to talk to the Lord about our situation. As I took my guitar down, it dawned on me that I was to lead worship at a church the next day. I was also committed to furnish some special music. I was having trouble coming up with something to sing, so I decided to write some music particularly for that service. All of a sudden 'Blessed Be the Lord God Almighty' just came out of my heart, lyrics and melody all at once. There was really no work involved.

"The next morning I went to the church, and as I stood up to present my song, I realized that I had completely forgotten it. I had not written it down, so I just could not remember it. Another song, which I had known for some time, came into my mind, so I sang that one. That experience left me more than a little frustrated.

"As I was walking home from the church, my new song came back to me, so I ran to the house and quickly put 'Blessed Be the Lord God Almighty' on tape. Two years after I wrote it, I did a singing tour in which I included the song, and it was very well received."

Bob's song is known in Europe as "Father in Heaven," the first three words of the verse. It is now making its way into hymnals, thus giving it an opportunity to become better known and loved by Christians everywhere.

The wonderful aspect of Bob's song is that it is threefold in its scope, as we recognize the marvelous attributes of God, extend our praise to him, and express our intention of making his name known in all the earth.

BLESSED BE YOUR NAME

VERSE

Blessed be Your name
In the land that is plentiful,
Where Your streams of abundance flow,
Blessed be Your name.

CHORUS

Every blessing You pour out
I'll turn back to praise.
When the darkness closes in,
Lord, still I will say,
Blessed be the name of the Lord,
Blessed be Your name.
Blessed be the name of the Lord,
Blessed be Your glorious name.

VERSE

Blessed be Your name
On the road marked with suffering,
Though there's pain in the offering,
Blessed be Your name.

In the Shadow of Tragedy

The LORD gave, and the LORD hath taken away; blessed be the name of the LORD.

JOB 1:21

Matt Redman has rapidly become one of the most respected worship leaders and songwriters in the praise and worship music genre and in youth revival movements around the world. Redman's songs, such as "The Heart of Worship" and "Better Is One Day," are regularly featured on countless praise and worship projects and at worship events in many countries.

Following is his own record of how he and his wife, Beth, wrote "Blessed Be

Your Name." This song, born out of the recognition of human suffering, has risen in popularity among Christians to the point that it is now sung by millions in many nations.

Matt said of the song, "Although the song wasn't born from any one particular circumstance, it is a song that stems from the story of our lives in general. Both my wife, Beth, and I had tough upbringings—a lot of different issues to do with fathers—and over the years we've come to realize that worshiping God is a choice, and the best choice we'll ever make.

"Trust is a beautiful act of worship. It says to God, 'I believe in you—in your unfailing goodness and greatness—no matter what season of life I find myself in.' So this is a song we'd wanted to write for years.

"There are a couple of other reasons that led to the song overflowing out of us. We were on sabbatical at the time in the USA, and the song was written in the shadow of the tragic events of 9/11—just weeks afterward. It struck me how little of a vocabulary we have in church worship music to respond appropriately in the dark times of life. No doubt being immersed in the spiritual and emotional climate of those days was an important factor in writing the song.

"It is really a song born out of the whole of life; a realization that we all face seasons of pain and unease. And in those times we need to find our voice before God. The church (and indeed the world) needs its songs of lamentation. The people of God have always had their laments. The Psalms are filled with a whole host of intense emotions and expressions toward God. So many of the psalms were birthed in times of suffering and struggle.

"The other element that led to the song being birthed at this time was rereading the book of Job. Many say this book is about suffering. I think it's really a book about something much grander—the sovereignty of God—of which 'suffering' is more a subcategory! At the end of chapter 1 we read, 'The LORD gave and the LORD has taken away; may the name of the LORD be praised' (v. 21 NIV). Or, as other translations word it, 'Blessed be the name of the LORD.'

> *By him therefore let us offer the sacrifice of praise to God continually, that is, the fruit of our lips giving thanks to his name.*
>
> HEB. 13:15

"I have to say that we've received more personal testimony feedback from this song than any other we've written. I have come across some of the harshest life circumstances I've heard of as people have e-mailed in their stories of how they've chosen to worship our amazing God even in some of the most difficult times of life. More than anything this reminds me of how much pain there is in the world, and about how important it is to be real, honest, and true (yet always remaining reverent) in the worshiping church."

One Christian organization that holds a massive amount of Matt Redman's attention and with which he travels a great deal is Passion Conferences, an American-based ministry to Christian college and university students, led by Louie Giglio.

Matt and his wife, Beth, make their home near Brighton, England. They have three children.

The most important aspect of our worship should be the giving of our complete attention to praising and glorifying our heavenly Father, no matter what the circumstances of the day may be. For it is in him, and him alone, that we live and move and have our being.

We can express our worship to God in many ways. But if we love the Lord and are led by His Holy Spirit, our worship will always bring a delighted sense of admiring awe and a sincere humility on our part.

A. W. TOZER

THE BLOOD WILL NEVER LOSE ITS POWER

VERSE

The blood that Jesus shed for me
'Way back on Calvary,
The blood that gives me strength
From day to day
It will never lose, its pow'r.

CHORUS

It reaches to the highest mountain,
It flows to the lowest valley.
The blood that gives me strength
From day to day,
It will never lose its pow'r.

VERSE

It soothes my doubts and calms my fears,
And it dries all my tears.
The blood that gives me strength
From day to day,
It will never lose its pow'r.

"If You're Gonna Play, Play!"

Forasmuch as ye know that ye were not redeemed with corruptible things, as silver and gold, from your vain conversation received by tradition from your fathers; but with the precious blood of Christ, as of a lamb without blemish and without spot.

1 PETER 1:18–19

In an interview a few years ago, Andrae Crouch related the following story:

"One day the call came to my father to preach at Macedonia Church, a small congregation about sixty miles from our home in Los Angeles. We had never heard my dad preach in a church—on street corners, in hospitals, and in other places, but not in a real pulpit in a church.

"My dad had been urged to preach at this little church on an interim basis, until they could secure a pastor. He was hesitant to do so but began to bargain with the Lord: 'If you will give Andrae the gift of playing the piano, I will be a full-time minister and figure out some other way to provide for my family.' He thought that there was not much chance of that prayer being answered and maybe he would not have to pastor that little church.

"During that first service my dad had called me up from the audience and asked, 'Andrae, if God gave you music, would you use it for his glory in your life?' I was only eleven years old and had never thought about it. There were no musicians in our immediate or extended family. I wouldn't have been more shocked if he had asked, 'Would you like to be an astronaut?'

"Three weeks later, during a service in that little church, as we were about to sing 'What a Friend We Have in Jesus,' my dad called out to me, 'Andrae, come up here.' He motioned to an upright piano nearby and said, 'Okay, if you're gonna play, play.' I said to myself, *What?* When the congregation began to sing, I found the right key and began to *play with both hands!*"

I asked Reverend Crouch to give me the story behind his song "The Blood Will Never Lose Its Power." Following is his amazing story:

"I was only fourteen years of age, three years following my initiation to the piano, and had been invited to a friend's home. It was Memorial Day, and there was to be a party with most of the guests being choir members. When I arrived the people were in the backyard barbecuing and generally having a good time. I was so shy and little—I was only four feet eleven inches tall until I was sixteen—I didn't want to go out there. I had seen some of them with cigarettes in their hands and generally acting in ways that were not Christlike. I didn't understand that and was so disappointed I began to weep.

"I then said to the Lord, 'God, I really love you. How can this be? I would love to write songs for you. If you will give me a song, I will live for you forever.' There was a large piano in the living room, and I began to play. The group in the backyard couldn't hear me. I then glanced toward the crowd and saw something that made time, it seemed, go into slow motion. I watched as they slowly poured red sauce onto the meat they were cooking. I couldn't hear for a few moments.

"Suddenly, in my mind's eye I could see Jesus carrying his cross up to Calvary, and I saw his blood. As I saw this scene, which had been prompted by the activities in the backyard, I said, 'Oh, the blood!' I then turned to my friend Billy Preston, also a pianist, and said, 'Play these chords.' And I began to sing, 'The blood that Jesus shed for me . . .' The people in the backyard heard me singing and came into the house. They began to weep as they came, and joined in my song."

Crouch's compositions have cut a wide path across Christianity for many years and have influenced several categories of sacred music.

Thank the Lord today for his precious blood, the blood that daily has the power to take away our sins—blood that will never lose its power.

BREATHE

A Dark and Desperate Time

For the bread of God is he which cometh down from heaven, and giveth life unto the world.

JOHN 6:33

Marie Barnett's song "Breathe" is not only popular in churches across America but has made its way into other countries with an unusually wide acceptance. It can be heard in great concerts, on television broadcasts, in prisons, and occasionally where soldiers work or wage war.

Marie told me, "I always wrote poems and simple songs, but I never thought of myself as a songwriter." In 1960, she became the fourth of five children born to Hector and Dianne Chenard in Concord, California. The whole family enjoyed music, and she grew up singing with them. She added, "I had very little music training. I only play guitar for myself—to write songs."

Marie continued, "I married a wonderful songwriter, John Barnett, who is a worship leader in the Vineyard Christian Fellowship in Mission Viejo, California. I began leading worship with him even before we were married."

Following is how Marie Barnett told of the writing of her famous song:

"It was a very dark and desperate time in my life. I had been working in a particular establishment for about ten years. I had been mentored in the business by the owner of the company, who was not a Christian. He and his wife began to have difficulties, and they ended up divorcing. He then took his own life. He left a note asking me to take over the business. It was a horrible situation. He had so many people who looked up to him. I didn't know what to do. I had never run a business before, and I was in a general state of confusion.

"My husband and I continued to lead worship at the Mission Viejo church. During a Sunday night service in 1995—I remember it so vividly—John and I had been leading the congregation in the song 'Isn't He?' by John Wimber. I have always loved that song as it leads us to fix our eyes on Jesus—isn't he so wonderful and beautiful? It goes into the names of Christ, names such as Prince of Peace.

"I was so captivated by the beauty of Jesus . . . and by the realization that I would be lost without him. I remember feeling that Christ was right in front of me. I began to think, *You are the air I breathe. You are my daily bread. I'm desperate for you! I have to breathe you in, and I must get a word from you or I can't live. I'm lost without you!*

"As we finished 'Isn't He?' John continued to play the chord progression of the song, and I began to sing what was in my mind, using another melody that was coming at the same time. As I repeated the phrases, the congregation began to sing along with me. And that night 'Breathe' was born. We then began singing it in our regular services at the church.

"Soon after that we were asked by Vineyard Music to do another recording. We agreed to do so and decided to include 'Breathe' in the list of songs for the project. After hearing the song, the producers at Vineyard decided that it wasn't the right style for a congregational worship album. They weren't planning to have us record 'Breathe,' but we believed so much in the song that they finally gave in and let us include it."

Five years later Brian Doerksen, whose story is told in "Come, Now Is the Time to Worship," put "Breathe" on an album in England with Catherine Scott singing it. The song had already been gaining in popularity in England, and this really helped it along. Marie told me that she and her husband did nothing to promote the song, but different singers—Michael W. Smith included—also recorded the song and began to use it.

The Barnetts make their home in Mission Viejo and are the parents of four grown children. "Breathe" was the first song that Marie wrote that received any notice.

We should daily remember that we have within our being the blessed Holy Spirit, who is our Teacher, our Sustainer, and our Comforter. God's Word should always be our daily bread.

CELEBRATE JESUS

VERSE

Celebrate Jesus, celebrate!
Celebrate Jesus, celebrate!
Celebrate Jesus, celebrate!
Celebrate Jesus, celebrate!

CHORUS

He is risen, He is risen,
And He lives forevermore.
He is risen, He is risen,
Come on and celebrate
The resurrection of our Lord.

© 1988 Integrity's Hosanna! Music
Gary Oliver

From My Special Place, the Kitchen

But for us also, to whom it shall be imputed, if we believe on him that raised up Jesus our Lord from the dead; Who was delivered for our offences, and was raised again for our justification.

ROMANS 4:24–25

What you are about to read is one of the most unusual interviews I have ever been a part of, and I have interviewed scores of songwriters. The story below was told to me by Gary Oliver as he sat in a booth eating lunch at a Luby's Cafeteria in Fort Worth, Texas. I was in Tucson, Arizona, at the time. Cell phones are terrific!

Gary Oliver was born in Beaumont, Texas, in 1956. His dad and mom took him to church regularly, and he began singing in church at age three or four. By age ten he was playing the piano in church services. Even with this strong church background, he was not truly converted until his early teen years.

Gary said, "At age thirteen, in a revival, I went to the altar and had one of the most powerful experiences with the Lord. I gave my heart to him, totally and completely. The Holy Spirit came into my life. It was awesome!"

In the early 1980s, Gary was made music director of Truth Church in Fort

38

Worth, Texas. During the next several years, he taught the congregation a new chorus each week—one that he had written. As was his custom, on Saturday night he would take his Bible and go to the kitchen, the only large room in the house that had space enough for the studio piano. He would read the Bible, pray, and sing out of his heart. There in that kitchen he wrote many of his one thousand songs.

He continued, "We were in a particular phase of ministry when we were trying to do some special things to enhance the children's ministry at Truth Church. One of the ladies who worked with the children's ministry came to me and said, 'Pastor Gary, we need to do something for our children so that they will understand the meaning of Easter. We are in a dilemma. We are working on a musical with the children, but all of the songs are slow and sad or too complicated for the kids. We want them to know that even though the cross was very sorrowful, there is joy in the resurrection and it is okay to celebrate Easter.' I said, 'You know what, we need to *do* something to let the kids know that it is good to celebrate Easter.' She replied, 'That would be awesome. Would you write a song for us so that we can teach it to the children?'

"I wrote a song in my special place, in the kitchen. I wrote it very simply so that children would understand that the reason we are celebrating is because Jesus is alive! Sure, he died on the cross. Without the cross we would have no resurrection. But we serve the only God who died and then rose again from the dead. He accomplished all that he came to earth to do. I wrote the song so that the children would realize that he lives forevermore.

"I'll never forget the Sunday we sang 'Celebrate Jesus.' As the children's choir was singing the song, the adult choir joined in and the whole place exploded. We sang the song for at least forty-five minutes. It interrupted the whole program. I knew then that the song was unique.

"Sometime later, in Stockholm, Sweden, just as I walked into the church I was visiting, they started singing 'Celebrate Jesus.' It blew me away. I began to weep as I thought how a song written by a young East Texas boy could go literally around the world and be sung in so many nations. It has been translated into Russian, Chinese, Japanese, Spanish, French, German, and several African dialects, just to name a few languages."

Gary has reminded us of the valuable and soul-stirring truth, that Christianity is the only way of "life" that is sustained by a risen Lord!

CHANGE MY HEART, O GOD

CHORUS

Change my heart, O God;
Make it ever true.
Change my heart, O God;
May I be like You.

VERSE

You are the Potter,
I am the clay.
Mold me and make me,
This is what I pray.

Eddie Espinosa © 1982 Mercy / Vineyard Publishing (ASCAP)
Admin. in North America by Music Services o/b/o Vineyard Music USA

Strolling the Aisles of a Target Store

*Create in me a clean heart, O God; and renew a right spirit within me. . . . Restore unto me
the joy of thy salvation; and uphold me with thy free spirit.*

PSALM 51:10, 12

I caught up with Eddie Espinosa, by way of his cell phone, while he strolled the aisles of a Target store in the Los Angeles area, shopping for a Mother's Day gift for his mother-in-law.

Eddie, born in Los Angeles in 1953, said, "At age fifteen, I was playing in a high school–age band. The bass player and his family were Christians, and they invited me to their church. On my third visit, the pastor taught from the Scripture the story of Jesus' encounter with the Samaritan woman at the well. After the lesson the pastor looked me square in the eye and asked, 'Would you like to drink of the Living Water?' I said, 'Yes,' and I was saved that very morning."

Now for the story behind Eddie's tremendous song, as he told it:

"The year was 1982. I had been a Christian since 1969, but I saw a lot of things in my life that needed to be discarded. The closer you get to the Lord, in all of his brightness, the better you can see the things in your life that need to be changed. But I had slowly become very complacent.

"I acknowledged my complacency, and at the same time I was like Paul the

40

apostle, who said, 'O wretched man that I am! who shall deliver me from the body of this death?' I prayed to the Lord, 'The only way that I can follow you is for you to change my appetite for the things that draw me away. You must change my heart!'

"Shortly thereafter, I was in my car on the way to my work, feeling a desire to draw near to God but with the wrestling still going on in my heart. Suddenly a melody and some words began to flood through my mind. As I stopped at a stop sign, I reached for something to write on, and the first thing I found was a small piece of yellow paper, which, by the way, I still have, and began to write as rapidly as I could. It was like taking dictation. I wrote the words on the paper and kept the melody in my mind.

"During those days I taught a weeknight home Bible study group. I shared my song with them, and someone from the group told the pastor that I had written a song that would be good to use during an altar call. The pastor asked me to play it for him, and afterward asked if I would share it with the congregation, which numbered about two hundred at that time.

"From that point on, I began to get reports that my song was being taught in San Diego, the Los Angeles area, and in many other places. Sharing a song in that manner was a common occurrence in those days. Vineyard Music decided to put 'Change My Heart, O God,' on an album, which became the vehicle that God chose to launch my song to a much wider audience."

At the time of this interview, Eddie is a counselor at Orange High School in Orange, California. As his other duties will allow, Eddie and his wife, Elsie, often travel as a team, leading worship in conferences and special services. They have two children.

As we have seen in this story, asking God to change us calls for a very definite and resolute decision—asking him to change our hearts, the control center of our beings, the place where we decide what we will think, say, and do.

COME INTO HIS PRESENCE

"Author Unknown"

Let us come before his presence with thanksgiving, and make a joyful noise unto him with psalms.

PSALM 95:2

The story behind this song, told to me by Lynn Baird in an interview in the early part of 2002, took place more than twenty years ago.

Lynn was born in 1952, in Phoenix, Arizona. He says of his conversion, "My earliest experience with the Lord was when I was about six years of age. I remember becoming convicted of my need for Christ while at church. So I went forward at the close of a morning service and shared my thoughts with the pastor. Following the service he took me to his office, where he led me to a personal knowledge of Christ as my Savior. I was then baptized."

In the early 1970s, while still a teenager and playing in a band, Unity, that he formed, Lynn also opened a coffeehouse, a place for young people to come, have refreshments, and hear Christian music along with a message from the Bible. It grew to the extent that a couple of hundred attended each weekend.

The band members of Unity started a very successful Bible study with those who frequented the coffeehouse. Out of this group a church was planted called Foundation Fellowship. Lynn became one of the pastors and was in charge of the music ministry. He often wrote songs for their worship on Sunday mornings. This gave him tremendous encouragement plus an outlet for his songwriting.

The writing of Lynn's most famous song took place during the early days of his ministry. He related it thus:

"In mid-1976, our family went to Oak Creek, in northern Arizona, a place where we had vacationed for years. We were staying in a mobile home in that resort area, surrounded by riverbeds and 'washes.' One day, while there, I decided to go for a hike. While walking through those wilderness places, the Lord dropped a melody and some lyrics into my mind. As soon as I was able to do so, I found something—I don't remember what—on which to write it all down. When I got to an instrument where I could play and sing the song, I became skeptical that it would even work, so I simply filed it away.

"Perhaps a year later, I pulled my song out of the files and played it for our praise band. Their response was positive, so we prepared to sing it during a Sunday morning service. It was so well received that we continued to sing it for five to six years—until it became old to us.

"In 1986, I was attending a leadership retreat in Scottsdale, Arizona. Before the start of the first morning session, a gentleman who was to be the worship leader for the retreat said to me and a few others standing near, 'Integrity has come out with a new praise and worship tape.' We all looked to Integrity and eagerly awaited those tapes to get more worship materials. I thought you would like to hear the tape,' he continued. He played it for us, and the first song on the tape was 'Come into His Presence.' I excitedly said, 'That is my song! I wonder how they got it!' All of us in that small group were just blown away. To add to my surprise, on the tape box, among the credits, the song was listed as 'author unknown.' To this day it has never been determined how they got my song, but they have since recognized me as the author."

"Come into His Presence" has extended the ministry of Lynn Baird a thousandfold. This, Lynn's only published song, is found in hymnals, in children's projects, on exercise tapes, on the *Songs 4 Worship* CD series, and in chorus books, just to name a few places. As I write this story, he continues to write songs for Abundant Life Community Church in Pasadena, California, where he is a pastor.

In Psalm 100, God lets us know that when we come into his presence he is pleased to have us praise him, sing to him, and be thankful to him—"Serve the LORD with gladness: come before his presence with singing. . . . Enter into his gates with thanksgiving, and into his courts with praise: be thankful unto him, and bless his name" (Ps. 100:2, 4).

Come, Now Is the Time to Worship

CHORUS

Come, now is the time to worship.
Come, now is the time to give your heart.
Come, just as you are to worship.
Come, just as you are before your God.
Come.

VERSE

One day every tongue
Will confess You are God.
One day every knee will bow.
Still the greatest treasure remains
For those who gladly choose You now.

Brian Doerksen © 1998 Vineyard Songs (UK/EIRE) (PRS)
Admin. in North America by Music Services

Hearing God's Invitation Near Wembledon

But the hour cometh, and now is, when the true worshippers shall worship the Father in spirit and in truth: for the Father seeketh such to worship him.

JOHN 4:23

Brian Doerksen was born into a very musical family in Abbotsford, just outside of Vancouver, British Columbia. Brian said, "I have been interested in music as long as I can remember. I started piano lessons as a child, but as soon as I was old enough to make my own decision, I, regretfully, quit.

"I grew up in a Christian home, and it wasn't as if I didn't know the truth of the gospel—I just didn't want to live it. But when I was fifteen years of age, probably as a result of my parents' prayers, I had one of those sovereign encounters with God. One night in my bedroom, the presence of God came into the room and I was convicted of my sin. I heard the Lord saying, 'Give me your whole life to serve me.' And I said yes. I began learning to play the guitar. I played for hours each day and started worshiping God in my room.

"It was not until I was the full-time music pastor at Langley Vineyard Christian Fellowship in British Columbia that I began to seriously write songs. I

44

was using songs from other sources but became convinced that we needed something else, other expressions to worship God."

I then asked Brian to give me the details surrounding the writing of his most famous song, "Come, Now Is the Time to Worship."

"Emotionally and spiritually the song came at the end of the darkest and lowest season of my life, the summer of 1977. We had tried a major ministry project that had failed. A group working with me, and I, lost over one million dollars. I lost our home.

"I moved to England and became the worship pastor of Southwest London Vineyard, meeting in the Elliot School. I had no other place to live and no job offers. I felt as if I was barely hanging on to my faith in God. My wife and I were severely tested both with our losses and with finding out that three of our six children had a condition called Fragile X syndrome, a form of mental retardation.

"One morning, within months of moving to London, I went for an exercise-prayer walk, as I often did. As I was walking through southwest London, very close to Wembledon Stadium, I heard this line, as clear as a bell, floating through the air, 'Come, now is the time to worship . . .' I thought, *Wow! The call of worship is being sounded all of the time and in all kinds of ways.*

"When I got home, I ran upstairs, sat down at the piano, found the key of the song I had just heard, and began playing it over and over again. Suddenly I realized that I was in my own dark time and that his call to worship doesn't just come to those who have it all together, who have no doubts or hard experiences, but it comes to all of us across the board.

"The song became like wings to lift me up from those shadows that had almost engulfed me. It was my private song for several days. I made sure of every word. I then brought it to my church. Within weeks of teaching it to our congregation, I began hearing reports of other churches singing it. Within months reports came of the song being sung in other countries. I soon heard that it was being sung in South Africa.

"Requests began to pour in asking permission to record 'Come, Now Is the Time to Worship.' Soon after that we moved back home to Canada, to the house I was raised in. We were able to purchase it from my parents."

Life is better now in Abbotsford for Brian, his wife, Joyce, and their children. At the time of this writing, Brian had just finished a new album of songs and had the joy of having one of his daughters play an instrument on the project.

Oh, that you and I were constantly in the mental and spiritual state that we, too, would hear God's invitation, "Come, now is the time to worship."

45

VERSE

Jesus is the Cornerstone,
Came for sinners to atone.
Though rejected by His own,
He became the Cornerstone.
Jesus is the Cornerstone.

When I am by sin oppressed,
On the Stone I am at rest.
Where the seeds of truth are sown,
He remains my Cornerstone.
Jesus is my Cornerstone.

CHORUS

Rock of Ages, cleft for me.
Let me hide myself in Thee.
Rock of Ages, so secure,
For all time it shall endure.
'Til His children reach their home,
He remains the Cornerstone.
'Til the breaking of the dawn,
'Til all footsteps reach His throne,
Ever let this truth be known,
Jesus is the Cornerstone.
Jesus is the Cornerstone.

The Newness Has Remained

Now therefore ye are no more strangers and foreigners, but fellowcitizens with the saints, and of the household of God; and are built upon the foundation of the apostles and prophets, Jesus Christ himself being the chief corner stone.

EPHESIANS 2:19–20

L ari Goss, a self-taught musician, has orchestrated and conducted the accompaniment for more Christian recordings than most any other person living today. Many of the leading music publishers and producers reach out for the services of this creative genius. But it was not until he had been elevated to a pinnacle of music acclaim among Christian musicians that the Lord decided to send a song around the world that he had given to Lari. Prior to that, he worked with the songs of other authors.

Goss was born in 1945, in Cartersville, Georgia. He and his siblings were reared by wonderful Christian parents. Although he started singing with his family as a child, he was not given the opportunity of extensive music training.

Lari, James, and Roni Goss, known for many years as the Goss Brothers, each had medium-range voices; therefore they had to resort to unusual, close harmonies. They were considered by leading musicians of the day to be far ahead of their time. At music concerts they usually started the performances, a place reserved for the less popular singers, or were the last to sing. Professional groups had a greater appreciation of their abilities than did the audiences. Consequently, backstage, it was a common sight to see groups of singers gathered around them to hear their awesome harmonies and chord progressions.

> *O come, let us worship and bow down: let us kneel before the* LORD *our maker.*
>
> Ps. 95:6

Lari began orchestrating songs at the age of sixteen, conducting his first recording session with thirty-five symphony players. Today he arranges and orchestrates music for the Brooklyn Tabernacle, Gaither Music, Lillenas, and Word, to name a few. As I interview songwriters, musicians tell me that they were more influenced musically by Lari and the Goss Brothers than by any other musicians.

I had the privilege of working closely with Lari for a time in Marietta, Georgia, where I was the minister of music and Lari was the pianist. I soon discovered that I had never met a musician with more creativity and talent.

Lari related the following story to me concerning one of his great songs:

"I had a melody that the Lord had given me that I called 'Cornerstone.' Yet I had no lyrics. At the same time I was studying the Word. [Lari is a conscientious student of the Bible.] I had been reading in the Scriptures where Jesus is presented as the Chief Cornerstone. I reasoned with myself that maybe I could put that thought with my melody. The lyrics of the song came strictly from the inspiration of the Word of God. Many of the phrases in the song are straight scripture.

"I continued to work the melody and the scriptures into each other. Then I went to the old hymnals to see what former writers had to say about Christ as a Stone or the Rock of our salvation. I borrowed a line from an old hymn—I don't even remember the song—'Where the seeds of truth are sown.' Then I turned to that old favorite song 'Rock of Ages.' It so ably depicts Christ as our Cornerstone, the Rock of Ages. My mind then went to our security in the Lord. That led me to 'Rock of Ages, so secure, for all time it shall endure. 'Til His children reach their home, He remains the Cornerstone.'

"No event or incident in my life influenced the song. It is strictly from the Scriptures."

Nancy Harmon was the first to record "Cornerstone," about two years after Lari had written it. The song was nominated for a Dove Award in 1978 and still continues to be a favorite everywhere. It has been put into music literature.

Whatever your lot in life, if you are a Christian,
you are secure in the knowledge that the Lord Jesus Christ
is the foundation and support of your very existence.

Listen, ere the sound be fled,
And learn there may be worship
without words.

HENRY WADSWORTH LONGFELLOW

DAYS OF ELIJAH

VERSE

These are the days of Elijah,
Declaring the Word of the Lord.
And these are the days
Of Your servant Moses,
Righteousness being restored.
And though these are days
Of great trials,
Of famine and darkness and sword,
Still we are the voice
In the desert crying,
Prepare ye the way of the Lord.

CHORUS

Behold He comes,
Riding on the clouds,
Shining like the sun,
At the trumpet call.
So lift your voice,
It's the year of Jubilee.
And out of Zion's hill,
Salvation comes.

Robin Mark © 1996 Daybreak Music, Ltd.
(Admin. in the US & Canada by Integrity Music, Inc.)

From the Church Kitchen to the World

*And they shall see the Son of man coming in the clouds of heaven with power and great glory.
And he shall send his angels with a great sound of a trumpet, and they shall gather together his
elect from the four winds, from one end of heaven to the other.*

MATTHEW 24:30–31

I cannot sit down and write automatically. God hasn't given me that gift," explained Robin Mark. "I write only when I feel I have something to say." As you continue to read, you will see how the Lord has in the past few years been moving Robin Mark into the forefront of the ministry of worship and praise.

Robin lives in Belfast, Ireland, with his wife, Jacqueline, and their three children, Catherine, David, and James. A successful businessman and lecturer at Queen's University, Robin has another gifting in life—that of worship leader and songwriter.

He said, "I didn't become interested in writing songs until I began to play in a Christian contemporary band. It was evangelistic in makeup, and we did outreach in and around Belfast." Invitations now come to Robin to minister in music in Europe, America, Canada, Australia, and the Far East.

Robin led me to a story on his Web site. "The song came from watching a television review of the year at the end of 1994. These were the years of the Rwandan civil war tragedies that claimed the lives of one million people. It was the year of the first ceasefire in Ireland. As I watched the review, I found myself despairing about the state of the world and began asking God if he was really in control and what sort of days were we living in.

"I felt in my spirit that he replied to my prayer by saying that indeed he was very much in control and that the days we were living in were special times. He was requiring Christians to be filled with integrity and to stand up for him just as Elijah did, particularly with the prophets of Baal. These are Elijah days.

"Those thoughts were in my mind when I came to church early one Sunday in 1995. We have two morning services, and the pastor spoke during the first service on the 'valley of dry bones' from Ezekiel. I took a prompt from this and in the thirty minutes between the services wrote down the words and chords to 'Days of Elijah' in the kitchen of our church building. As we were about to close the second service, I presented the song to the church, and we sang it together as our worship.

"Maybe one day I will hear the call to go into full-time ministry. Maybe the business will decline. Maybe I'll need to find work elsewhere. All I know is, his ways and thoughts are higher than ours. He knows the plans he has for each of us, and the paths we are to take. Listen for the call, and no matter how strange it may seem, go where he leads you to go, work 9 to 5, and worship 24/7.

"I now have been graced to take on the role of director of worship at Christian Fellowship Church, my home church. My songs have gone from Belfast to all over the world. God's call was a good one!"

"Days of Elijah" was launched on a meteoric flight around the world with the publishing of a CD, *Revival in Belfast*, recorded by Robin Mark and the Christian Fellowship Church in Belfast, Northern Ireland.

It is refreshing to hear from someone who is not afraid to follow the call of the Lord and to trust in him completely. God says to each of us, "Trust in the Lord *with all thine heart; and lean not unto thine own understanding. In all thy ways acknowledge him, and he shall direct thy paths" (Prov. 3:5–6).*

DRAW ME CLOSE

VERSE

Draw me close to You;
Never let me go.
I lay it all down again
To hear You say
That I'm Your friend.

CHORUS

You're all I want;
You're all I've ever needed.
You're all I want;
Help me know You are near.

VERSE

You are my desire;
No one else will do,
'Cause nothing else
Could take Your place,
To feel the warmth
Of Your embrace.
Help me find the way;
Bring me back to You.

The Ministry Had Gotten in the Way

Draw nigh to God, and he will draw nigh to you.

JAMES 4:8

The affecting melody of "Draw Me Close" carries the message deep into the mind and heart.

Kelly Carpenter, the song's author, was born in Walnut Creek, California, in 1958. His parents, Robert and Ida Mae Carpenter, made sure there was music in the house for Kelly and his siblings. He said, "Mom informally gave me piano lessons, but I became bored with the piano books and began to play other things. I would try to make up songs even at an early age.

"I grew up in a Lutheran church. When I was sixteen, I went on a weekend Young Life retreat in Northern California. In an evening service, someone presented a message of salvation in a way that was different than how I had learned it in our church. I was saved at that retreat.

"During my high school years, I fell away from the Lord, and by the time I was nineteen or twenty years old, I was really trying to make it in the secular music world. But by age twenty-one, I realized that I was making a mess of my life, so I decided to go back to school. I wanted to have something to fall back on in case the music thing didn't work out. At North Seattle Community College I became friends with some Christian young people. They had a wonderful influence on my life.

"In June 1980, I rededicated my life to the Lord. By that time I had met Merrilyn, the young lady I was to marry two years later. After I rededicated my life to the Lord, I began to be involved with other Christian musicians who played contemporary Christian music. Merrilyn and I then began attending the Northshore Vineyard at Mount Lake Terrace, Washington. It eventually became the Vineyard Christian Fellowship in Kirkland. We were there for about eleven years.

> *"My mouth shall speak the praise of the Lord: and let all flesh bless His holy name for ever and ever."*
>
> Ps. 145:21

"In 1992, I became a worship leader at the Kirkland church. The former worship leader had left, and I was asked to take his place. Actually, I coordinated all of the worship ministry. This was a daunting task for me—in a church with an attendance of six hundred—and that would later figure into the writing of 'Draw Me Close.' I felt as if I had been thrown into the deep end of the pool and had to sink or swim.

"Merrilyn had the strength that I lacked. I could keep the music end going, but pastoring was an area that I was not prepared for. She helped tremendously with that part of my ministry.

"In January 1994—I had been worship leader for about eighteen months—I came home one day from church with the realization that I had been tremendously driven to prove myself and to make this thing happen. I felt overwhelmed and beaten down. I was pushing extremely hard to keep everyone happy and make the music program work.

"Suddenly a song began pouring into my heart. The pivotal part of the song said, 'I lay it all down again, to hear You say that I'm Your friend.' The time and effort that I was putting into my ministry had gotten in the way of my relationship with the Lord. I was willing to lay all of the ministry things aside if I could feel close to the Lord again. How the song sounds today is exactly how it sounded that day. The melody and the lyrics were all given to me in about a twenty-minute span.

"I sent the song to my friend Andy Park, who was preparing to record his album *The River Is Here*. He decided to put my song on his album and asked that I come and play keyboard on the project. That CD helped to send my song on its way."

It is now sung in other nations of the world, as well as in thousands of churches in the United States.

Every morning, you and I should draw close to the heart of our heavenly Father, and all through the day never wander farther than his fingertips.

"*The more beautiful and elabo*
becomes, the greater is the dang

C. B. Moss

Firm Foundation

Jesus, You're my firm foundation.
I know I can stand secure.
Jesus, You're my firm foundation.
I put my hope in Your holy Word,
I put my hope in Your holy Word.

VERSE

I have a living hope;
I have a future.
God has a plan for me,
Of this I'm sure, of this I'm sure!

VERSE

Your Word is faithful,
Mighty in power.
God will deliver me,
Of this I'm sure, of this I'm sure!

Disappointment Turns to "Living Hope"

Nevertheless the foundation of God standeth sure.

2 TIMOTHY 2:19

Jamie Harvill was born in California in 1960 and received his education at the University of Mobile. Nancy Gordon, who wrote a number of songs with him, is a native of Mobile, Alabama, born there in 1955. They met during a series of services at a small church in Mobile in 1988 where Jamie was the song leader and Nancy had been invited to play the piano.

Nancy was already an experienced songwriter, while Jamie only had aspirations to write songs—he had tried his hand at it but had never been published. The two of them decided to make an effort at writing some songs together. Their first opportunity came when they were asked to submit some songs for a country album about to be produced. They wrote what they thought was an absolutely fantastic

song, "The Belle of the Ball," a song that affirmed the love between a father and his daughter.

Their song was accepted for an album on which Suzy Luchsinger, Reba McEntire's sister, was to sing. Suzy loved the song, and everything seemed to be in order for it to appear on the project, but in the end, "The Belle of the Ball" was cut from the list. Jamie and Nancy were both disappointed—big time. Jamie said, "We found that the saying is true, 'It's not final till it's on the vinyl.'"

During a subsequent phone conversation, they found themselves discussing their bafflement and disappointment that the song was rejected. Nancy told me, "Just that morning I had been reading in the Scriptures and saw a phrase in the *Living Bible*, 'I have a living hope.' When I read that, a deep desire welled up within me to sing those words."

Jamie told Nancy, "We were wrong to put so much hope in men. We need to pick up and go forward." Nancy then said, "We have a living hope!" Jamie answered, "And we have a future." Nancy said, "Our conversation was like a volleyball game of encouragement. We were both aware that we had placed our hope in a song we had written and not in our God.

"Through the ministry of encouragement, Jamie and I actually talked ourselves into the song 'Firm Foundation.' Almost line for line we were exhorting one another not to be discouraged in the circumstances but to put our hope in God's holy Word. Most of the lyrics were written over the phone.

"Afterward we got together a couple of times to tweak the song. I can still remember Jamie's wife, Brenda, commenting to us, 'Well, country music didn't get a good song, but the church got a great one!'"

The song first appeared on an Integrity album called *Firm Foundation*. From there it has been woven into the worship of millions of Christians in thousands of churches in our nation and in other lands.

Nancy told me, "When I heard a chorus of thousands of ladies at one of the Women of Faith gatherings sing 'Firm Foundation,' I was so moved I had to sit down. It is truly amazing how a song can be carried in the Spirit to people and places we will never see or go. We are continually blessed by the stories we hear about the powerful encouragement the song has been to people everywhere. We're forever grateful that we worked through our disappointment with the 'living hope' of God's eternal Word, and we still celebrate the joy of having written this song."

Shaun Alexander, a Seattle Seahawk and National Football League's Most Valuable Player for 2005, quotes the lyrics of "Firm Foundation" in his book *Touchdown Alexander*, published in 2006 by Harvest House.

How settling to our hearts when we realize that underneath are the "everlasting arms" that sustain our very lives—our present and our future.

FOREVER

VERSE

Give thanks to the Lord
Our God and King;
His love endures forever.
For He is good, He is above all things;
His love endures forever.
Sing praise, sing praise,
Sing praise, sing praise.

CHORUS

Forever God is faithful,
Forever God is strong.
Forever God is with us,
Forever, forever.

VERSE

With a mighty hand
And an outstretched arm,
His love endures forever.
For the life that's been reborn,
His love endures forever.
Sing praise, sing praise,
Sing praise, sing praise.

The Word Is "Strong"!

O give thanks unto the Lord; for he is good: for his mercy endureth forever.

PSALM 136:1

Forever" is one of many songs written by Chris Tomlin, a talented songwriter and worship leader who travels the world over and yet finds time to be involved with his local church responsibilities at Austin Stone Community Church in Austin, Texas.

In a recent issue of *Time* magazine, Belinda Luscombe wrote, "According to CCLI, Tomlin, 34, is the most often sung contemporary artist in U.S. congregations every week . . . that might make him the most often sung artist, anywhere."

The *Time* article quoted Chris as saying, "I try to think, *How do I craft this song in a way that the person who's tone-deaf and can't clap on two and four can sing it?* I hope that when someone hears a CD of mine, they pick up their guitar and say, 'OK, I can do that.'"

Chris's recounting of the writing of "Forever" follows, as he told it to me.

"'Forever' was a song I started to write while a student at Texas A&M University. I began this task shortly after the writing of 'We Fall Down.' I wrote most of the lyrics, but I couldn't finish it. It seemed to take forever to write 'Forever.'

"One day as I was reading Psalm 136, I was blown away by that passage of Scripture. It really moved me as I read 'for his mercy endureth forever' at the close of each verse.

> *All the earth shall worship thee, and shall sing unto thee; they shall sing to thy name.*
>
> Ps. 66:4

I could imagine that during Bible times when people were led in this psalm they would respond, all together, at the end of each verse by saying 'for his mercy endures forever.' I wanted to capture that approach musically—to sing a line and have the people respond with 'His love endures forever.'

"I wanted desperately to complete the song, but it was so difficult. I had people tell me, 'That is going to be a great song.' That went on for four years. I had a sense in my heart that the song would be something special if only I could finish it.

"I went to lead worship at a summer camp, and one afternoon during free time I decided to work on the song. I had said to myself, 'I need to finish this song.' So I began singing, 'Forever God is faithful'; repeatedly I sang, 'Forever God is faithful.' I wanted to follow that line with the same phrase, except for the last word. I worked for several afternoons on the song, singing it all the way through only to get to the last word and stop. No matter how hard I tried, I could not come up with a suitable word for the closing of the song.

"Janet Reeves, the wife of our bass guitarist, was in the room across the hall. She had heard me, each afternoon, repeatedly get to the last word and stop. She knocked on the door, and as I went to the door, she said, 'The word is *strong.*' *That's it!* I thought. That was the word I needed to finish my song. We began to use the song in our concerts and worship services with a great response from the audiences. We then included it in an album of songs.

"A year later, at some gathering, someone handed me a copy of Michael W. Smith's *Worship* album. 'Forever' was the lead song on the project. I had no idea that he had recorded it. That greatly helped 'Forever' to be known across the nation."

Band members who work with Chris are Dan Carson (electric guitar, backup vocals), Jesse Reeves (bass guitar, harmonica, backup vocals, co-songwriter), and Travis Nunn (drums, loops). Nunn replaced Ryan Sandlin as drummer sometime in 2004. Chris and the band developed while working with the Harvest Ministry at The Woodlands (Texas) United Methodist Church in the late 1990s. He is one of the main worship leaders in Passion Conferences, led by Louie Giglio, and many of his songs are featured on their albums.

When it is declared by the angel of the Lord that "time shall be no more," you and I will just be beginning to realize the extent of God's love and mercy.

Worship is more than singing beautiful songs in church on a Sunday. It is more than instruments and music. As a true worshiper, your heart will long to worship Him at all times, in all ways and with all your life.

DARLENE ZSCHECH

GIVE THANKS

VERSE

Give thanks with a grateful heart,
Give thanks to the Holy One,
Give thanks because He's given
Jesus Christ His Son.

CHORUS

And now let the weak say, "I am strong"
Let the poor say, "I am rich
Because of what the Lord has done for us."
And now let the weak say, "I am strong,"
Let the poor say, "I am rich
Because of what the Lord has done for us."

What a Song!

*Giving thanks always for all things unto God and the Father in the name
of our Lord Jesus Christ; submitting yourselves one to another in the fear of God.*

EPHESIANS 5:20–21

Many stories can be told of the blessing "Give Thanks" has been to Christians worldwide. The flight of the song has been dramatic and even unusual at times. In Uzbekistan, a country just north of the war-torn land of Afghanistan, a group of Uzbeks are singing a Christian song they recently learned. This is an unusual sight in a unique country. One photographer said, "Uzbekistan, crossroads of Asia, is an elusive mixture of Soviet industrial atheism, Islam, and the Orient. Crossing the Kyzyl Kum desert in a Lada left a lasting impression." The group is singing Henry Smith's "Give Thanks," which had traveled from America to this extraordinary place.

While in his teens, Henry Smith Jr. picked up his brother's guitar, ordered from the Sears catalog, and began to learn to play it. His songwriting ventures started during those years and have lasted until the present. Of the nearly three hundred songs he has written, only one has been published—that's right, only one, but what a song!

Henry went on to study at King College in Bristol, Tennessee, earning a degree in psychology. He also studied at Union Theological Seminary and earned a master of divinity degree.

I was delighted with the following story he related to me:

"I had been writing a lot of songs, but in 1972, while a sophomore in college, the Lord seemed to increase his blessings as he poured out his Spirit upon me. I began putting psalms to music, which revitalized my songwriting.

"In 1978, at the Williamsburg New Testament Church, in Williamsburg, Virginia, where I was attending, the pastor taught us from the Scriptures how Jesus became poor in order that we might be made rich in him. I remember that some other scriptures were woven into his lessons, making it a good background for a song. Later, in my apartment, I wrote the song 'Give Thanks.'

"Shortly thereafter, my wife, Cindy, and I, although at that time we were not married, sang the song at the church. We repeated it a number of times over a period of several weeks. There happened to be a military couple who attended the church for a while who carried songs learned in the United States back with them to Germany. As far as I know, that is how my song got to Europe. It did a lot of traveling before Integrity Music picked it up and published it. It is a 'God thing' that the song has become so widely known.

"In 1986, eight years after the writing of the song, a friend brought a cassette tape to me and said, 'Listen to this song and see if you have ever heard it.' After listening to it, I said, 'I wrote that song!' My friend had ordered the *Hosanna!* tape from Integrity Music, and 'Give Thanks' was listed as 'author unknown.' I then called Integrity and told them that I had written the song. Their response was 'Good! We have been trying to find you.' I then signed a writer-publisher agreement with them. Now, more than fifty companies have recorded 'Give Thanks,' and it has been published in a number of books."

"Give Thanks" is one of the most widely used songs in churches in the United States. I think I can understand why so many people in impoverished lands love this song.

At the time of this writing, Henry and Cindy reside in Mechanicsville, Virginia, and have two children, Shari and Joshua. He is a small-group worship leader at the Mechanicsville Christian Center.

Every good thing with which we have to do, or which we possess, is a gift from our heavenly Father. He wants us to be so grateful that we will enter his gates with thanksgiving and come into his courts with praise.

GOD OF WONDERS

CHORUS I

God of wonders beyond our galaxy,
You are holy, holy.
The universe declares Your majesty;
You are holy, holy.
Lord of heaven and earth,
Lord of heaven and earth,
Lord of heaven and earth.

VERSE

Lord of all creation,
Of water earth and sky,
The heavens are Your tabernacle.
Glory to the Lord on high.

VERSE

Early in the morning,
I will celebrate the light.
When I stumble in the darkness,
I will call Your name by night.

Good Morning, Astronauts!

*The heavens declare the glory of God; and the firmament
sheweth his handywork.*

PSALM 19:1

Good morning! That song was for Rick. It was 'God of Wonders' by Steve
Green." An answer came back from Rick, "Good morning. Thank you. We
can really appreciate the lyrics of that song up here. We look out the window and
see that God truly is a God of wonders!"

That was the conversation between Mission Control in Houston, Texas, and Rick Husband, an ardent Christian and commander of the space crew as they orbited the earth in the space shuttle *Columbia*. This was the second voyage during which "God of Wonders" had been played in space.

A few days later, on February 1, 2003, President Bush declared to the world that the crew of the shuttle *Columbia* did not return safely to Earth. *Columbia* had disintegrated and fallen in bits and pieces over the southern part of the United States.

As a California lad, only six years of age, Steve Hindalong saw a painting of Jesus knocking at a door. He was told that it represented Jesus knocking at our heart's door. He went to his mom and said, "I want Jesus to come into my heart." She helped him to understand, and he prayed and asked Christ to come in.

He wrote his first song at age eleven and later participated with youth music groups at his church, all the while wanting to become a lyricist. You may remember him as a member of a touring Christian music group called the Choir.

Marc Byrd was born and raised in Eldorado, Arkansas. He is a self-taught musician who started playing guitar at age thirteen. After his college days and then several years of touring with a Christian band, Common Children, he came to a crossroads in his life. He told me, "I didn't know what the future held for me or even where the next penny was coming from. So I grabbed my Bible on a Friday in 1999 and spent the entire weekend reading the Psalms, accompanied only by my guitar. I basically spent those days restoring my life to the place where I was when I first came to the Lord. It was a time of singing to God with a childlike heart.

"Worship always brings peace and healing to me. I believe we were created for that purpose. The beginning of 'God of Wonders' came out of the Psalms during that weekend. I had the music and a few phrases, one of which was 'You are holy.'"

> *All nations whom thou hast made shall come and worship before thee, O Lord; and shall glorify thy name. For thou art great, and doest wondrous things: thou art God alone.*
>
> Ps. 86:9–10

Steve Hindalong continued the story: "Marc brought me the music for 'God of Wonders' during the time that I was beginning to do an album called *City on a Hill*, a worship project. He strummed the chord progressions to me, and the hair stood up on my arms. It gave me a chill. It just felt really vast to me. To this point most of my songs were introspective and personal, but I told Marc, 'This song sounds to me as if it should be like . . . 'God of wonders, beyond all galaxies.' That was my reaction to the feeling the music gave to me.

"It took several days, working together, to finish the song. I mostly wrote the lyrics and Marc mostly wrote the music. We had often worked closely on projects. We were like brothers and had written a lot of songs together."

"God of Wonders" was first recorded in 2000, on that *City on a Hill* album. Since then scores of artists have recorded it, one of whom was Steve Green. It has gone like a meteor around the world in several languages. Choirs, praise teams, and church congregations worldwide have made it one of their favorite worship songs.

The lyrics of this song bring us to the glorious realization that we serve and are loved by a God of wonders. Though he created and controls all the universes beyond our galaxy, he also cares for you and me as though we were the only ones in his keeping. And we can call on him at any time.

Worship gives us courage, makes prayer a power, makes God's promises a reality, and changes our attitudes.

LEE ROBERSON

God Will Make a Way

CHORUS

God will make a way,
Where there seems to be no way.
He works in ways we cannot see.
He will make a way for me.
He will be my guide,
Hold me closely to His side,
With love and strength
For each new day,
He will make a way.
He will make a way.

VERSE

By a roadway in the wilderness He'll lead me,
And rivers in the desert will I see.
Heaven and earth will fade,
But His Word will still remain.
He will do something new today.

© 1990, 2006 Integrity's Hosanna! Music
Don Moen

To Strengthen a Grieving Mother

I will even make a way in the wilderness, and rivers in the desert.

ISAIAH 43:19

Many songs that are meaningful to Christians were born during a dark period in someone's life. A deep tragedy was the background for one of Don Moen's most influential and widely known songs. The message in the lyrics and the beauty of the melody have caused it to cross over from the genre of praise and worship to other categories of Christian music.

The following is how Don related his story to me about his song:

"My wife's sister and her husband, Craig and Susan Phelps, were involved in a car accident during a ski trip they were taking from their home in Oklahoma to a resort in Colorado. Way out somewhere in the Texas panhandle their van was hit by an eighteen-wheeler. The truck hit a rear panel of the van with such force that all four of their children were thrown out.

"The children had just left their seats, where they were buckled in, to lie down for a nap on a 'bed' positioned in the rear of the van. In the darkness only the crying of their severely injured children made it possible for Mom and Dad to find them—all except one—their nine-year-old son, Jeremy, who they finally located lying by a nearby fence. He was already dead. His neck had been broken.

"Craig, a medical doctor, picked up his son and tried to revive him, but God said to him, 'Jeremy is with me. You deal with those who are living.' They sat for forty-five minutes, out in the wilderness, waiting for an ambulance.

"They asked me to sing at the funeral, so I boarded a plane the next day, March 19, 1987, and headed for Oklahoma. As I sat on the plane, wondering what I should say to them, I began to read in the book of Isaiah. My eyes went to chapter 43, verse 19, 'I will even make a way in the wilderness, and rivers in the desert.' Instantly, the Lord gave me a song to sing to them. I sketched it out on a legal pad, intending to sing it at the funeral, but they had already planned to ask me to sing Henry Smith's 'Give Thanks,' so I sang their request instead.

"After the funeral, I was sitting with them, holding them in my arms. I cried with them, and through my tears I said, 'The Lord gave me a song for you.' And I began singing, 'God will make a way . . . where there seems to be no way.'"

Don continued, "I made a taped copy of the song for Susan to play on her small cassette player just above her kitchen sink. I knew that when all of the people had gone, and everything was said and done, that there would be days when she needed to hear that God was working in ways she couldn't see."

God does work in many ways that we do not understand. Young Jeremy's friends heard that he had become a Christian before the accident. Many of them began to ask how they might know Christ so that they could go to heaven when they died.

Jeremy's mother later related how she made a quick decision between the time she got out of the van and the time they found her son. She knew that she had to make a choice between becoming bitter and angry and accepting God's plan for their family at that time. Good things happened as a result of making the decision to embrace God's will no matter what that would mean in their lives. She later agreed that God really did make a way for them.

At first Don protested F. G. Baldwin's suggestion that the song be recorded, citing that it was "much too simple." But after discussing it with the staff at Integrity, the song was placed in an album titled *Eternal God*.

In times of trial, and especially in times of extreme trial, we need to be assured that we have a God who loves us and will provide for our every need.

GREAT AND MIGHTY

Great and mighty is the Lord our God,
Great and mighty is He.
Great and mighty is the Lord our God,
Great and mighty is He.
Lift up your banner let the anthems ring
Praises to our King;
Great and mighty is the Lord our God,
Great and mighty is He.

Great and mighty is
Great and mighty is
Great and mighty is He.

© 1984, Sound III, Inc.
Marlene Bigley

I Sat There and Cried

Who is this King of glory? The LORD strong and mighty, the LORD mighty in battle.

PSALM 24:8

To have your song be used as a musical opening for a Billy Graham Crusade would an honor indeed. That is what happened with Marlene Bigley's "Great and Mighty." The flight of the song into the hearts of millions of people has been truly amazing, especially when you consider its humble birth. Only the Lord could have caused that to happen.

Los Angeles, California, said hello to Marlene in 1952. She had a humble beginning, but great things were in store for her. Just like thousands of other children, she had taken piano lessons but had grown tired of them and stopped playing. When only eight years of age, she had aspirations of teaching music, but that was due to the admiration she held for her choir teacher.

Marlene told me of her yielding to Christ and her songwriting efforts. "I had made a profession of faith in Christ when I was thirteen, but I made an absolute and total commitment to the Lord at age nineteen. I became aware of worship at age twenty-one, and a year later I began to have a real desire to become a worship leader.

"My father passed away when I was twenty-two, about the same time as the birth of my second child. He had left me a small insurance policy, with which I purchased a used upright piano. I only remembered a few chords from my childhood days of piano lessons, but I began with those and tried to improve my playing. I would also rock my children and make up songs and sing to them.

"At that time I was attending the Christian Center Chapel in Claremont, California. The pastor was Tony Alward. He often would walk around the church saying, 'God, you are so great and you are so mighty. You are so great and you are so mighty.' Every service we attended we would hear him say those words.

"One morning, after I had put my children down for a midmorning nap, I sat down at the piano to have a time of worshiping the Lord. All of a sudden I began singing a song I had never sung before—'Great and mighty is the Lord our God, great and mighty is He,' and on and on. I picked up a paper napkin nearby and wrote it all down. I then began to cry and ask myself, 'What just happened here?'

"I called my pastor's wife, who led worship at the church, and told her about the song. She said, 'Well, let's introduce the song to the church.' They allowed me to teach the song to the choir, who sang it for the congregation. The church exploded with it! The message seemed to bring a sense of hope and assurance to the people. People began to tell me how they would sing the song at home and at work.

"The song traveled so swiftly that someone, not knowing who wrote the song, put it on an album of songs and listed it as 'author unknown.' It was a new time and things were happening fast in the Christian music community. It took quite an effort for me to get the copyright secured.

"Through a series of circumstances, I met Melva Lee who was a teacher at Christ for the Nations, a Christian college in Dallas, Texas. They had new songs introduced to them in their weekly chapel services. They would then put many of the songs on tapes and send them to many places around the country and to other nations. My song was put on one of those tapes and is now sung by millions of Christian worshipers in thousands of churches. It is now in hymnals.

"The most memorable time for me to hear the song performed was on television as I watched the opening of a Billy Graham Crusade."

Marlene taught voice for ten years at Christ for the Nations Institute. She has traveled extensively as a worship leader and singer. On one occasion she had the opportunity to sing at a gathering in the White House.

We can only imagine the might and power of our heavenly Father.
It is glorious to live under his wing of protection and provision in
our time of need. Indeed, "great and mighty is He."

GREAT IS THE LORD

VERSE

Great is the Lord,
He is holy and just.
By His power we trust in His love.
Great is the Lord,
He is faithful and true.
By His mercy He proves He is love.

CHORUS

Great is the Lord,
And worthy of glory!
Great is the Lord,
And worthy of praise!
Great is the Lord!
Now lift up your voice;
Now lift up your voice.
Great is the Lord!

A Dynamic Writing Duo

Great is the LORD, and greatly to be praised.

1 CHRONICLES 16:25

Michael W. Smith saw Debbie Davis walk by as he read a magazine during a visit to a record company in Nashville, Tennessee. It was love at first sight. He called his mother and said, "Mom, I just saw the girl I am going to marry!" "Really! Who is she?" his mother asked. His excited reply was, "I don't know. I'll have to call you back." He quickly learned her name from others in the building and went looking for her. He spotted her coming out of the ladies' room and readily introduced himself.

Michael was already into music in a big way, but little did he realize that he had just seen the young lady who would write songs with him, give birth to their five children, and be a devoted companion and mother.

Little did Debbie realize that she would become the wife of the man who would later become one of the most notable singers and songwriters in the world of praise and worship music, and that millions of people would sing the songs they would write together.

Following their meeting at the record company, Michael and Debbie began to date a couple of days later. Michael remembers, "We were engaged three and one half weeks later and were married four months afterward." During the engagement period, they wrote their first song together, Debbie the lyric and Michael the musical setting.

For more than two decades the Smiths have continued a music ministry that has extended throughout the United States and abroad—Debbie writing lyrics and Michael composing music, recording, singing in concerts from coast to coast, and writing more songs, many of which become favorites soon after they are presented. The Smiths, who have five children, are active in their church.

Debbie related the following story to me concerning one of their early efforts in songwriting:

"I always enjoyed being around the keyboard with Michael. Sometimes at night we would light a candle. We would often open the Bible and God would inspire our hearts with a particular passage of Scripture.

"We wrote many praise choruses and worship songs during these evening sessions. Although many of them were never used or heard by others, we greatly enjoyed writing them together. They were the expressions of our hearts, in response to the treasures we gleaned from God's Word.

> *Who shall not fear thee, O Lord, and glorify thy name? for thou only art holy: for all nations shall come and worship before thee . . .*
>
> REV. 15:4

"During one of those late-evening writing sessions in 1982, God led us to a particular passage of Scripture that we both thought would be the base for a good song. I wrote a few lines of the lyric as Michael was working on the music. We worked very closely together, and the words and the musical setting came together at the same time. We were delighted with the song God had given us, and Michael thought it was something that he would like to share with others, especially the people of the church where we attended at that time.

"Michael often led worship at the church, so during one of the services, he taught the song to the congregation. The congregation seemed greatly moved to a spirit of worship as they sang 'Great Is the Lord.'"

She continued, "I remember I was so overwhelmed as I heard that great crowd lifting their voices in praise as they sang our song. The massiveness of the people around me sounded like a large choir. I felt so blessed to be used in that way."

During those days Michael was working on his first album, *The Michael W. Smith Project,* and he decided to include "Great Is the Lord." Since the release of that album, the song has gone on to circle the globe again and again. It continues, year after year, to be among the favorite songs used in churches across America.

In this song we are reminded of several attributes of our heavenly Father: he is just, and our justifier; he is love, and he loved us before the foundation of the world; he is faithful, and how greatly we are sustained; he is holy, and we can only imagine but never quite comprehend the extent of his holiness.

"One becomes superstitious whenever the means of worship are permitted to eclipse the object of worship. A crucifix may supplant the Lord."

ANONYMOUS

HALLELUJAH

VERSE

Your love is amazing, steady and unchanging,
Your love is a mountain firm beneath my feet.
Your love is a myst'ry, how You gently lift me,
When I am surrounded, Your love carries me.

CHORUS

Hallelujah, hallelujah, hallelujah,
Your love makes me sing.
Hallelujah, hallelujah, hallelujah,
Your love makes me sing.

VERSE

Your love is surprising, I can feel it rising,
All the joy that's growing deep inside of me.
Ev'ry time I see You, all Your goodness shines through,
I can feel this God song rising up in me.

Brenton Brown | Brian Doerksen © Vineyard Songs (UK/EIRE)

An Untimely Announcement

Behold, what manner of love the Father hath bestowed upon us,
that we should be called the sons of God.

1 JOHN 3:1

In another story in this volume—for the song "Come, Now Is the Time to Worship"—you will find some very unusual and interesting biographical information about Brian Doerksen. So let me briefly tell you about Brenton Brown. He is a native of South Africa, who grew up with a passion for the guitar. He also studied law and politics as a college student in Cape Town.

His intellectual prowess gained him a Rhodes Scholarship to study for two years at Oxford University in England, beginning in 1996. Once there he joined the Vineyard Church and became very active in the music ministry of the church as a worship leader. While in England he met Brian Doerksen, who had moved there from Canada and was very active in ministry as a worship leader. Brian, older and more experienced, actually became a mentor and guide for Brenton.

Brown met a young lady, Jude, also from South Africa, who was to later become his wife. A short time after that they moved back to South Africa to seek help with some medical issues. They later moved to Malibu, California.

In the meantime Brian and his family had moved back to Canada, where he continued to pursue his ministry of songwriting and leading worship in many places all over the world. One day in February 2000, before he had married Jude, Brenton visited the Doerksen home in Canada. At this point I'll let Brian continue the story, just as he gave it to me in a recent interview.

"Sometimes single people don't entirely understand family life. We have six children, and Isaiah, our youngest son, about eight months old at the time, became very upset at something and began to cry. It was one of those days when my wife had reached her exasperation point, and she had brought Isaiah to me in the living room to see if I could comfort him.

"Brenton came rumbling into the room with an announcement, 'Brian! Brian! I have this wonderful idea for a song, but it doesn't have a chorus! I feel that it is a great song, something special, but I don't know how to finish it.' He starting playing and singing, 'Your love is amazing, steady and unchanging.' My first instinct was to say, 'Buddy, can't you tell that this is not a good time for that? I'm trying to comfort my son. I'm in the middle of family life, and you just don't really get it, do you?'

"Brenton continued to sing the first verse, fairly close to the way it is at present. When he finished the verse, he said, 'I have no idea what to do next.' So I said, 'Why don't you sing, "Hallelujah, hallelujah, hallelujah, Your love makes me sing," and then repeat that one more time?' His jaw dropped, and he protested, 'You can't sing a chorus with just the words "Hallelujah, Your love makes me sing"!' Then I said, 'The church needs some fresh songs about the love of God. The word *halle-lujah* is a God word. This God word, *hal-le-lu-jah*, is a word all about who God really is. It works the same in all languages.'

"Brenton walked out of the room. Later we discussed the song and tried different things for the next two days. I then told him, 'I know I thought of the chorus on the spur of the moment, but I really believe it needs to be that simple.'

"Then, together, we wrote a second verse. The word *God* in the second verse is a direct reference to the word *hallelujah* in the chorus. It is the love of God that makes us sing. While doing concerts all over the world, I sing that song and tell the story of how we wrote it, and how even in the midst of a unique situation we can still be inspired by the Lord and write such a song. When people hear the story, they seem to better understand the song and its real meaning."

When God extends his love through his Son, Jesus, we joyfully accept it. He then gives us a song, causing us to sing and make melody in our hearts to the Lord.

HALLELUJAH, PRAISE THE LAMB

CHORUS

Hallelujah, praise the Lamb.
Hallelujah, praise the Lamb.
My heart sings His praise again,
Hallelujah, praise the Lamb.

VERSE

From the moment man first disobeyed the Father,
We were then held captive by our sin.
The law of God demanded a sacrifice
Restoring to Himself His own again.

Dawn Thomas | Gary McSpadden | Pam Thum © 1984 Designer Music
(Admin BMG Music Publishing) /Lehsem Music, LLC
(Admin. Lehsem Music LLC)

Singing and Dancing in the Kitchen

I will bless the LORD at all times: his praise shall continually be in my mouth.

PSALM 34:1

At a very early age, Pam Thum began traveling and singing in the revival meetings of her parents, Bruce and Ruth Thum. She and her mom, who played several instruments, wrote songs together during her childhood.

"I remember when I was in my teen years, and still traveling with Mom and Dad, we were staying in an apartment owned by a church, in Miami, Florida. I had traveled my entire life, and I remembered that I had said good-bye to so many friends along the way—friends I probably would never see again here on the earth. A sadness came over me that was so heavy. I was normally a happy person, but I couldn't seem to handle this weight.

"I tried to pray, and it didn't seem to work. It was so overwhelming. I remember that my parents just didn't know what to do about my problem. It seemed so abnormal. When they went to sleep, I was still up. I went to the kitchen and began walking around in that little space.

"I remember hearing in my mind the words of David that I had read in the Psalms, 'I will bless the LORD at all times: his praise shall continually be in my mouth.' It took all my strength just to talk out loud, but I began to say, 'I love you,

Jesus.' Then I began to sing it. It was so hard to sing. As I was singing various phrases to the Lord, suddenly out of my mouth came 'Hallelujah! Praise the Lamb,' and on and on through what is now the chorus. The melody came with it.

"I then felt the weight lifting off of me. The heaviness left. I felt joy and strength stirring in me again. I sang that chorus again and again; it must have been for two hours. I was laughing and crying and dancing around the kitchen. The presence of God seemed to dispel all of the sadness. Strength and joy were back again! The following morning my parents had me share that chorus with the church, and they responded so joyfully."

Several years later Pam became a member of Gary McSpadden's team of songwriters. You will meet Gary in another story in this book—the song "Jesus, Lord to Me." Gary was a singer, songwriter, and music producer. Pam showed her chorus to Gary, who said, "You need verses to go with this chorus." Pam tried again and again to write some verses, but it never seemed to work. Finally, Gary said, "If it is all right with you, I would like to try to write some verses to this wonderful chorus." Pam said, "I would love for you to do so, because I want this to be a complete song."

Gary added, "I sat down one day and wrote verses that I thought would be good for the chorus. I took it in a completely different direction than Pam had first taken it. After I finished I took the verses to Dawn Thomas, another of our writers, and asked her to help write some music for the 'verses' section of the song. Pam already had the words and the music for the chorus. Dawn agreed to help, and so we wrote the music and then took the completed song back to Pam. She helped us make a few changes, but basically the song was complete."

Soon after that, "Hallelujah, Praise the Lamb" began to appear on album projects by singers such as the Talleys, the Brooklyn Tabernacle Choir, and Gary McSpadden, to name a few. Those recordings helped to spread the song around the United States. It was later sung by the one-thousand-voice choir of the Billy Graham Crusades, with the congregation joining in on a repeat of the chorus.

These days only the chorus of the song is universally sung by church congregations, worship gatherings, and revival campaigns.

As this song suggests, try singing to the Lord with your whole heart, not just with your voice—"singing and making melody in your heart to the Lord" (Eph. 5:19).

He Has Made Me Glad

VERSE

I will enter His gates with thanksgiving in my heart;
I will enter His courts with praise.
I will say this is the day that the Lord has made.
I will rejoice for He has made me glad.

CHORUS

He has made me glad;
He has made me glad;
I will rejoice for He has made me glad.
He has made me glad;
He has made me glad;
I will rejoice for He has made me glad.

A Mountain Girl's Triumph

This is the day which the LORD hath made; we will rejoice and be glad in it.

PSALM 118:24

In her childhood in the late 1920s, Leona Bruce and her family were "land poor" people who lived, much like the pioneers, in the Appalachian mountain range, with no plumbing or electricity. They grew their own food, which, in those mountains, came at a cost of hard labor.

Leona told me in 2001, "I worked long hours, along with my brothers and sisters and our parents, just to survive. At age thirteen I was one of eleven children. To make matters worse, my father was a strict disciplinarian who would severely discipline us for the smallest matter that caused him displeasure. As a small, sensitive child, I developed a spirit of fear that shaped my life. Our father, who never hugged us or displayed any affection toward us, once saw me sucking my thumb and threatened to cut it off with his razor. It frightened me almost beyond words.

"We often lacked proper clothes for those cruel winters in the mountains. My mother, a godly woman, was our only source of encouragement. Since my sisters

80

and I were older, to help her we would care for the babies who were coming one after the other. We loved that part of our work.

"After graduating from high school, in order to make a living, I made my way to the factories of Detroit, Michigan. I spent three years in the defense plants, and from there went on to college to train to be a beautician.

"I moved to California and, after a short engagement, married Robert Von Brethorst, with whom I had two children, a son and a daughter. Robert left us when the oldest was not yet three years of age. His only financial contribution to our survival was some rent money. I was once again thrown into a state of fear and depression, not knowing how I would be able to care for my children.

"My son became very ill, and during the sickness I bargained with God by saying, 'God, if you will heal my child, I'll give you the rest of my life.' The Lord healed my son, and I was delivered from the spirit of fear. Not long after that I was called into a ministry of prayer, which I still participate in to this day.

"After my children were grown, I began to write songs and poems and spend a great deal of time in prayer and fasting. One day, after reading 2 Chronicles 5:11–14, where the glory of the Lord came down into the midst of the children of Israel during the dedication of the temple, I prayed, 'Lord, if you would do that for a people who were still under the Old Testament law, what would happen if we had the Holy Spirit in our lives today?' I then said, 'Lord, I will enter your gates with thanksgiving in my heart and go into your courts with praise.'"

On Leona went until she had finished a song based on Psalm 100 and Psalm 118:24. She continued, "Shortly afterward, I sang the song to our Sunday school class at Bethany Chapel, where I was attending. As I did so, I felt that the whole of me was being lifted. My song has now gone around the world, and my provision has been far beyond anything I ever expected or dreamed."

Contrary to what has been reported, Leona never learned to play any kind of musical instrument. She told me that Doug Hamblin, an organist at the church, wrote the music out for her so that she might present it to a publisher. Maranatha Music published her song and has seen it used in an unusual manner, blessing the hearts of millions of Christians. The royalties Maranatha Music has sent to Leona have provided for much of her living expenses during the past quarter century. "He Has Made Me Glad" is her only published song.

In 2 Chronicles 5, when the children of Israel lifted their voices to praise and thank the Lord, then and only then did he manifest his glory in their presence.

HE IS EXALTED

VERSE

He is exalted;
The King is exalted on high,
I will praise Him.
He is exalted, forever exalted,
And I will praise His name.

CHORUS

He is the Lord,
Forever His truth shall reign.
Heaven and earth,
Rejoice in His holy name.
He is exalted;
The King is exalted on high.

"My Songs Are Like Children"

Thine, O LORD, is the greatness, and the power, and the glory, and the victory, and the majesty: for all that is in the heaven and in the earth is thine; thine is the kingdom, O LORD, and thou art exalted as head above all.

1 CHRONICLES 29:11

Twila Paris continues to write songs because, in her own words, "My songs are like children who will grow and expand and do things I could never do. They make their way around the world as they are being used for the purpose that God gave them. A song that was given to me in a time of worship is now offered back to him on a Sunday morning in a small church on a faraway island. 'He Is Exalted' has gone far beyond the people who know my name."

Twila, a PK, was born in Fort Worth, Texas, in 1958, into the home of evangelist Oren Paris and his wife, Inez. She grew up with music all around her, starting her singing experiences at the age of two in her dad's services. As she grew older, her dad, a pianist of extraordinary talent, began to teach her music and challenge her creativity. She wrote her first recorded song at age seventeen and included it on one of her albums at age twenty.

After finishing high school, Twila enrolled for one year in the discipleship program of Youth With A Mission (YWAM), thinking that she would enter college the following year. One year turned into two, and by then she was already writing and recording songs, so she continued in her music ministry.

Those thoughts brought us to the real reason for the interview, and so I asked Twila to share the circumstances surrounding the writing of "He Is Exalted."

"As was my custom, I was sitting at the piano in my parents' home worshiping the Lord for a period of time. I would usually start singing—one of my songs or a song written by someone else that happened to be meaningful at that particular point in my life. As I was there before God, 'He Is Exalted' was given to me by my heavenly Father. I recognized the moment and knew that this 'gift' from the Lord was something extra special. It was like taking dictation.

"I first sang 'He Is Exalted' in a Sunday service at the YWAM base in Arkansas. I became a worship leader there a number of years ago. The song was well tested before it was first recorded in 1985. Several years later I became aware that a lot of people in churches across the country seemed to know my song. It wasn't a big splash, but it gradually made its way from town to town.

"One day I was watching a network television news show, and the story being reported was of a religious nature. During their comments they cut away to a congregation singing 'He Is Exalted.' For several moments it was almost surreal. It took me a few seconds to realize, 'Hey, that's my song.'" She then added, "I hope I never get used to hearing my songs."

In the twenty years that Twila has been writing, the Lord has given her approximately two hundred songs, most of which have been recorded or published. This story space does not permit the many awards and accolades that came to Twila Paris and her songs. When she thinks of the ministry of songwriting the Lord has graciously given, her mind goes to the impact the songs have had on the world—and she is grateful.

She and her husband, Jack Wright, reside in Elm Springs, Arkansas, and continue their involvement with Youth With A Mission. On April 29, 2001, after sixteen years of marriage and many sincere prayers, God blessed their lives with their first child, Jack Paris Wright.

One of Twila's favorite verses of Scripture, the essence of her songwriting, is Romans 11:36, which says, "For of him, and through him, and to him, are all things: to whom be glory for ever."

He Is Here

He is here, hallelujah.
He is here, amen.
He is here, holy, holy.
I will bless His name again.
He is here, listen closely.
Hear Him calling out your name.
He is here, you can touch Him.
You will never be the same.

© 1990 Kirk Talley Music
   Kirk L. Talley

"I Had Trouble Stopping in Time"

For where two or three are gathered together in my name, there am I in the midst of them.

MATTHEW 18:20

Although Kirk Talley's name is synonymous with Southern Gospel music, he has made a tremendous contribution to the genre that we call praise and worship music. In addition to the song that is the subject of this story, he has written in that vein "Magnify Him" and "Triumphantly the Church Shall Rise." He is a singer, a songwriter, and a promoter of the contributions of other songwriters.

Talley's experiences are legendary, first as a member of a family singing group, the Talleys, then with a number of other touring groups, and as a soloist and songwriter. The major portion of his Christian influence will forever be his songwriting—the blending of a biblical message with a beautiful melody. When the voice of Kirk Talley is silent and still, his songs will live on in the hearts of Christians as they continue to worship God using his creations.

Kirk was born into a musical family in Whitesburg, Tennessee. He related to me in an interview, "My dad was a song leader and my brother was a pianist, so we sang locally at our little church."

Kirk came to know the Lord at age thirteen at his home church. He said, "After the preacher had given his sermon, he gave an invitation for people to receive Christ. The Lord spoke to my heart, and I knew I needed to trust Christ as my Savior, and that is what I did."

I asked Kirk to give me the story behind "He Is Here," and the story follows.

"In 1990, I had been in Nashville, Tennessee, for a weeklong convention. A number of wonderful things happened that week that were very impressive to me. Then very early on Sunday morning, with the victories of the week still fresh in my mind, I began to drive toward a location in Georgia where I was to sing in the evening church service.

"As I made my way down the interstate on that beautiful morning, I began talking to the Lord, thanking him for all that he had done—for the things I had learned the past week—and for the moving of the Holy Spirit in our lives. Suddenly a song began coming to me. I had trouble stopping in time to get all that the Lord was giving to me. I had to write very rapidly. It was all finished in about ten minutes.

"I stopped on the way at a church were a group of my friends were to sing during a morning service. Before the service began, I gathered the group around me at the piano and said, 'I want you to hear something that I just wrote.' I played and sang the song for them. They loved it! I knew right then that it was a good song, but I had no idea that churches would soon pick it up and begin singing it.

"At that time I was singing with the Talleys, a group made up of Roger and Debra Talley, my brother and sister-in-law, and myself. We were about to make an album on the Word label. 'He Is Here' was put on that album. That year, 1991, it won a Dove Award for Song of the Year."

Since that time it has been placed in at least one major hymnal and has become a favorite of audiences all across the United States.

Kirk continues to crisscross the United States, singing his songs and occasionally writing a new one. He can often be seen on national television programs.

Our lives would be much happier, fuller, and more victorious if we would keep in mind that he is really here—all of the time.

The Heart of Worship

VERSE

When the music fades,
All is stripped away,
And I simply come,
Longing just to bring
Something that's of worth
That will bless Your heart.

CHORUS

I'm coming back
To the heart of worship,
And it's all about You,
All about You, Jesus.
I'm sorry, Lord,
For the thing I've made it,
When it's all about You;
All about You, Jesus.

VERSE

I'll bring You more than a song,
For a song in itself
Is not what You have required.
You search much deeper within
Through the way things appear;
You're looking into my heart.

No Band to Lead Us

And I, brethren, when I came to you, came not with excellency of speech or of wisdom,
declaring unto you the testimony of God. For I determined not to know any thing among you,
save Jesus Christ, and him crucified.

1 CORINTHIANS 2:1–2

Following is Matt Redman's own record of the writing of his famous "The Heart of Worship":

"A few years back in our church, we realized some of the things we thought were helping us in our worship were actually hindering us. They were throwing us off the scent of what it means to really worship. We had always set aside lots of time in our meetings for worshiping God through music. But it began to dawn on us that we'd lost something. The fire that used to characterize our worship had somehow grown cold.

"In some ways, everything looked great. We had some wonderful musicians and a good-quality sound system. There were lots of new songs coming through too. But somehow we'd started to rely on these things a little too much, and they'd become distractions. Where once people would enter in no matter what, they would now wait to see what the band was like first, how good the sound was, or whether we were 'into' the songs chosen.

"Mike Pilavachi, the pastor, decided on a pretty drastic course of action: we'd strip everything away for a season, just to see where our hearts were. So the very next Sunday when we turned up at church, there was no sound system to be seen and no band to lead us. The new approach was simple—we weren't going to lean so hard on those outward things anymore. Mike would say, 'When you come through the doors of the church on Sunday, what are you bringing as your offering to God? What are you going to sacrifice today?'

"At first the meetings were a bit awkward: there were long periods of silence, and there wasn't too much singing going on. But we soon began to learn how to

> *I will praise the LORD according to his righteousness: and will sing praise to the name of the LORD most high.*
>
> PS. 7:17

bring heart offerings to God without any external trappings we'd grown used to. Stripping everything away, we slowly started to rediscover the heart of worship.

"After a while, the worship band and the sound system reappeared, but now it was different. The songs of our hearts had caught up with the songs of our lips. Out of this season, I reflected on where we had come to as a church and wrote 'The Heart of Worship.'"

The song is a confession that we have made worship something other than a recognition of the majesty and deity of Christ himself. And so we return to the real "heart" of worship—Jesus Christ the Lord. Matt's songs have been recorded by some of the leading worship leaders and Christian recording artists in contemporary Christian music.

Two Christian organizations that hold a massive amount of Redman's attention and with which he travels a great deal are Passion, an American-based ministry to Christian college and university students, led by Louie Giglio, and Soul Survivor, a youth-oriented ministry with offices in seven countries, headed by Mike Pilavachi. Their main headquarters are in West Sussex, England. Matt also related, "My real passion lies with Heartofworship.com, a training resource for lead worshipers."

The most important aspect of our worship should be the giving of our complete attention to praising and glorifying our heavenly Father. For it is in him, and him alone, that we live and move and have our being.

Our worship here is a mere prelude to the great praise service in the future when we stand in God's presence. But sometimes when we join with others in vibrant worship, we experience an echo of paradise on this earth.

DENNIS FISHER

HERE I AM TO WORSHIP

VERSE

Light of the world,
You stepped down into darkness,
Opened my eyes, let me see
Beauty that made this heart adore You;
Hope of a life spent with You.

CHORUS

So here I am to worship,
Here I am to bow down,
Here I am to say that You're my God.
And You're altogether lovely,
Altogether worthy,
Altogether wonderful to me.

VERSE

King of all days
Oh so highly exalted,
Glorious in heaven above.
Humbly You came to the earth You created,
All for love's sake became poor.

"I Pushed It Out of My Mind"

At the name of Jesus every knee should bow, of things in heaven, and things in earth, and things under the earth; and that every tongue should confess that Jesus Christ is Lord, to the glory of God the Father.

PHILIPPIANS 2:10–11

Tim is a man most definitely running in the right direction. Behind these fresh new songs is a faithful heart." That was said of Tim Hughes by his good friend Matt Redman.

Tim Hughes was born in High Wycomee, a small town just outside of London, England. Tim said, "Because my dad was a pastor, I grew up in church. I always kinda believed in God, but a very significant thing happened for me when I was eleven years old. I went to a conference and had the opportunity to observe people who were very passionate about singing. It dawned on me that they weren't singing *about* someone or something, but they were singing *to* someone. That really challenged me. I made a commitment to take Jesus as my Lord and Savior.

"It was during my sixteenth year that the worship pastor at my dad's church asked me to get involved in the music ministry, playing guitar and singing background vocals. I think he saw a potential and wanted to encourage me. It was a safe place to learn. As I grew older, I began to lead worship in the youth group and occasionally in the church services. Then the worship pastor moved to another location and I took over the leading of a large portion of the worship in church."

I asked Tim to tell me about the writing of his famous song "Here I Am to Worship." Following is his story:

"I actually wrote the song while I was at Sheffield University. During that time I had been thinking and meditating on the cross. I began to read several scriptures but seemed to concentrate on Philippians chapter 2—about Christ's humility and how he took upon himself the attitude of a servant and how he humbled himself and became obedient to death on a cross. I was challenged with the wonder of who God really is and his sacrifice for us.

"I sat down in my room and began worshiping him as a response to those thoughts. It was then that the initial inspiration of the song came. I began, 'Light of the world, You stepped down into darkness . . .' and on and on until I had two verses finished. I then began to try to write a chorus that I thought would be an appropriate response to the verses. I tried and tried but could not finish the song. I didn't know where to take it from there. I became so frustrated that I put the song away and pushed it out of my mind.

> *Give unto the LORD the glory due unto his name: bring an offering, and come before him: worship the LORD in the beauty of holiness.*
>
> I CHRON. 16:29

"About six months later I was in my room worshiping when I thought of the verses again and said to myself, 'I really do need to finish that song.' I began flipping through ideas of melodies and lyrics that I had stored on a mini disc player. I came across a melody that I had saved, which sounded quite simple, and yet the feeling I sensed as I played it seemed to complement my verses perfectly. I wanted the chorus to be a response to our Lord's amazing sacrifice.

"I began to ask, 'How are we going to respond to that great happening? Do we bow down? Do we scream out? How do we say, "You are altogether lovely—you are worthy"? Sometimes we don't know how to respond even though we desperately want to. As I finished the song, I finally felt as if the pieces had all come together and it all was complete."

Tim recorded "Here I Am to Worship" on his album of the same title. The song won a Dove Award in 2003 as the Inspirational Recorded Song of the Year.

Tim Hughes lives in Watford, England, and at the time of the interview was engaged to be married very soon.

Truly, when you and I see Christ in all of his matchless love, expressed though his great sacrifice on Calvary, we, too, will say with Tim, "Here I am to worship and bow down." Christ will become to us "altogether lovely, altogether worthy, and altogether wonderful."

*The whole person, with all his senses,
with both mind and body, needs to be involved
in genuine worship.*

JERRY KERNS

HERE WE ARE

CHORUS

Here we are in Your presence,
Lifting holy hands to You.
Here we are praising Jesus,
For the things He's brought us through.

VERSE

I don't have the words to tell You how I feel;
I just don't know what I can say.
I'm not worthy to speak Your holy name,
Yet You tell me You love me just the same.

VERSE

I never thought that it could be this way,
And I never thought I'd be the one.
But You found me dying in my sin,
And You looked at me with love and took me in.

© 1978 Going Holm Music
Dallas Holm

When Contemporary Wasn't "Cool"

I will praise thee, O LORD, with my whole heart; I will shew forth all thy marvellous works.

PSALM 9:1

Dallas Holm was the first contemporary artist to win Dove Awards for Song of the Year, Songwriter of the Year, and Male Vocalist of the Year. He was born to Howard and Viola Holm, in St. Paul, Minnesota, in 1948. One of his songs, "Rise Again," has set chart records that have not been surpassed for more than a quarter century and counting. However, this particular story concerns another of his very popular compositions.

Although Dallas was raised by Christian parents, by age sixteen he was playing in rock bands for dances and parties that they could never approve of. But, Dallas said, "when I became a Christian, along with the commitment of my life to the Lord came a commitment of my music—I would only write for him."

He also said, "My interest as a young Christian was in contemporary music. I

94

felt that there must be some way to use drums and electric guitars to serve the Lord. At that time the term *contemporary Christian music* had not even been invented, but I remember going to jails, rest homes, street corners, and small conservative churches in the St. Paul area, to present the 'praise' music of our small band. On more than one occasion, our engagements were cut short in churches by the pastors who would graciously explain why we couldn't—or shouldn't—do that kind of music in church. To borrow an expression from our country music friends, 'Dallas was contemporary when contemporary wasn't "cool,"' especially in some areas."

In 1970, David Wilkerson, an evangelist who wrote *The Cross and the Switchblade*, asked Dallas to join him in his youth crusade ministry as soloist and song leader. By 1976, they had formed a band, Dallas Holm and Praise, as part of the Wilkerson team.

I asked Dallas to tell me how he came to write "Here We Are," and the following is his response:

"I consider 'Here We Are' the first praise and worship song that I consciously wrote. Although a lot of my music falls into the genre of praise and worship, I really didn't think of it in those terms.

"I was actually doing a radio interview in Carlinville, Illinois, in 1974, when the disc jockey asked me a couple of questions that were kinda out of left field: 'Where did music come from, and what should be the primary function of music?' As I thought about my answers, I realized that a lot of my music was evangelistic or testimonial, yet I said, 'The primary purpose of music is to bring praise, worship, and honor to the Lord. It is something that pleases God.'

"Sometime later, as I thought on those things, I prayed, 'Lord, I want to write something that you want to hear. I come from a testimonial and communicative base in my music thus far, but I want to say words and write songs that please you.' I began the process of writing another song, and the outcome was 'Here We Are.'

"That was a big moment in my musical life. It opened a doorway of musical expression for me, which I go through occasionally and write songs just for the Lord—not for people."

In 1976, "Here We Are" appeared on *Tell 'em Again*, the second album of Dallas Holm and Praise. It got a lot of radio play and appeared in several publications, and in the process made its way around the United States and into other countries.

Dallas summarizes his goal in life thus: "When I stand before the Lord, it won't be how many records I've sold, or how many people saw me in concert. What we do for him is never as important as who we are 'in' him. That's all he's measuring."

There are times when we consciously recognize that
we are in the presence of God, but lest we forget, because of his
omnipresence we are always and forever where he is.

High and Lifted Up

VERSE

Jesus said if I be lifted up,
I will surely draw all men unto Me.
So as Moses raised the serpent in the wilderness,
So high and lifted up must Jesus be.

VERSE

See Him on the cross, His eyes of love
Looking down on all who stood and watched His shame.
As they mocked Him and they scourged Him
God turned His eyes away,
While high and lifted up He took the blame.

CHORUS

High and lifted up, the loving Savior,
High and lifted up for all to see.
Reconciling God and man forever,
High and lifted up on Calvary.

© 1993 Homeward Bound Music
Dianne Wilkinson

"I Began to Paint Word Pictures"

And I, if I be lifted up from the earth, will draw all men unto me.
JOHN 12:32

Occasionally a song comes along that crosses all boundaries and will not be confined to one genre of Christian music, contemporary praise and worship, traditional, or Southern Gospel. Such is this Dianne Wilkinson song. She began her music career at age twelve, and through her life span as a wife, church pianist, faithful church member, Sunday school teacher, and businesswoman, she has been a dedicated servant of Christ.

Blytheville, Arkansas, is home for Dianne. She was born there in 1944. Her grandmother strongly suggested that she start taking piano lessons when Dianne was only eight years old. She did so, and progressed so rapidly that she was soon playing the piano for church services, and continues to do so. The church members certainly know of her fame as a songwriter, but they love her mostly for her faithful service to her church family. She told me, "I have always had a music ministry in my church, and that is my calling."

Early in Dianne's songwriting career, the Lord led her into serious study of the Word of God. This has resulted in the writing of songs that were true to the Word of God, and in quality teaching for her Sunday school class.

In the following twenty years, Dianne wrote close to three hundred songs. Some of them have become standards—songs such as "We Shall See Jesus" and "Boundless Love," seemingly favorites of all who hear or sing them. Thousands of artists have put her songs on their albums, tapes, and CDs.

One day as Dianne sat in church, the pastor preached on John 3:14, where God said, "And as Moses lifted up the serpent in the wilderness, even so must the Son of man be lifted up."

Let's let Dianne finish her story:

"I began to think about the cross, and how Christ was lifted up, giving his life for each of us that we might be saved. I also began to think of how he would be lifted up a second time, not on a cross, but in all of his glory. As I began to write, I wanted to contrast the two, and so I began to paint word pictures. After I developed the two scenes in my mind, it didn't take long to put it on paper.

"I showed the song to pianist Roger Bennett, who graciously informed me that it still needed some work. Roger felt that the melody that I had written for the chorus would be difficult to harmonize. I was hesitant at first because I usually didn't rewrite after I have finished a song. But I prayed about it and thought, *Lord, maybe we do need to put a tweak here and there.* I only slightly changed the first line or two of the chorus.

"The Cathedrals made the decision to record it. In fact, they chose my song 'High and Lifted Up' as the title song for their new project. Lari Goss, who wrote 'Cornerstone,' and who had done all of the orchestrations and produced the complete work, was present in the studio during the recording. It was a class act from beginning to end. The following year it received the *Singing News* Fan Award as Song of the Year."

Tom Fettke has arranged this song for choirs, and it has been presented all over the United States to audiences who were thrilled and spiritually lifted up. It is indeed a powerful worship song.

"High and Lifted Up" will help you to place Christ in his rightful place in your heart and mind.

His Name Is Wonderful

His name is Wonderful,
His name is Wonderful,
His name is Wonderful,
Jesus my Lord.
He is the mighty King,
Master of everything,
His name is Wonderful,
Jesus my Lord.

(BRIDGE)
He's the Great Shepherd,
The rock of all ages,
Almighty God is He.

Bow down before Him,
Love and adore Him,
His name is Wonderful,
Jesus my Lord.

A Crooked Halo and a Rare Christmas Day

For unto us a child is born, unto us a son is given: and the government shall be upon his shoulder: and his name shall be called Wonderful, Counsellor, The mighty God, The everlasting Father, The Prince of Peace.

ISAIAH 9:6

I have interviewed scores of songwriters, but few interviews have been more enjoyable than the one in the late 1980s with Audrey Mieir of California. She has since passed away, but her songs live on in the hearts of Christians everywhere. She was not only a great composer but also a marvelous organist, pianist, and choral director.

Audrey Mieir directed very talented choral groups, such as the Phil Kerr Singers, and she made herself available to small churches as well. It was in a small California church that her most famous song was written. It all happened on Christmas Day, one of those rare Christmases that came on Sunday. Audrey was forty-three years of age at that time.

As the children prepared for their annual Christmas pageant, the angel's halo was a little crooked and the shepherds had their pants rolled up under their dads' bathrobes. But something wonderful was about to take place. A beautiful song was soon to be born. Following is Audrey Mieir's story just as she gave it to me:

"We wanted to do something special in our little church, Bethel Union Church in Duarte, California. The pastor was my brother-in-law [Dr. Luther Mieir]. We were using the young people in a Christmas presentation. Mary was a teenage girl, and the angels were young boys. The baby was a doll.

"The whole place smelled of pine boughs, which we used to decorate the church. The atmosphere was charged. I so often have thought that I could hear the rustling of angels' wings. It seemed that the whole room was filled with the presence of the angels of God.

"I looked down at the little children, and they were sitting there with open mouths, thinking, as they listened to the soft organ music. I looked around at the older people, and they were wiping tears away, remembering many other Christmases gone by.

> *If any man speak, let him speak as the oracles of God; if any man minister, let him do it as of the ability which God giveth: that God in all things may be glorified through Jesus Christ, to whom be praise and dominion for ever and ever. Amen.*
>
> I PET. 4:11

"The pastor stood up and slowly lifted his hands toward heaven and said, 'His name is Wonderful!' Those words electrified me. I immediately began writing in the back of my Bible. As I wrote, I was thinking that God had something he wanted said. I wrote a simple chorus and sang it that night for the young people around the piano. They sang it immediately. It wasn't hard for them to learn. I never dreamed that it would go any further, but it has traveled around the world in many languages."

Audrey said of the writing of this song that she considered herself only a channel and not otherwise involved. She gave God all of the praise and glory for using her to give the world such a praise chorus.

One day, sometime later, she met music publisher Tim Spencer, who told her that she had written a good song but that it needed a bridge. At that time she didn't know what he meant. He explained to her that she could cause the song to be much more of a blessing with an extension to the chorus she had written.

She had been on her way to lunch when she met Spencer. While still in the restaurant's booth, during lunch, she opened her Bible and went over some names of Christ in the concordance and wrote them down on a napkin. Later, in her office, she finished the song.

Audrey Mieir was born in Pennsylvania in 1916. She began her songwriting career at age sixteen. How thankful we should be that God chose to use her talents to praise him with this simple and powerful song.

Why not make this song meaningful in your life today?
Make the Lord Jesus Christ your great Shepherd, to lead your
every step, the Rock on which you rest secure, and the Master of
every area of your life. He is truly our almighty King.

Without worship, we go about miserable.

A. W. TOZER

HOLY GROUND

VERSE

As I walked through the door, I sensed His presence,
And I knew this was the place where love abounds.
For this is a temple, Jehovah God abides here,
We are standing in His presence on holy ground.

CHORUS

We are standing on holy ground,
And I know that there are angels all around.
Let us praise Jesus now,
We are standing in His presence
On holy ground.

VERSE

In His presence there is joy beyond measure,
And at His feet peace of mind can still be found.
If you have a need, I know He has the answer;
Reach out and claim it, child,
You're standing on holy ground.

"No Sir, but I'm Fixin' To"

But now in Christ Jesus ye who sometimes were far off are made nigh by the blood of Christ.
EPHESIANS 2:13

Geron Davis related the following unusual story about his song "Holy Ground:"

"When I was nineteen years of age, my dad was pastor of a church in Savannah, Tennessee. The church had progressed and grown to the point that a new sanctuary was needed. When we were about two months from the completion of a beautiful new church auditorium, my dad asked, 'Son, would you write a song for us to sing during the first service in our new building?' I replied, 'Okay, Dad.' Well, a couple of weeks went by, and I had not written the song. My dad asked, 'Son, how about it? Do you have a song for us?' I said, 'No, Dad, but I'll write one.'

"I was busy traveling from place to place, singing with some of the young people from our church. But Dad was insistent; he desperately wanted me to write the song for the opening of the new building. He kept bugging me. I was like, 'Dad, just chill out; I'll write a song.'

"Well, Saturday night came, the night before the first service in the new building, and I still had not written a song. We had worked all day at the church, getting everything ready. It wasn't a large church, only a couple hundred members, but people were there working, putting last-minute touches on everything.

"After all of the church members had gone, and only Dad, Mom, and I were left, we began to check all of the Sunday school rooms and the offices, making sure that those areas of the church complex were in readiness for the big day. My dad turned to me and asked, 'Do you have a song for us?' I used a good ol' Southern term and said, 'No sir, but I'm fixin' to.'

> *Enter into his gates with thanksgiving, and into his courts with praise: be thankful unto him, and bless his name.*
>
> Ps. 100:4

"I went into the new sanctuary, dimmed the lights, and sat down at the new grand piano. I began to think, *What do we want to say when we come into this building tomorrow to have a service for the first time?* I began to hum a bit and softly sing some lyrics that were coming to me. As I began to write the lyrics down, they kept coming about as fast as I could write. Within fifteen minutes I had finished the entire song.

"Someone asked me later, 'Did you realize that you had written something powerful?' I replied, 'Are you kidding? I was nineteen years old, it was midnight, and I wanted to get to bed.' I was too young to recognize the greatness of what God had done. I was just happy the song was finished.

"Early the next morning, I taught my song to my brother, Jeff, seventeen, and sister, Alyson, eleven, who often sang with me. We sang it for the opening church service.

"My dad was happy because I had written a song for us to sing. My mom cried because she thought her kids never sounded better. The congregation responded unbelievably to 'Holy Ground.' I said to myself, 'Well, it's a highly emotional day.' It was our first Sunday in the new building, and we appreciated what had happened, but we had no idea what would really happen to the song over the coming years. Even so, the events of the morning made for a memorable birth for my song."

Geron, Jeff, and Alyson continued to sing "Holy Ground," launching it on its flight around the world. It grew in popularity, even to the point that it was used during the funeral of President Bill Clinton's mother. Barbara Streisand, who was in attendance at the funeral, was so taken by the song, she recorded it and put it on her next CD. It shows no signs of slowing down as it becomes one of the most popular and well-known Christian songs in the world.

The goal that all of us should strive to reach is to live in such a way as to recognize that the place whereon we often stand is "holy ground," the place where God can meet with us and teach us his ways. He is with us, and in his presence there is fullness of joy. Live today as if you are truly standing on holy ground.

A glimpse of God will save you.
To gaze at Him will sanctify you.

MANLEY BEASLEY

HOLY IS THE LORD

VERSE

We stand and lift up our hands,
For the joy of the Lord is our strength.
We bow down and worship Him now;
How great how awesome is He.

(PRE-CHORUS)

And together we sing,
Ev'ryone sing,

CHORUS

Holy is the Lord God Almighty;
The earth is filled with His glory.
Holy is the Lord God Almighty;
The earth is filled with His glory,
The earth is filled with His glory.

(BRIDGE)

It is rising up all around;
It's the anthem of the Lord's renown.
It's rising up all around;
It's the anthem of the Lord's renown.

"I Was Floored, Right There in the Grass"

Holy, holy, holy, is the LORD of hosts: the whole earth is full of his glory.

ISAIAH 6:3

As noted in another story in this volume—"Forever"—in a November 2006 *Time* magazine article, Belinda Luscumbe estimated that more people were regularly singing songs written by Chris Tomlin than any other songwriter in the world.

Louie Giglio, founder and director of the Passion Conferences for college-age young people, was instrumental in the birthing of the worship song "Holy Is the Lord." While flying from Waco, Texas, to Atlanta, Georgia, in 1997, the Lord spoke to Giglio's heart about starting this national ministry to students. Thousands of young people flock to these meetings. Chris Tomlin is one of the major worship leaders.

In an interview in 2005, Chris told me the following story about the writing of "Holy Is the Lord":

"I was reading Isaiah chapter 6 in my home during a devotional time. As I read in verse 3, 'Holy is the LORD of hosts: the whole earth is full of his glory,' I picked up my guitar and began to sing those words. Those lines and the melody that came to me were all that I had.

"Sometime later—the year was 2003—I was preparing to lead worship at a Passion Conference that was to be held on a large ranch outside of Dallas, Texas. I sensed that God was putting this song, though incomplete, on my heart for this particular meeting. They were expecting between twenty and thirty thousand people for that conference.

"Louie Giglio, who I sometimes write songs with, and I had gotten together for a weekend. I said, 'Louie, I have this song, "Holy Is the Lord," and I feel that it is for the upcoming Passion Conference.' He was in the throes of planning for the meetings. After I sang the chorus for him, he began to give me a number of ideas that were in his heart. Among other things, he helped me with the phrase, 'It's rising up all around. It's the anthem of the Lord's renown.'

"I took his suggestions and ran with them. Although I was having some questions in my mind, I basically felt that this song was from the Lord and should be used for the meetings. I had never played it completely through at that time, and I really didn't know if it was a good song.

"I arrived at the Passion Conference and found that I was to follow a preacher named John Piper, a gifted communicator and writer. I was to lead worship following his message. While he was on the stage speaking, I was behind the platform on my knees in the grass. I was praying, 'Lord, I want to lead these people in the right way, with the right songs. You just show me what to do.'

"John Piper walked onto the stage, took the microphone in his hand, and said, 'Students, God has put a message for you on my heart. It is from Isaiah chapter 6—"Holy, holy, holy, is the LORD of hosts: the whole earth is full of his glory." ' That floored me, right there in the grass. I thought, *God put a song in my heart two months ago. He knew I will follow John Piper, and he put the same message on both our hearts.* At that moment it was confirmed in my heart that I was to use that song. We played it for that day, but it is a song for all days. It seems to be a repeating anthem of heaven."

When you and I see God, through his Word, in all of his holiness—as Isaiah saw him—we, too, will say, "Woe is me! for I am undone; because I am a man of unclean lips, and I dwell in the midst of a people of unclean lips: for mine eyes have seen the King, the LORD of hosts" (Isa. 6:5).

HOLY SPIRIT, THOU ART WELCOME

CHORUS

Holy Spirit, Thou art welcome in this place.
Holy Spirit Thou art welcome in this place.
Omnipotent Father of mercy and grace,
Thou art welcome in this place.

VERSE

Lord, in Thy presence there's healing divine.
No other power can save Lord but Thine.
Holy Spirit, Thou art welcome in this place.
Thou art welcome in this place.

VERSE

Fill all the hungry and empty within;
Restore us, oh Father, revive us again.
Holy Spirit, Thou art welcome in this place.
Thou art welcome in this place.

David Huntsinger | Dottie Rambo ©1977 John T. Benson Publishing Co. (ASCAP) / Bridge Building Music, Inc. (BMI) (Administered by Brentwood-Benson Music Publishing, Inc.)

"What Song Were You Whistling?"

Cast me not away from thy presence; and take not thy holy spirit from me.

PSALM 51:11

David Huntsinger grew up in Los Angeles, California. His parents had moved there from Indianapolis, Indiana, in 1955, when David was only ten days old. When he was eleven years of age, his parents bought a piano from their family doctor for sixty-five dollars. David said, "I had never known that I was interested in music at all, but with the coming of the piano, suddenly the interest was there. I was in love with it! I played constantly." Within a year David was playing at church services. This went on until he graduated from high school.

David became a Christian in an Assembly of God in Norwalk, California. Music was extremely important to the congregation, and it ranged from traditional church music to that of Ralph Carmichael and Audrey Mieir. One day his mother bought a very early recording of the Rambos, and David played it over and over. He said, "As a kid, I liked their music."

David attended the University of California at Long Beach for two years, after which he began playing piano for the Rambos—Dottie, Buck, and Reba. He had been playing for a group called the Monarchs. He was recommended by Andrae Crouch, who had seen David playing piano on television. Crouch said, "I've seen this kid on TV, and I don't know his name, but he's really good." The necessary contacts were made, and David was soon playing for the Rambos. He continued with them for three years.

Huntsinger said, "I loved observing the songwriting of Dottie Rambo." He worked with Reba (Rambo) McGuire on a record project called *Lady*, which contained a number of her songs. It was a number one album for an extended time.

David and Dottie together wrote a very popular children's musical, *Down by the Creek Bank*. It was ironic, because Dottie's songwriting started by a creek bank when she was a small child. You can learn more of her early life in the stories of her songs that appear in this volume.

While David was with the Rambos, Dottie would often watch the television ministry of Rex Humbard in Akron, Ohio. She noticed that Reverend Humbard would open his program with "Holy Spirit, thou art welcome in this place." She remarked to David, "That would be a good title for a song. Let's write one."

David told me, "I remember that we were on their bus, and Dottie wrote the lyric very quickly. I then began to work on the music. I said to her, 'I think it would be good to have a verse.' I had already been thinking of a melody. Dottie then wrote an additional lyric. It all happened, initially, in an hour or two at the most. On the Rambo's next record, they included 'Holy Spirit, Thou Art Welcome.' We also began to use it in the concerts. It took off very quickly. It was published in sheet music and in a choral arrangement and began to be sung very widely in churches.

"Not long after the song was written, I went to Canada to play a concert. While at the airport picking up my luggage, I heard a gentleman nearby whistling a tune. I listened long enough to be sure that he was whistling the tune I thought he was. I then broke into his music and engaged him in a bit of conversation. I asked, 'Sir, I am interested to know the name of the song you were whistling.' He said, '"Holy Spirit, Thou Art Welcome." We sing it at our church.' I said, 'I wrote that song with Dottie Rambo.' He looked at me like, *No way!* That was the first time I had heard anyone outside our concerts sing—or whistle—the song after we wrote it. That experience I will never forget. The song has now gone around the world."

I love "Holy Spirit, Thou Art Welcome" because it addresses the blessed third person of the Trinity, the heavenly Guest, who has taken up his abode in the hearts of those who know Christ as Lord and Savior. He is our Comforter, our Guide, and our Teacher.

HOSANNA

Hosanna, hosanna,
Hosanna in the highest!
Hosanna, hosanna,
Hosanna in the highest!

CHORUS

Lord, we lift up Your name
With hearts full of praise;
Be exalted, oh Lord my God.
Hosanna in the highest!

VERSE

Glory, glory,
Glory, to the King of kings!
Glory, glory,
Glory, to the King of kings!

Nothing Has Changed

Hosanna; Blessed is he that cometh in the name of the Lord.

MARK 11:9

Very often, when I talk with songwriters, I hear statements such as, "I was reading the Scriptures in my devotions," or "As I read the Scriptures, a very wonderful phrase just leaped off the page," or "As I read that passage of Scripture, I was blown away!" It is so refreshing that many of these writers are moved and inspired by the Word of God to pen our worship songs. This story is about a particular, very meaningful word from the New Testament.

Carl Tuttle, who for many years has lived in California, was born in Natick, Massachusetts, in 1953. He was introduced to the world of music in high school while participating in school plays. While still in high school, he began playing the guitar and has become an accomplished musician and singer.

Carl came to know the Lord at the age of twelve. By this time his family had moved to California. His older sister, a dedicated Christian, invited Carl to a Sunday school picnic, something he had never heard of prior to that moment. He told me, "It was there that I came into contact with Protestant Christians for the first time in my life." One of those persons was John Wimber, former keyboardist for the Righteous Brothers, and he had been saved two years earlier. Wimber had led Carl's sister to the Lord prior to that time.

During Carl's teen years, he began to hone his skills as a musician and to write songs. He was influenced by Ralph Carmichael, an outstanding songwriter and orchestra leader. Then, at age twenty-three, he became the worship leader of a church started in his sister's home.

Carl was later involved in the worship ministry of the influential Vineyard Christian Fellowship of Anaheim, California. John Wimber was pastor of the church at that time and often joined with Carl in songwriting ventures. Carl had the following to say about the composing of "Hosanna":

"I was in the living room of my home, and I picked up my guitar and began to play around with some chords. All the while I had a picture of this scene in my mind—Christ on a donkey making his way into Jerusalem while people threw palm branches in his path and shouted, 'Hosanna!' *Hosanna* was a word of adoration and praise, but it also had a deeper meaning—recognizing this one as Deliverer or Savior. Soon a melody and the lyrics came together. Actually, it all happened in about five minutes. I don't remember changing a single thing about it from that moment forward.

"For some reason, I had a strong feeling in my heart that this song would be widely used. I had been involved with music for quite some time, and I remember thinking, *This song will become well-known.*

"I called the gentleman who was leading Vineyard Music at that time and said, 'I think I've got something here.' I played it for him over the phone, and he said, 'Put it on tape and send it right away.' The next thing I knew, we were recording it and it was on its way. That was in 1984. It became the title song for the album on which it was placed."

"Hosanna" is now sung in other countries of the world and has been translated into many languages.

Carl, at the time of this writing, is the worship leader and outreach director of Faith Community Church in Thousand Palms, California.

The next time you sing "Hosanna," remember that we not only lift up his name, but we recognize him as and thank him for being our Savior!

How Excellent Is Thy Name

How excellent is Thy name, O Lord;
How excellent is Thy name.
Heaven and earth together proclaim,
How excellent is Thy name.
How excellent is Thy name, O Lord;
How excellent is Thy name.
Heaven and earth together proclaim,
How excellent is Thy name.

VERSE

I look into the midnight blue
And see the work You've done;
Your children raise a perfect praise,
While enemies hold their tongue.
Creation shows Your splendor,
Your reigning majesty,
And yet I find You take the time
To care for one like me.

Longing for Lyrics for My Music

O LORD our Lord, how excellent is thy name in all the earth!

PSALM 8:1

Dick and Melodie Tunney have a wide variety of musical interests in ministry, as duet performers, solo artists, producers, arrangers, composers, and studio musicians. They met while singing in Truth, a touring music ensemble. During those days, Mel began to seriously try her hand at songwriting, with at least one of her songs being recorded by Truth, which was a great encouragement.

One day while at a particular church, Dick came upon Mel in one of the church classrooms, sitting at a piano, laboring over a composition she had started. Dick offered some suggestions, and then and there began a very successful song-writing duo. They continued traveling with Truth for about eighteen months.

It would not be possible in the small space available to report on the Tunneys' many successful projects and awards. They have made a major impact on the genre of contemporary worship music.

Dick and Mel shared the following story concerning the writing of "How Excellent Is Thy Name":

Dick said, "In 1981, I was on the road playing for a touring group. Mel and I had only been married for a year. The lead singer in the ensemble, Paul Smith, was a lyricist of some talent, and we repeatedly said to each other, 'We must write something together.' But we just never got around to it.

"The parents of Paul's wife had a cabin on a lake not too far from our home, and he invited us to come to the cabin for a fish fry to be held several days from that time. We accepted the invitation, and upon arriving back in town from a visit with friends, drove straight out to their cabin. In the weeks prior to that, Mel had composed a melody that she had no lyrics for, not even an idea.

"As we were leaving the fish fry, Paul said, 'Wait a minute. I have some lyrics that I want to give you. He had a verse about half finished, with a chorus that was taken from Psalm 8:9. During the thirty minutes it took us to drive home, Mel said, 'I've got it!' After we reached our home, we finished the project in about two hours. We completed the lyrics for the verses, put the music with it, and the whole thing made sense to us."

Mel added, "The musical setting came first, and the lyrics went with it perfectly. Usually we pretty much get the lyrics and the melodies at the same time, but this time it was different. I wrote the music and then said to myself, *I don't have a clue what is going to happen to this.*" They were delighted that they finally had something that would fit with the superb musical setting.

Dick added, "When we showed the song to Greg Nelson [the famed song-writer and composer of 'People Need the Lord'], he said, 'If you increase the length of the chorus, I think Larnelle Harris will cut it.' Mel quickly said, 'We can do that.' Harris did in fact record the song, and it won a Dove Award for Song of the Year in 1987. God was really blessing what we were doing, and it was a wonderful period in our lives."

The name of the Lord our God excels all other names.
His name alone is worthy of our praise. We should say with the psalmist,
"Let them praise the name of the Lord: for his name alone is excellent:
his glory is above the earth and heaven" (Ps. 148:13).

How Great Is Our God

VERSE

The splendor of the King,
Clothed in majesty,
Let all the earth rejoice;
All the earth rejoice.
He wraps Himself in light,
And darkness tries to hide,
And trembles at His voice,
And trembles at His voice.

CHORUS

How great is our God,
Sing with me,
How great is our God.
And all will see how great,
How great, is our God.

VERSE

And age to age He stands,
And time is in His hands.
Beginning and the End,
Beginning and the End.
The Godhead three in one,
Father, Spirit, Son,
The Lion and the Lamb,
The Lion and the Lamb.

Rewrite the Verses and the Melody!

Bless the LORD, O my soul. O LORD my God, thou art very great;
thou art clothed with honour and majesty.

PSALM 104:1

How Great Is Our God," written by Chris Tomlin, Jesse Reeves, and Ed Cash, is wonderful in its simplicity. The truths developed in the lyrics are timeless in scope. The song, which went through several rewrites, ultimately has as its roots Psalm 104. In the Old Testament, the psalms and songs were used to declare the greatness of our God.

In the stories behind "We Fall Down" and "Forever," included in this volume, you'll find some biographical information about Chris Tomlin. Jesse Reeves, who has traveled with Chris as his bass guitarist since 1997, was born in Arlington, Texas, in 1975, and became interested in music at age fifteen. He says about his conversion experience, "I was saved at a Christian concert in which a local band, Judah, ministered in 1990. I was raised in church but didn't have a personal relationship with Christ until that time." He has written, mostly with Chris, twenty to thirty songs.

Ed Cash, songwriter and music producer, was born in Charlotte, North Carolina, where he accepted the Lord at age five. In a recent interview, he said, "I walked through a very big wilderness as a teenager and was called into the Lord's purpose at age twenty-one." He also worked as a studio musician on a number of projects. He did not get involved with "How Great Is Our God" until it was brought to him in Nashville, where he works as a producer.

> *. . . in the midst of the church will I sing praise unto thee.*
>
> HEB. 2:12

Ed has written or cowritten two hundred songs. He often helps songwriters finish their songs. Such was the case with "How Great Is Our God." He told Chris when the song was brought to him, "It doesn't have a bridge, something to tie the verses and the chorus together." So that was his contribution to the song.

Jesse says of the writing of "How Great Is Our God," "I had originally written three verses for this song, but I didn't have a chorus. I gave what I had written to Chris to write a chorus." The chorus came after Chris had been reading Psalm 104, concerning the greatness, splendor, and majesty in which God wraps himself.

Chris said, "I started singing a little chorus, 'How great is our God.' The truth behind the song is that it is timely, and yet it is timeless. It is something we need to be singing during such a time as this, declaring the greatness and worthiness of our God. As we look around our world, I think the song is important because it gathers us together and points our hearts in the right direction. The verses are very simple, and hopefully they magnify our Lord as they amplify the chorus. What a beautiful picture from the Psalms as our God wraps himself in light and darkness cannot hide from him. I also feel that the melody that carries these truths is from God."

Jesse added, "When we went to record the song, the producer, Ed Cash, and others involved with this project, which included Louie Giglio of the Passion movement, all decided that they liked the chorus, but that the verses needed more work. For the rewriting of the verses, Louie suggested that we write them as declarations of the might, power, and majesty of God. We even rewrote the melody used for the verses. Our song really got a makeover before it was recorded. Ed Cash was very instrumental in the revamping of our song.

"Many times since then, after we have finished singing this song, the crowd continues to sing the chorus. We then find ourselves joining back in with the audience."

This song won a Dove Award in 2006 as Song of the Year. At the time of this writing, "How Great Is Our God" has risen to the number two spot on the Christian Copyright Licensing International's (CCLI) Top 25 Songs list in the United States.

Our finite minds cannot fathom the infinite wisdom, majesty, and glory of our heavenly Father. Even in the prayer Jesus taught us to pray, we declare to him, "Hallowed be thy name."

When God's people begin to praise and worship Him using the biblical methods He gives, the Power of His presence comes among His people in an even greater measure.

GRAHAM TRUSCOTT

How Great Thou Art

VERSE

O Lord my God, when I in awesome wonder
Consider all the worlds Thy hands have made.
I see the stars, I hear the rolling thunder,
Thy pow'r throughout the universe displayed.

CHORUS

Then sings my soul, my Savior, God, to Thee,
How great Thou art, how great Thou art!
Then sings my soul, my Savior, God, to Thee,
How great Thou art, how great Thou art!

VERSE

When Christ shall come with shout of acclamation,
And take me home, what joy shall fill my heart.
Then I shall bow in humble adoration,
And there proclaim, my God, how great Thou art!

While Lightning Flashed

O LORD, how great are thy works!

PSALM 92:5

How Great Thou Art" is loved by followers of contemporary worship music (at the time of writing it is number twenty-seven on the CCLI Top 100 Songs list), by people who favor traditional Christian music, and by those who love Southern Gospel. It has been recorded by thousands of singers—some in all three categories.

I have learned about it from extensive research and from a personal friend, Victor Nischick, who visited the home of the English missionary who brought the song to the English-speaking world.

The life of this great hymn began in 1886 on an estate in southern Sweden. A young preacher, Carl Boberg, was caught in a thunderstorm while strolling across the beautiful grounds. He was in awe as he watched the sky go from gray to black and then back to a beautiful blue again.

He later put his response to this display of nature in the form of a poem that he titled "O Store Gud" ("O Great God")—a poem of adoration and praise. It was then set to a Swedish folk tune. In 1907, Manfred von Glehn translated it into German, and five years later a Russian pastor, Reverend Ivan Prokhanoff, translated it into the Russian language.

English missionary Stuart Hine was born in 1899, in Hammersmith Grove, a small hamlet in England, and was dedicated to the Lord by his parents in a Salvation Army meeting. He was led to Christ by Madame Annie Ryall, on February 22, 1914, and was baptized shortly thereafter.

> *My praise shall be of thee in the great congregation.*
>
> Ps. 22:25

In 1931, Hine and his young wife went as missionaries to the Carpathian area of Russia, then a part of Czechoslovakia. There they heard a very meaningful hymn that happened to be a Russian translation of Carl Boberg's Swedish song.

Hine found himself in a thunderstorm one day as he strolled through the Carpathian Mountains. While the lightning flashed and the thunder rolled through the mountain range, his mind went to the Russian hymn that he had heard. English verses began to form in his mind, verses that were suggested by portions of the Russian translation. He wrote a second verse sometime later as he roamed through the forests of Rumania with some of the young people of that region. He completed a third verse before returning to England.

Stuart Hine and David Griffiths visited a camp in Sussex, England, in 1948, where displaced Russians were being held. Only two in the whole camp were true Christians and would profess their belief. The testimony of one of them, and Hine's anticipation of the second coming of Christ, inspired him to write the fourth stanza of his English version of the hymn.

Hine wrote a book titled *Not You, but God* that presents two additional, optional verses that he copyrighted in 1953 as a translation of the Russian version. Dr. J. Edwin Orr introduced Hine's "How Great Thou Art" in the United States in 1954. Three years later it began its orbit around the world by way of the Billy Graham New York Crusade.

In my possession is a prized copy of "How Great Thou Art" in the Russian language. All four of the men who helped bring us this song—Boberg the Swede, Von Glehn the German, Prokhanoff the Russian, and Hine the Englishman—carefully preserved the awesome message of the song.

I personally held a letter in my hand from Hine's daughter, Sonia, dated March 16, 1989, which contained the somber news that Stuart Hine had died peacefully in his sleep two days before. He was ninety-two years of age. His memorial service was held at the Gospel Hall on Martello Road, Walton-on-Naze, Essex, England, on March 23, at two o'clock in the afternoon. Thus in quiet dignity ended the life on earth of a man whose long years had been dedicated to serving the Lord.

God's majestic creations all testify to God's greatness. As we look around us at the things he has made, we, too, stand in awe of the Creator, the Power of all the universes. And just think—this great God has chosen to live in my heart and yours and in all who have accepted his gift of love, making Christ Lord in their lives.

As we come to worship our God,
we must always be calling upon Him
for the cleansing of our hearts.

LEE ROBERSON

I Am

VERSE

VERSE

I am the Root of David,
The Bright and Morning Star.
I am the Lion of Judah,
I Am, I Am.

CHORUS

I am Alpha and Omega,
The Beginning and the End,
The First and the Last,
I Am, I Am.
I am faithful and true;
I am the Word of God;
I am the Lamb;
I Am, I Am.

VERSE

I am the King of kings and Lord of lords;
I am Holy, Holy Lord God Almighty,
Which was and is and is to come;
I am that I am the Lord.

Michael W. Smith | Wayne Hilliard © 1980 Bridge Building Music, Inc. (BMI)
(A Division of Brentwood-Benson Music Publishing, Inc.)/Designer Music Group, Inc.
(SESAC) (A Division of Brentwood-Benson Music Publishing, Inc.)

"I've Got It!"

And God said unto Moses, I AM THAT I AM: and he said,
Thus shalt thou say unto the children of Israel, I AM hath sent me unto you.

EXODUS 3:14

The majestic song "I Am" had its beginning with two great musicians, Wayne Hilliard and Michael W. Smith. "I Am" has been used to lift great throngs of people, live and by way of television, to a glorious awareness of who our heavenly Father really is—as much as man is capable of doing so. The names of God used in the song describe to us the greatness of our heavenly Father.

Michael Whitaker Smith was born in Kenova, West Virginia, on October 7, 1957, to Paul and Barbara Smith. He soon was given the nickname Smitty. He attended Marshall University for a time, and in addition to his schoolwork played with some local bands in the Huntington, West Virginia, area. He dropped out of school and headed for Nashville, hoping to strike it big in the music industry. After an emotional crisis, he gave up the alcohol and drugs that had plagued him since his college days and rededicated his life to Christ. He then began playing keyboards for Christian musicians.

One such musician was Wayne Hilliard. Born in Danville, Virginia, in 1946, Hilliard became interested in music early on in life. He said, "My parents were very musical, so I grew up singing in a trio with them from the age of seven." He was saved at age eleven and later went to Wesleyan Bible College and John Wesley University in High Point, North Carolina. He started out majoring in music but switched to theology, which was greatly helpful in later songwriting ventures. He told me, "I needed the biblical background because so many songs today are trite. I am tired of songs with no substance."

Wayne told me the story of the writing of "I Am." "Michael had come to Nashville and was doing some one-night gigs. He was playing keyboards in the country music field, had met with little or no success, and had been treated rather shabbily. Randy Cox of Paragon Music sent him to me to see if I could use him. I was amazed when I heard him play. I tried to act cool about it. I really didn't want to tell this guy how great he was. Although he looked ragged around the edges, I hired him on the spot.

"After traveling together for a period of time, one night very late I was studying on the titles or names of Christ. I began to write, 'I Am the Root of David, the Bright and Morning Star' and so on. I had no intention of writing a song, but as I stood up and looked at what I had on paper, the names seemed to fall into verse form. I thought, *Oh my! This could be a great song.*

"The next morning I called Michael and said, 'I have a great idea for a song.' Right there, over the phone, I read him those lyrics. He called me back in about two hours and said, 'I've got it!' I answered, 'You have what?' He said, 'I've got that song!' He was ecstatic! He played it for me, right there over the phone.

"We got together with Randy Cox of Paragon, and as Michael played and sang the song, Randy began to weep. Paragon quickly took the song and put it in choral form. It met with wonderful success. We recorded it in 1980 on the album *Changes* for Zondervan on their Milk and Honey label. Others soon began to sing it and record it, groups as well as soloists, one of which was Gary McSpadden.

"Prestonwood Baptist Church in Plano, Texas, developed a complete cantata around the song. They televised the musical, and when I saw it, I was blown away. The song has now been translated into approximately forty languages."

It truly is wonderful to serve a God who is . . . and was . . . and is to come!

I CAN ONLY IMAGINE

VERSE

I can only imagine
What it will be like when I walk by Your side.
I can only imagine
What my eyes will see when Your face is before me.
I can only imagine.

CHORUS

Surrounded by Your glory what will my heart feel?
Will I dance for You Jesus or in awe of You be still?
Will I stand in Your presence or to my knees will I fall?
Will I sing hallelujah, will I be able to speak at all?
I can only imagine, I can only imagine.

VERSE

I can only imagine
When that day comes, and I find myself standing in the Son.
I can only imagine
When all I will do is forever, forever worship You.
I can only imagine.
I can only imagine.

© 2001, 2002 Simpleville Music
Bart Millard

A Song Ten Years in the Making

Eye hath not seen, nor ear heard, neither have entered into the heart of man,
the things which God hath prepared for them that love him.

1 CORINTHIANS 2:9

While working with the youth in a church in Florida when I was nineteen years of age, I mentioned to my grandmother that I wanted to start a band. Her response was, 'Well, mercy me! Why don't you get a real job?'" Bart Millard laughed as he told me that story on March 4, 2005, adding, "We stuck with the name MercyMe to remind us that one day we may have to get a real job."

Bart continued, "I was born in Greenville, Texas, in 1972. Since early childhood I was always interested in music. My music training, as I grew up, consisted of singing to the radio. I would love to have learned to play an instrument, but it never happened."

I asked Bart about his conversion experience, and he said, "I came to know Christ when I was thirteen years of age at a camp called Glorieta in New Mexico. I have faithfully attended church since that night. It was a vivid moment in my life.

"My first attempt at songwriting happened when I was nineteen years of age. I was entered into a Christian music competition for which I sang a Steven Curtis Chapman song. They liked how I sang, but in their critique they said, 'Unless you start writing your own songs, it is difficult to make a career of it.' I had never really thought of making a career of it at all. I wanted to be a youth pastor. But the idea of writing songs has really stuck with me, and a lasting earthly influence has been my dad, Arthur Millard, who became ill with cancer in my late teen years."

In the mid-1990s Bart helped form MercyMe. One of their greatest hopes during the early years of their music career was that they could stay afloat and support their families. And then came "I Can Only Imagine," which was put on their CD project *Almost There*. In less than a year, it had become a record-breaking collection, being certified gold and rapidly moving toward the platinum

> *God came from Teman, and the Holy One from mount Paran. Selah. His glory covered the heavens, and the earth was full of his praise.*
>
> HAB. 3:3

level. "I Can Only Imagine" won a Dove Award as Song of the Year in 2002, and Millard won a Dove Award as Songwriter of the Year in that same year as its author.

When Bart was nineteen, cancer ended his dad's earthly life. Bart grappled with the oft-heard comment, "Your dad is in a better place. He wouldn't leave heaven and come back to this earth even if he were able." Bart confessed that though he heard such statements, they didn't mean much to him at the time. He realized, and truly believed, that his dad was in heaven, but he struggled with the loss.

He began to scribble, "I can only imagine," on most anything he could find to write on. He accepted the fact that his dad was in a better place, yet he found himself wondering time and time again about the things his dad was experiencing in God's presence.

A decade after the loss of his dad, Bart was using an old journal, trying to write some lyrics for a project planned by MercyMe. They would later title it *Almost There*. The old journal was a place that he had written, many times over, the phrase "I can only imagine." Thoughts of his dad and heaven once more began to flood his mind, and in less than ten minutes he had written his now famous song. Putting it on paper took only minutes, but it had been nurtured in his heart for those ten years.

The song and a subsequent video featuring "I Can Only Imagine" have struck a vibrant chord in the hearts and lives of thousands of hurting people. It is being used in memorial services and countless other ways to bring healing to God's people.

God has blessed us greatly with an ability to imagine. It is wonderful beyond our language to express—God's gift that allows us sweet, mental visualization of our heavenly home and of seeing our blessed Savior.

If we are going to worship in Spirit, we must develop a spirit of worship.

MICHAEL CATT

I Could Sing of Your Love Forever

Over the mountains and the sea,
Your river runs with love for me.
And I will open up my heart,
And let the Healer set me free.
I'm happy to be in the truth,
And I will daily lift my hands.
For I will always sing
Of when Your love came down.

CHORUS

I could sing of Your love forever.
I could sing of Your love forever.
I could sing of Your love forever.
I could sing of Your love forever.

(BRIDGE)

Oh I feel like dancing;
It's foolishness I know.
But when the world
Has seen the light,
They will dance with joy
Like we're dancing now.

The Lyrics Tumbled Out

O that thou hadst hearkened to my commandments! then had thy peace been as a river, and thy righteousness as the waves of the sea.

ISAIAH 48:18

Although born into a sports-oriented home, Martin Smith, at age twelve, was able to push those things into the background because the guitar held more and more interest for him. Martin said, "When I began learning guitar, I started writing songs as part of the process—silly little songs about falling in and out of love as a twelve-year-old. The songwriting kept progressing in me, and at age sixteen I began writing songs about my faith."

Martin Smith was born in Essex County, England, just north of London, in 1970. Martin said of his salvation experience, "When I was only eight years of age, our family went on holiday in Cornwall, in the west country of England. I began chatting with my parents about spiritual matters and became aware of sin. I wanted to address the problem in my life. With their help and counsel, I became a Christian."

In a recent interview, I asked Martin to tell me of the writing of his now famous song, the subject of this chapter. The story, in his own words, follows.

"In 1993, I was again on holiday with my family in a place called Devon, also in the west country of England. One evening I was sitting outside our accommodations, which overlooked the mountainside, the valley below, and a winding river. I began thinking about God's love and how in the Bible his kindness and provision is often likened to a river.

"Suddenly the lyrics began tumbling out of me and the whole song wrote itself really. Other songs I have written have taken a long time, but not this one. I first played it to my sister-in-law, Sarah Smith, and asked, 'Do you like this? What do you think of this?' She said, 'Yes, not bad.' And so I accepted that and turned my thoughts to other things. I didn't think about my song again until the following week when I was preparing to lead our congregation at the Arun Community Church in singing, 'I Could Sing of Your Love Forever.' The response was great! People latched on to it pretty quickly.

> *Sing forth the honour of his name: make his praise glorious.*
>
> Ps. 66:2

"I don't think anyone thought of the song as a global classic, since it was just one of the songs that we sang at church. Our band used it as we went out from place to place to lead worship or to give a concert. After a couple of years, we stopped singing it. It became an old song to us. It was not until an American group, SONICFLOOd, picked it up in 1999 that it kinda mushroomed.

"It is always amazing when you see that one of your songs has a life and that something you have written in the privacy of your own home is suddenly becoming a part of the establishment. It is quite unusual when it happens, yet it is a great thing and you are amazed that God has done it."

Since the early days of his music ministry, Martin has been the lead singer for a group called Delirious?—a worship band that had its beginning in 1996 and now sings all over the world. The group was a part of the Arun Community

Church worship ministry and later was very active in the church's monthly outreach service called Cutting Edge.

I asked about the unusual name of the group, and Martin said, "In the dictionary *delirious* means to be wildly excited about something. So we feel we are excited about God in our lives. We are trying to encourage the presence of God to be found in our generation. It is quite an odd name, but we went for it."

Martin, his wife, Anna, and their four children live in England. When he is not traveling with Delirious?, Martin can be found leading the congregation at his home church where he is one of the worship leaders.

May it be the desire of every one of us to sing of the love of our blessed Savior forever. His love truly has no boundaries, no beginning, and no ending.

God is to be praised with the voice, and the heart should go therewith in holy exultation.

CHARLES H. SPURGEON

I Exalt Thee

"Could You Present Another Song?"

For thou, Lord, art high above all the earth: thou art exalted far above all gods.

PSALM 97:9

Pete Sanchez was born in Houston, Texas, in 1948, to Bonnie and Pete Sanchez Sr. He was one of eight children, and music became important to Sanchez early in life. He said, "I grew up in a broken and disadvantaged Hispanic home. The church became a refuge for me. A kind church organist took me under her wing and encouraged me. I started learning to play the piano at about age seventeen."

Pete is now the dean of education for Integrity Worship Institute. In an interview in late 2001, I asked Pastor Sanchez to tell me just how he came to write his very popular song.

"It was during one of those quiet times with the Lord that I came across a rather obscure verse, when thinking of the whole body of the Psalms, Psalm 97:9, 'For thou, LORD, art high above all the earth: thou art exalted far above all gods.' I wrote a tune so that I could sing those words.

"In 1975, during my quiet sessions with the Lord, I would often sit at the piano and sing the first half of what is now the song 'I Exalt Thee.' Each time I worshiped him in that manner, that song would come out. I often sensed that something was lacking at the end of the song, but I didn't know just what. But I seemed to be content with what the Lord had already given me. After all, I was the only one hearing or singing it, nor was I concerned that anyone else would ever hear it.

"The following year, sometime in the spring, I was waiting one Sunday morning for my wife to finish getting dressed for church. As was my habit, I sat down at the piano and began to sing. This time, as I got to the end of my song, I stepped into 'another room.' A new chorus for the song was given to me. I knew as I began to sing it that something special was taking place in my life. It was a very powerful moment.

"When I finished it, I thought, *Well, something just happened, but I don't know just what.* I continued to think that the song was only for me, for my private times with the Lord, so I didn't mention it to anyone else. My wife, Karen, and I went on to the New Testament Baptist Church in Houston that morning. As things happen that are orchestrated by God, when I reached the church, I was asked to present some special music, so I sang 'I Exalt Thee.' It had a profound effect on the congregation, which really surprised me.

"I didn't sing it again until a few weeks later when I was asked to attend a songwriters conference in Mississippi. Each of the songwriters, and there were about thirty-five of us, were asked to present three of our songs. I was the last person to present a song. I presented two of my 'well-written' compositions, and the people politely clapped and seemingly expressed some appreciation.

"I was then asked, 'Do you have another song you could present?' The only fresh thing I had was 'I Exalt Thee.' I began to sing my new song, much like the two previous songs, with no visible response. But when I came to the chorus, it was like someone had set off a bomb in the room. People jumped to their feet and sang with their full voices, many of them with their hands in the air. I had never intended to share it except, perhaps, on some special occasion."

One of the greatest blessings concerning his song that has come to Pete Sanchez Jr. was when he heard a tape recording of a Francis Schaeffer conference overseas. People were singing "I Exalt Thee" in ten different languages all at the same time.

When we come into the presence of the Lord to praise and exalt him, he brings joy and strength into our lives. "In thy presence is fulness of joy" (Ps. 16:11). "The joy of the LORD is your strength" (Neh. 8:10).

I Give You My Heart

Reflections Following an Accident

With my whole heart have I sought thee: O let me not wander from thy commandments.

PSALM 119:10

Reuben Morgan is rapidly becoming one of the most powerful songwriters of our day. Although most of his time is spent in the worship ministry of the ten-thousand-member Hillsong Church in Sydney, Australia, his influence for Christ is now being felt around the world. His worship songs are among the most popular in the United States and a number of other countries. High-profile recording artists are putting his compositions on their CDs, further spreading the songwriting ministry of this talented Aussie.

Though Reuben grew up in a Christian home, he made a decision to pursue the things of God for himself when he was in high school. He began to read ancient Christian writings that led him toward Christ, and he was drawn to listen to praise and worship music, which heretofore he had not enjoyed. The "Christianity" that Reuben grew up with soon became a living encounter with the Lord Jesus and a passion that was consuming.

He was involved with musical activities from primary school age, and his love for music seemed to grow as he became older. In Papua, New Guinea, where he grew up, he began writing songs by age ten or eleven. He learned some basic elements of playing the guitar from a female missionary but soon grew tired of practicing songs that his teacher assigned and began making up his own. He later attended the Institute of Music in Sydney, majoring in guitar.

A week following Reuben's involvement in a serious automobile accident, he began thinking of the need to be completely surrendered to the plan and purpose of God. He later confessed that while he found himself truly aware of God's presence at the time, he also yearned for "God's way" in his life. In the process of discovering God's unfolding plans, Reuben prayed and continues to pray, "Lord, I give you my heart . . . have your way in me." "I Give You My Heart" was soon on paper ready to be used in the worship experiences of God's people.

Shortly after Reuben's move to Sydney to study at the Institute of Music, he began attending Hillsong Church. There he came under the direct influence and guidance of Darlene Zschech, one of the most widely known and effective worship leaders in the world.

"I Give You My Heart" was first used during one of the Saturday night services at Hillsong. The congregation received it enthusiastically and responded well to its message of consecration to the Lord. The pastor in charge of that service asked that it be used the following Sunday night, where again it was sung very powerfully during the altar call, with the hearty participation of the congregation.

"I Give You My Heart" was first published and recorded by Hillsong Publishing in 1995 on an album titled *God Is in the House*. Since then it has been included in many recorded projects of singers and musicians in other lands.

The song is a prayer that burns in Reuben, and he has been amazed to hear stories and testimonies of the way it has ministered to people's lives, influencing many of them into a personal place of surrender before the Lord.

Although Reuben's compositions are primarily for Hillsong Church, numbers of them, as has been stated, are sung and enjoyed around the world. Each week you will hear others of Reuben's songs used at the Sydney church, and many of them have become a part of the live church recordings each year. Since 1995, they have published and recorded more than forty of Reuben's "gifts" from the Lord.

At the time of this writing, Reuben continues his writing and his ministry as one of the primary worship leaders at Hillsong.

Someone has said, "Christ will be Lord of all, or he will not be Lord at all."
Jesus wants nothing less than our full surrender—the control of our hearts.

I Love You, Lord

CHORUS

I love You, Lord,
And I lift my voice
To worship You.
O my soul, rejoice!
Take joy my King
In what You hear.
May it be a sweet, sweet sound
In Your ear.

From a House Trailer by the Highway

Grace be with all them that love our Lord Jesus Christ in sincerity.

EPHESIANS 6:24

As a sixteen-year-old, Laurie Brendemuehl wrote a song she titled "Loving Unconditionally." This started her on a journey of songwriting that would become a part of her daily quiet times with the Lord.

By age twenty-four she had met and married Bill Klein, and the Lord had given them their first child, a little girl. Bill was a student at Central Oregon Community College studying forest technology, and . . . well, let me have Laurie tell you the story as she told it to me.

"It was a dark time in my life. We had no extra money, no friends nearby, no church home, and my husband was busy all of the time with his studies. I didn't drive, so I couldn't get away. We lived by a highway in a mobile home, so I couldn't even put the baby in a stroller and go for a walk. Our only neighbors were people long retired and tired of life. When I needed some encouragement, there was no extra money for long distance calls to family or friends. I was lonely. The only thing I was committed to was trying to get up each morning before our baby, then a toddler, and spend some time with Jesus. I knew that was where the 'life' was.

"I would normally get out my Bible and my guitar and begin praying and singing songs. I seemingly was trying to help the Lord get me out of my depressed condition—trying to find strength to face the day. But I could only do that for so long.

"One morning I had gotten up early and was sitting with my Bible and my guitar. I realized that I didn't have anything in me to give to Jesus. I knew the right thing to do was to give him praise, but I just didn't have anything in me to offer him. I was so empty. So I prayed and said to the Lord, 'If you want to hear me sing, would you give me something that you would like to hear?'

"I started strumming on the guitar, and the first two lines came out of my mouth with absolutely no effort. They just came as a gift from heaven. I sang them again, and they felt kinda good, so I scribbled them on a piece of paper just in case I would want to remember them and sing them again. Those words meant a lot to me.

"I wondered if I could play the melody again—if I would even remember—because a lot of times I write songs and soon forget them. I played and sang the two lines again. They were still there, in my mind. The last two lines just followed as effortlessly as the first two had come. It was a gift from God that just wrote itself.

"Though it is a very simple song, it changed everything for me. When you are in a dark valley and the Lord gives you light, it makes all the difference, and you keep growing.

"Sometime later a pastor friend took my song to a national church convention in California and sang it for them. It became their theme song. As a result, it went home with pastors from all over the world, and within a year we were getting phone calls from people wanting permission to use the song."

Then Laurie shared with me the following heartwarming account:

"The most meaningful time that I ever heard anyone sing my song was in the fall of 2000 while my husband and I were in Discipleship Training School at Youth With A Mission in Lakeside, Montana. Late one night in the dormitory, I heard a baby crying somewhere down the hall. I slipped down the hall to the outside of the door just to pray for the baby, that it would be able to sleep. As I was praying outside the door, I heard the mother singing a song, but the little one kept crying. She then sang 'I Love You, Lord,' and while she was singing, the baby fell asleep. She, of course, had no idea the person who wrote the song was outside her door."

The psalmist, under the inspiration of the Holy Spirit, said, "Exalt the LORD our God, and worship at his holy hill; for the LORD our God is holy" (Ps. 99:9).

I Pledge Allegiance to the Lamb

Verse

I have heard how Christians long ago
Were brought before a tyrant's throne;
They were told that he would spare their lives
If they would renounce the name of Christ.
But one by one they chose to die,
The Son of God they would not deny.
Like a great angelic choir sings,
I can almost hear their voices ring.

Chorus

I pledge allegiance to the Lamb,
With all my strength with all I am.
I will seek to honor His commands.
I pledge allegiance to the Lamb.

Ray Boltz © Word Music, LLC/ Shepherd Boy Music (Admin. By Word Music, LLC)
All Rights Reserved.

A Perfect Number One Song

*I am not ashamed: for I know whom I have believed, and am persuaded that he is able to keep
that which I have committed unto him against that day.*

2 Timothy 1:12

A "Hoosier," Ray Boltz as a young lad had a variety of musical interests, which included piano, organ, and woodwind instruments. He, like so many others in their late teens, became interested in rock music and the problems of American society. Woodstock culture and the Vietnam War protests were foremost in his mind.

In an interview he told me, "At age nineteen, I was kind of messed up on drugs and alcohol. I had really gone in the wrong direction. Then one day I attended a Christian concert by a group called Fishermen from Anderson University. At that concert I made a commitment to the Lord that totally changed my life. After I gave my heart to the Lord, I began writing very positive songs about my faith and about what Christ had done in my life. I finally knew the answers to some of the questions I had been asking."

138

Ray told me the following story concerning the writing of "I Pledge Allegiance to the Lamb," which took place in 1994:

"My oldest daughter, about sixteen years of age at the time, was involved with a youth missions group, Teen Mania. They were scheduled to go on a mission trip to Africa, and she wanted to make the trip with them. It made me nervous to think of my daughter traveling to Africa, but after talking with Ron Luce, the leader of the group, my wife and I decided to let her go.

"Ron asked me to write a song for the group to sing in Africa, and so I wrote a song that I titled 'I Will Tell the World.' He then asked if I would film a video for the song, and would I like to film it in Botswana, Africa? I consented to do so and soon found myself on my way to Africa with the group. The program was called *Allegiance*. The drama asked the question, 'Who is your allegiance to? Is it to God, or is it to someone or something else?'

"I watched the audiences in the villages of Botswana as the teens presented their programs. The people realized that the kids were not there for political reasons, or for money, or to con anyone. They were there to deliver a message. Consequently they were enthusiastically received by the African people.

"On the way home, as we were somewhere over the Atlantic, I began to question my own allegiance. I thought about all of the people who had given their lives for Christ. I asked myself, 'What if you were put in that position? What would your choice be?' I said to myself, 'I hope my allegiance would be to the Lamb.' And so I began to write, and I continued until I had the chorus complete.

"After we returned to America, I went into the studio and recorded the song. The very next year it won a Dove Award as Inspirational Song of the Year. 'I Pledge Allegiance to the Lamb' made music history in that it topped inspirational music charts as a perfect number one song, receiving one hundred points, a first for the *CCM Update* publication."

To stand on a platform in the Mall of America singing "I Pledge Allegiance to the Lamb" to an audience of 1.3 million men was a wonderful experience in the life of Ray Boltz. Very few people have had that experience! But I'm glad that it came true for Ray Boltz.

Have I given my whole being—mind, soul, and body—to the Lord Jesus Christ? Does he have my complete allegiance? It is not enough just to answer in the affirmative; we must make it so with our very lives.

I Sing Praises

VERSE

I sing praises to Your name, O Lord,
Praises to Your name, O Lord,
For Your name is great
And greatly to be praised.
I sing praises to Your name, O Lord,
Praises to Your name, O Lord,
For Your name is great
And greatly to be praised.

VERSE

I give glory to Your name, O Lord,
Glory to Your name, O Lord,
For Your name is great
And greatly to be praised.
I give glory to Your name, O Lord,
Glory to Your name, O Lord,
For Your name is great
And greatly to be praised.

From the Music Library of Heaven

He hath put a new song in my mouth, even praise unto our God:
many shall see it, and fear, and shall trust in the LORD.

PSALM 40:3

Terry MacAlmon was born in Poughkeepsie, New York, in 1955 and was considered by some to be a child prodigy. He began playing the piano at age three and continued to develop on his own until age eight when his parents, Edward and Roberta MacAlmon, coaxed him to take piano lessons. Terry said, "That was a disaster that lasted for about two months." By age eleven he was the church pianist for the First Assembly of God in Lexington, Kentucky.

Terry later became a student at the University of Kentucky, where he studied voice. In addition to piano, he played trumpet for a number of years. He said of his songwriting, which began at age eighteen, "I began to write songs, completely on my own, under the inspiration of the Lord."

Following is Terry's story concerning the writing of "I Sing Praises" as he told it to me:

"In 1986, I was serving as worship pastor at the Resurrection Fellowship church in Loveland, Colorado. As was our custom, the ministry leaders of the church would meet for prayer thirty minutes before each service. One Sunday evening, during one of our prayer times, I was quietly worshiping the Lord when suddenly the Lord gave me a song. I often say, 'It was as if the Lord went over to the music library of heaven and took something out of the *I* file and dropped it right into my heart.' I began to quietly sing, 'I sing praises to your name, O Lord. . . .' Realizing that this was a new melody and new lyrics that the Lord was giving me, I took a piece of paper from my Bible and jotted down the words and a rough melody line as the song was being given to me. I then placed the paper back into my Bible.

> *Praise ye the* LORD. *Sing unto the* LORD *a new song, and his praise in the congregation of saints.*
>
> PS. 149:1

"Later that evening I was sitting at the piano leading the music portion of the service. When I came to a transition period, where I usually go from more upbeat melodies to the slower more worshipful songs, I sensed the Holy Spirit saying to me, 'Teach the new song.' Something then said to me, '*That song?* There's nothing to that song. It has no substance and it's too simple.' I felt that Satan was trying to get me not to share what the Lord had given me. I sat there and stared at the keys for what seemed an eternity, trying to decide whether to sing it or not sing it. About two thousand people were awaiting my decision, although they had no idea what was going through my mind.

"Finally, I went with the more positive urge and said, 'Folks, I would like to teach you a song that the Lord gave to me just before the service tonight,' and I began to sing, 'I sing praises to your name, O Lord. . . .' Immediately I sensed victory in my heart, because the people began to sing with me almost before I had sung through it the first time. We sang it again and again. God used his song and my timid, reluctant obedience to bless his children with the music of heaven.

"I had a small band behind me, and the bass player, Neal Marchman, stepped up to me following the service and said, 'Pastor Terry, when you taught "I Sing

Praises" tonight, the Lord showed me that song being sung in nations all over the world.' I smiled and said, 'Neal, thank you, but you're crazy!' Well, we continued to sing it for approximately two years before I submitted it to Integrity Music. They liked the song and included it on an album titled *Enter His Gates*. That started it on it way."

Terry receives reports that "I Sing Praises" is also being sung in other lands such as England, Canada, Mexico, China, Russia, Argentina, and the Philippines, just to name a few. Its popularity still seems to be on the rise.

In a portion of Terry's song, the lyrics bring us back to
1 Chronicles 16:25, which says, "Great is the Lord, and greatly to be
praised." Praise his name, anywhere you can commune with him,
because he truly is "greatly to be praised."

We only learn to behave ourselves
in the presence of God.

C. S. Lewis

I STAND IN AWE

VERSE

You are beautiful beyond description,
Too marvelous for words,
Too wonderful for comprehension,
Like nothing ever seen or heard.
Who can grasp Your infinite wisdom?
Who can fathom the depth of Your love?
You are beautiful beyond description,
Majesty enthroned above.

CHORUS

And I stand, I stand in awe of You,
I stand, I stand in awe of You.
Holy God to whom all praise is due,
I stand in awe of You.

Mark Altrogge © 1988 People of Destiny Int. / Pleasant Hill Music

His Best Move Was Back Home

Let all the earth fear the LORD: *let all the inhabitants of the world stand in awe of him.*
PSALM 33:8

At age fourteen I became excited about the Beatles. I was not a Christian at the time, so I wanted to play guitar, get into a band, and be just like them." It was not until ten years later that through the influence of Mark Altrogge's parents, Julian and Jonalee Altrogge, his interests were turned toward spiritual things.

After six months of guitar lessons, Mark, still in his early teens, formed a small band and taught the other members of the group to play their parts. This led to an attempt to make a career of rock and roll music, which lasted until he was twenty-four years of age.

I asked Mark to tell me of his conversion experience, and he told me the following story:

"In 1974, during a Bible study, which had as the subject genuine repentance, I truly realized what it meant to surrender my life to the Lord, and I wholeheartedly turned my life over to Christ. I soon realized that I would have to give up the rock and roll band. We were playing in places and using music that I knew were not glorifying God, so I quit the band and began to follow the Lord."

Mark continued, "The year 1980 was a notable year in my life. I was married in February of that year, and since I had a degree in art, I was an itinerant instructor, traveling to five different schools, teaching art to six hundred elementary students. During that same year, Brent Detwiller became pastor of our church, which had been started from a Full Gospel Business Men's Bible Study, and I was asked to be the worship leader." Several years later Mark became the senior pastor of the church—Lord of Life Church in Indiana, Pennsylvania.

During our session, Mark shared with me the details surrounding the writing of his most unusual song.

"In 1988, I had been studying the attributes of God. Several books were influential in my life at the time: *The Holiness of God* by R. C. Sproul, *The Knowledge of the Holy* by A. W. Tozer, and particularly *The Attributes of God* by Stephen Charnock. The writings of Charles H. Spurgeon were also very meaningful.

"I began to reflect on the beautiful truth that God is infinite in each of his attributes—in his beauty, his holiness, and his wisdom. He is unsearchable! We will never come to an end of learning new things about him—even throughout eternity.

"I was playing my guitar as I thought on those things, trying to write a song capturing the thoughts of my heart. The first phrase came quite quickly—acclaiming the beauty of God and the marvel of his being. Then came my response to his beauty, a feeling of awe. I had an idea for the chorus, so it took me quite a time to work out the complete song—several days. In all of my songwriting, I have only had one song come completely at one sitting.

"I am grateful for the assistance of two friends, Bob Cauflin and Steve Cook, who made suggestions, strengthening the song. At the recommendation of David Clydesdale, I later wrote the second verse, to be used in a musical he was writing."

Mark first used "I Stand in Awe" in the church he pastors, and from there it has made its way around the world, becoming one of the most requested songs in churches of the United States.

He continues to write songs, along with fulfilling his duties as senior pastor of Lord of Life Church. Mark and his wife, Kristi, have three sons, Stephen, David, and Jonathan, and one daughter, Beth.

Mark's song brings to our minds the realization of the beauty and the majesty of our heavenly Father, which we will only be able to fully realize when we stand before him in our heavenly home. Then we will know, even as we are known.

I Want to Be Where You Are

Maybe Playing Violin Isn't So Bad After All

*He that dwelleth in the secret place of the most
High shall abide under the shadow of the Almighty.*

PSALM 91:1

I 've had enough! I quit! I don't know if I want to be a violinist anymore, or even a musician." That declaration was made by Don Moen in 1960 in Jackson, Mississippi, where he had just played his violin in the opera *Carmen*. As he left the concert hall, he proceeded to drive back to the University of Southern Mississippi in Hattiesburg, pick up his luggage, get into his car—with his tuxedo still on—and drive straight through to Minnesota.

A week later he was a lumberjack in the frozen Superior National Forest. He drove a bulldozer, working with a logger who had a long beard with brown icicles that formed on it when he spit tobacco juice.

Don related to me: "After a few months of that, sometimes in thirty below zero temperatures, sitting on a bulldozer, I thought, *Maybe playing a violin isn't so bad after all.*" So back to college he went, and this time to Oral Roberts University. Several years later, in 1984, Michael Coleman, president of Integrity, Inc., approached Moen about coming on board with Integrity Music.

I asked Don to tell me how he wrote "I Want to Be Where You Are," and the following is his story in his own words:

"In 1987, I was writing the musical *God with Us.* It was going to be a journey from the outer court to the inner court of the tabernacle of Moses. I had studied for about eighteen months on this subject, becoming familiar with the furnishings of the tabernacle and how they were symbols. In my studies I learned that Christ was revealed in all of these things.

"For the opening number, I wanted a song that would tell about all of the tribes of people coming up to Zion to worship the King. I sat down at the piano to write about all of those things, and then asked myself, *How am I going to write about this journey and make it into a musical?* My fingers fell on the keys, and I suddenly was playing the musical setting that you know today as 'I Want to Be Where You Are,' and the words came with the melody. It just popped out of me.

"I then thought, *Now, I have to start over, because the musical cannot start like that. The bridge of the song doesn't even rhyme.* I was simply sketching out things I wanted to say at the time—things that were in my heart. I decided that if I ever wanted to use the song for some other purpose, I would come back and rewrite the lyrics because they didn't work. I literally threw it aside, thinking, *This is not the big anthem that I was looking for.*

"Sometime later I was at a church in Oklahoma, the church where my brother-in-law and his family attend—the ones for whom I wrote 'God Will Make a Way.' I had gone out to visit them. They had a small church, and they graciously asked me to sing something. I had carried my legal pad on which I had sketched out the words of 'I Want to Be Where You Are.' I explained to the people how I had written the song, and then I sang it.

"Numbers of people came up to me that day and said, 'That is the cry of my heart. I want to be where Christ is.' It impacted people, not because it was a well-crafted song, but because it resonated with a lot of people that God was inviting us to himself, and they wanted to be where God is, and to dwell in his glory. I think that is why the song has become so popular. A lot of people identify with it."

We are unworthy, in our own flesh, to come before God to worship him, but the blood of Jesus Christ has cleansed us and made us new creatures. We come boldly into his presence solely because God has ordained it so.

I WILL GLORY IN THE CROSS

VERSE

I boast not of works nor tell of good deeds,
For naught have I done to merit His grace.
All glory and praise shall rest upon Him,
So willing to die in my place.

CHORUS

I will glory in the cross, in the cross,
Lest His suffering all be in vain.
I will weep no more for the cross that He bore;
I will glory in the cross.

VERSE

My trophies and crowns, my robe stained with sin,
'Twas all that I had to lay at His feet.
Unworthy to eat from the table of life
'Til love made provision for me.

Dottie Rambo © 1978 John T. Benson Publishing (ASCAP)
(Administered by Brentwood-Benson Music Publishing, Inc.)

It All Started Down by the Creek Bank

*God forbid that I should glory, save in the cross of our Lord Jesus Christ,
by whom the world is crucified unto me, and I unto the world.*

GALATIANS 6:14

A brilliant career began in the rural town of Madisonville, Kentucky, when Dottie Rambo was only eight years of age. She came home one day and began to quote a poem to her mother who was cooking in the kitchen. She had just come from the creek bank, one of her favorite places to visit, where she had composed the verses. Her mother was moved to tears as she heard the poem.

Since that creek bank experience, God has given Dottie hundreds of songs, many of which are sung by people around the world and have been recorded by thousands of artists. Scattered among those triumphs were periods of heartaches and disappointment. Yet out of these dark days came some of her most blessed songs. During an interview she told me that she and her family were going through some rough times in the mid-1970s. She related it to me in the following fashion:

"We were doing a lot of concerts, competitive concerts, making a lot of money. Suddenly I realized that I was not living close to the Lord. I was not writing under the anointing of the Holy Spirit. I also realized that I had never done anything to merit all of this goodness, recognition, and fame.

"I then began to study the scriptures where Paul said that he didn't glory in himself [Gal. 6:14]. I came back to the realization that all I have is because of the grace of God and the cross of Christ.

"During this time we went to Holland to do a number of concerts. When we got off the plane, people met us and took us to this little, quaint hotel. As we rode along, they informed us that while we were there, singing in the concerts, we were not to sing about the cross of Christ. I looked at the young man who was escorting us and asked, 'Do you mean that we are not allowed to sing about the cross to these Christians?' He said, 'No, they consider it gory. They don't want to hear about the blood or the cross.' I then looked at him—I was old enough to be his mother—and said, 'Son, if you won't tell them you told me this, then I will pretend I don't know it. Because I *will* be singing about the cross and about the blood of Christ.'

"We sang in the concert that very night 'He Looked Beyond My Fault and Saw My Need.' People were weeping all over the audience, even the man who sent the message that we were not to sing about the cross of Christ. The Lord really seemed to move in the hearts of the people.

"We went back to the little hotel that evening and to bed. I lay there in the darkness and began to weep. I said, 'God, I apologize that we wouldn't want to hear about the blood of Christ, his cross, and his grace. I really apologize.' As I lay there, the Lord began to give me a song. I kept it all in my heart until the next morning when I awoke to write it down."

The song that she wrote as she lay there in the darkened room has a thought not expressed in any other musical composition that I have ever heard: "I will weep no more for the cross that He bore, but I will glory in the cross."

Dottie Rambo, following great periods of sickness and surgeries, continued to travel across our nation, singing her songs and blessing the hearts of Christians until her tragic death on May 11, 2008, in a bus accident. She told me, "I asked the Lord to let me, at least once each year, write a song that will speak to the hearts of Christians everywhere." She certainly did.

I, too, have nothing in which to glory, save in the blessed truth of the death, burial, and resurrection of our blessed Lord. By his marvelous grace he included you—and me—in his kindness.

I WORSHIP YOU, ALMIGHTY GOD

I worship You Almighty God,
There is none like You.
I worship You, O Prince of Peace,
That is what I want to do.
I give You praise,
For You are my righteousness.
I worship You Almighty God,
There is none like You.

"What Do You Mean, a Check?"

*O LORD, there is none like thee, neither is there any God beside thee,
according to all that we have heard with our ears.*

1 CHRONICLES 17:20

At age eighteen Sandra Corbett Wood enrolled in Christ for the Nations Institute in Dallas, Texas. It was a special time for her as she saw many wonderful praise songs birthed during her time there, with numbers of them circling the globe. She said, "I remember when I first arrived at the school, they divided us into groups of four in order for us to get acquainted with other students. Marty Nystrom, author of 'As the Deer,' was part of my group of four. I also became with friends with Tommy Walker, who wrote 'Mourning into Dancing,' and our families still keep in touch. I'm thankful to have had that time in my life."

Following is Sondra's story of how she wrote her very special song:

"On a Saturday morning, while a student at CFNI, I had gone to the music building to worship and pray. The singing group that I was a part of, which went out to represent the school, was going the following morning to minister at a local church. I wanted to be prepared by praying for the service and the people who would attend. I also wanted to spend some time in the presence of the Lord, singing to him. I had no intention of writing a song, nor was it even on my mind.

"I sat down at a piano in one of the rooms and began to pray and sing. I felt a strong sense of the presence of the Lord. I began to sing, 'I worship You, Almighty God, there is none like You.' When another line came out of my mouth, I thought to myself, *I'm getting a song here!* I ran out of that little room to the office and asked someone for a pencil and paper, and quickly jotted down the words and the chords to the song that I had just played and sung.

"The song came directly from prayer and a desire to commune with the Lord. It was my response. God is the focus of the song. It is a prayer to him expressing our desire to praise him and to recognize his righteousness. I gave the song to one of the worship leaders, who taught it to the students at a chapel service. They learned the song very readily and sang it joyfully.

"After graduating from CFNI and returning to my little Kentucky town of 175 people, including cats and dogs, my mailbox began to fill up almost on a daily basis with requests to use my song. It had been recorded by Word Records. A friend told me that my song was listed on the cassette tape as 'author unknown.' I phoned Word and politely told them that I was the author of the song. The person at Word said to me, 'Ma'am, just because you say you wrote a song doesn't mean we are going to send you a check!' I said, 'What do you mean, a check?' I thought to myself, *Is money involved?* I hadn't thought of that. I was only excited that my song was being used. Shortly after that phone conversation, I received my first royalty check in the mail. I was amazed at God."

Sondra and her husband, John Wood, have two children and reside in Madison, Wisconsin, where she is the worship leader of Bethesda Christian Fellowship. She also works in the children's ministry, singing and writing songs for the little ones.

God invites us to come to a place of worship, a place where you are aware
that he is with you. You speak to God and God speaks to you (Ps. 95).
It's by God's invitation, not simply an act of your will.

I'm Glad I Know Who Jesus Is

VERSE

In a little town called Bethlehem
So many years ago,
They told Him there was no room in the inn.
But they had no way of knowing
That they had turned away
The Lamb of God who would
Take away their sins.

CHORUS

I'm glad I know who Jesus is,
I'm glad I know who Jesus is.
He's more than just a story;
He is the King of Glory.
I'm glad I know who Jesus is.

(BRIDGE)

He's the Alpha and Omega,
The Beginning and the End.
He's a Counselor, Deliverer to me.
He's the Everlasting Father.
He is the King of glory.
I'm glad I know who Jesus is.

A Song for the Old-Timers

I am the Alpha and Omega, the beginning and the end.

REVELATION 21:6

I have interviewed many songwriters who, at times, didn't think the song they had just written was worthy of very much attention. Many of them have come to realize that the Lord is the one who raises up a song and causes it to bless the hearts of Christians. Such was the song in this story.

Geron Davis was born in Bogalusa, Louisiana, in 1960, into the home of Pastor Gerald and Patricia Davis. As a child he would listen to recordings of his favorite singers, whose arrangements were done by Lari Goss, composer of "Cornerstone," and try to pick out their intricate harmonies. Now, as an accomplished musician, Geron has ministered with the choirs of such great churches as Christ Church in Nashville, Brooklyn Tabernacle in New York City, and Prestonwood Baptist Church in Dallas.

Geron told me the story behind the writing of "I'm Glad I Know Who Jesus Is."

"I was serving as minister of music in a large church in Alexandria, Louisiana. We were making plans for our 1990 Christmas musical, a time when many people from the community would come in and enjoy the Christmas music with us.

"I had a group of older singers in the choir, a quartet of very experienced people who were loved by the people and whom I wanted to present in some manner during the program. I would, from time to time, find things that were good for them to present.

"I wanted this quartet to do something original, never heard before, and so I sat down and wrote 'I'm Glad I Know Who Jesus Is.' I literally wrote the song in fifteen minutes. I taught it to them that evening, and they loved it! When they sang it during the musical, the people loved it! I really didn't know what to think of the song myself, because the Old Timers Quartet could sing out of the phone book and people would love it.

> *O come, let us sing unto the* LORD: *let us make a joyful noise to the rock of our salvation.*
>
> PS. 95:1

"A month or so later, the Nelons, good friends of mine, called me and asked if I had any songs that I thought they might be interested in. They, along with the producer, Lari Goss, were searching for new songs to put into an upcoming project, and they needed a few more things to listen to and consider. I said, 'Yes, I have some songs that I can send to you.' So I sat down at the piano and recorded four songs to send to them. The last song I put on the tape, I almost didn't include— 'I'm Glad I Know Who Jesus Is.' And then I thought, *You know what? That song has a Southern feel, and they might like it,* so I put it on the tape.

"They recorded the song and put it on their new album. They 'singled' two or three songs from the album and sent them to radio stations, but not 'I'm Glad I Know Who Jesus Is.' Sometime later they recorded another album and tried in the same manner to get some reaction from it. But a funny thing happened: the stations went back to the former album and began to play 'I'm Glad I Know Who Jesus Is.'

The response was so great that the radio stations contacted the record company and the Nelons and said, 'We love "I'm Glad I Know Who Jesus Is." We're getting a large number of requests for it.' After hearing that, the record company went back to the former album and released my song as a single. It soon went to number one with the radio stations and number one on the *Singing News* charts."

The goal of every Christian should be to get to know our Savior, in all of his love and mercy. We should realize afresh and anew each morning who Jesus really is, draw close to his heart, and all through the day never wander farther than his fingertips.

When I worship, I would rather
my heart be without words than
my words be without heart.

LAMAR BOSCHMAN

It's Still the Cross

It's not conservative or liberal
However they're defined;
It's not about interpretations
Or the judgments of the mind.
It's the opposite of politics,
Power, and prestige;
It's about a simple message
And whether we believe.

CHORUS

It's still the cross;
It's still the blood of Calvary
That cleanses sin
And sets the captive free.
It's still the name,
The name of Jesus that has pow'r
To save the lost.

The Life of an Overcomer

*For the preaching of the cross is to them that perish foolishness;
but unto us which are saved it is the power of God.*

1 CORINTHIANS 1:18

Niles Borop III has very few peers in the songwriting world. In spite of very poor health since childhood, he developed into a man of enormous creativity. He has written more than thirteen hundred songs. Some six hundred of them have been published. The subject of this story is a joint effort between Niles and three other men, and what a song!

Niles was born in Aiken, South Carolina, in 1956, the son of Dr. Niles Borop Jr. and his wife, Meta. Niles became a very industrious teenager, giving his heart to Christ at age fourteen. It may sound strange, but two years before his conversion, he sensed that God wanted him to preach the gospel. During those early years, he began to study guitar and write songs. He wanted to communicate his biblical messages, so he sang at any invitation and to anyone who would listen.

Niles holds a degree from Mercer University, a Baptist school in Macon, Georgia, where he graduated with honors after accomplishing a triple major—speech, dramatic arts, and education. Some years later his time spent at a graduate school figured into the writing of "It's Still the Cross."

Niles told me the following story, which took place in 1987:

"I found out that I was losing my only kidney, and that I faced the prospect of death without a transplant. Quite frankly, all of the worldly successes became meaningless very quickly. I had no idea that my sisters could donate, or if they would. It was a breaking time for me. So I packed up all of the awards and put them in a closet and left them there for five years. I needed to perceive that my worth and value are not based on what other people think, but on what Christ has called me to do and whether or not I am obedient to him." In 1991, Niles's sister Catherine lovingly donated one of her kidneys to him.

I asked Niles to tell me about the writing of "It's Still the Cross," and following is what he offered:

"I am a graduate of Vanderbilt Divinity School, a very liberal place. But that course of study put a burning in my heart to communicate that we are not to lose sight of the foundation of our faith. It boils down to something very simple: it is still the blood and the sacrifice of Christ on the cross that redeems us and sets us free. It allows us to have an unfettered relationship with the heavenly Father. We must not displace or elude the fact that it is the compassion and love of Christ, as he willingly gave himself for us, that makes all the difference.

"'It's Still the Cross' was, in reality, written by several people, Buddy Mullins, Luke Garret, Mike Harlen, and myself—a group process. Mullins had brought the basic concept and the seed thought to me at an earlier meeting. I then met with Luke and Mike and shared with them what Buddy's ideas were about this subject.

"I basically wrote the verses and the chorus from Buddy's concepts, and Luke and Mike did a masterful job in musically interpreting what the Lord had given in the lyrics. The verses are very intense, while the chorus gives the bottom line remedy for all problems of the heart."

Christ took a thing to be despised—a cross—a place of sorrow, shame, and death, and made it a badge of honor.

Jesus Is Lord of All

VERSE

All my tomorrows, all my past,
Jesus is Lord of all.
I've quit my struggles, contentment at last,
Jesus is Lord of all.

CHORUS

King of kings, Lord of lords,
Jesus is Lord of all.
All my possessions and all my life,
Jesus is Lord of all.

VERSE

All of my conflicts, all my thoughts,
Jesus is Lord of all.
His love wins the battles I could not have fought,
Jesus is Lord of all.

"You Missed My Bat Again!"

*To this end Christ both died, and rose, and revived,
that he might be Lord both of the dead and living.*

ROMANS 14:9

The purpose of this story is twofold: (1) to let you see the heartbeat of the songwriters as they struggle to make Jesus Christ Lord of their lives, and (2) to let Gloria Gaither tell you about the writing of this wonderful worship song.

"I began writing in high school and entered numbers of speech contests, winning many of them. In one of the contests, an oration earned for me a trip to Washington where I met President Dwight Eisenhower." These activities and accomplishments led to a college scholarship for Gloria.

She continued, "As I sought God's will for my life, I always remembered the advice and counsel of my mother, who said, 'God's will for your life is God's will for this minute. Don't ask God for any more information until you know what you know to do now. Then do it with everything you've got.'

"When our children were small, we were talking a lot about the lordship of Christ. Just how do you prioritize? What may be important to us may not be what God wants to dwell upon at that particular time.

"I remember one notable event during those times. It was June and the week of Amy's third birthday. To celebrate she wanted to have a cookout down at the creek. She planned her own menu: hot dogs and hamburgers, corn on the cob, green beans, watermelon, and raspberry cake.

"The afternoon of the big affair, Grandma and Grandpa were the first to arrive. Benjy, then almost two, had a brand-new ball and bat and wanted Grandma to play ball with him. So while Amy waited for the cousins to climb into the wagon we had hitched to the garden tractor, Benjy and Grandma went on down to play ball.

"I watched Grandma pitch the ball to Benjy who was up to bat. Suddenly the peaceful mood was shattered as Benjy threw his bat to the ground, stomped his feet, and yelled at the top of his lungs, 'Grandma! You missed again! You missed my bat again!' It turned out to be that kind of day for this little guy. By the end of the day, with all the playing, running, fighting, and crying, Benjy was exhausted.

> *Bless the* LORD, *O my soul: and all that is within me, bless his holy name. Bless the* LORD, *O my soul, and forget not all his benefits . . .*
>
> PS. 103:1-2

"He held his arms up to me and said, 'Carry me, Mommy,' so I carried him up the hillside and to the house. He was all hot and dirty, and he went to sleep on my shoulder before I got him to the top.

"I took him to his room and laid him on his green bedspread. How dear he looked—his blond hair all plastered to his forehead, ketchup on his nose, a grubby little baseball clutched tightly in one hand! How I loved him! I took the baseball from his clenched fingers and smiled to myself as I remembered what he had said earlier about missing his bat. I became aware of some struggles of my own, some areas in my life that I needed to relinquish.

"There had been times when I acted like a spiritual two-year-old. Times when I had stood with my own neat little set of needs and longings and desires in my hand

and, in my own more subtle and sophisticated way, shouted to my children, and to my husband, and to the church and others around me, 'You missed my bat!'

"So that day beside a sleeping little boy, I knelt and gave it all up to Jesus: our precious children, our marriage, our hopes and plans and dreams and schemes, my fears and failures—all of it. Once more the peace and contentment came as I began to cease the struggling.

"As soon as we relinquish one area of our lives, God seems to make us aware of new unsurrendered areas. This process caused us to write 'Jesus Is Lord of All.' The verses tell of the struggle. I was convicted, and I prayed, 'Lord, you know I just need to make one big decision here. I don't need to make all of these decisions. I just need to say, "You are Lord of all."'"

The song has now gone around the world and been translated into scores of languages.

Recognizing many of the conflicts and needs in our lives often calls for the wisdom that only God can give to his children. He has admonished us, "If you lack wisdom, just ask me for it."

As John 4:23 says, its time, as worshipers of God, to give him all we have. For when he is exalted, everything about me is decreased.

JESSICA LEAH SPRINGER

JESUS, LORD TO ME

VERSE

If I had seen the sunset
On the day that Jesus died
And felt the glow of the sunrise
When the tomb was opened wide,
Would I have known You?
Could I have seen that
You were more than just a man?
You were Lord and King,
But now I know You and I can see
That You are Lord of all,
And You are Lord to me.

CHORUS

Jesus, Jesus, Lord to me;
Master, Savior, Prince of Peace;
Ruler of my heart today;
Jesus, Lord to me.

Gary McSpadden | Greg Nelson © 1981 River Oaks Music Company/Yellow House Music

If I Had Watched Jesus Die

And Thomas answered and said unto him, My Lord and my God.

JOHN 20:28

The Lord brought two prominent musicians together and used their individual, dedicated, and unique abilities to craft a song that has been a blessing to untold multitudes of Christians—a song born right out of the Scriptures.

Mangum, Oklahoma, is the hometown of Gary McSpadden. He was born there in 1943. His parents, Boyd and Helen McSpadden, later moved to Lubbock, Texas. Gary grew up in an extremely musical family. His mom and dad were songwriters with at least one of their compositions, "Heaven," becoming quite popular after being recorded by George Beverly Shea and a number of others.

As a youngster, Gary, like many other children, took his salvation for granted. But, he says, "on my fourteenth birthday I gave my heart completely to Christ. I made an exchange with God. I gave him nothing, and he gave me everything."

Gary sang as a soloist in the church from the age of ten. His voice began to mature and improve to the point that he was brought to the attention of Hovie Lister, manager of the Statemen Quartet. At age eighteen he was invited to sing with that Southern Gospel group for a period of about five months, during a medical leave of Jake Hess. He later sang with a number of traveling groups, two of which were the Bill Gaither Trio and the Gaither Vocal Band.

I asked Gary to tell me how "Jesus, Lord to Me" was written. Following is his story:

"I was reading the Bible one day and was thinking of Thomas in terms of his doubting. We all have our 'Thomas' moments. I tried to put myself in Thomas's shoes and asked myself, *What would I have thought if I had watched Jesus die, and later they had come to me and told me, 'He's alive'?* I might have concluded, *These people are nuts*, depending on my level of belief. Then, in my imagination I could hear Thomas say, after placing his hands in the wounds of Jesus, 'Now I know you, and now I see that you are Lord of all, and you are Lord to me.'

"I then wrote, 'If I had seen the sunset on the day that Jesus died, and felt the glow of the sunrise when the tomb was opened wide. Would I have known You, could I have seen that You were more than just a man, that You were Lord and King? But now I know You, and I can see.' Even though we might have an occasional 'Thomas' moment, we must personally get to the place where we believe in Christ's death, burial, and resurrection, with all of our hearts. Then we can sing with sincerity, 'Jesus, Lord to me.'

"As I completed the writing of the lyrics and had a portion of a melody, I concluded that I wanted someone of the talent and statue of Greg Nelson to have a part in this project with me, so I invited Greg to my home. I shared the lyric with him, and we talked briefly about the idea that I had concerning a melody. Nothing further was done with the song at my home that day. Greg took the lyric and the ideas that I shared with him and later wrote the musical setting, just as you see it in print today.

"Afterward, while on a cruise, I had an opportunity to show the new song to Sandi Patty, who liked it and agreed to record it. That helped to launch it on its way around the world. Many others have recorded 'Jesus, Lord to Me,' and it now appears in hymnals and has been translated into other languages."

I can only be a victorious Christian when I come to the full realization that Christ's death was for me, personally, as well as for every other individual who has come into the world.

JESUS, NAME ABOVE ALL NAMES

From the Washhouse to the World

Behold, a virgin shall be with child, and shall bring forth a son, and they shall call his name Emmanuel, which being interpreted is, God with us.

MATTHEW 1:23

Of the approximately twelve songs Naida Hearn wrote—she wasn't quite sure how many when I spoke with her—only one has been published. But what a song! She wrote it as she was nearing her fortieth birthday. She was born in New Zealand in 1931.

So great was Naida's interest in the different names of Jesus mentioned in the Bible that she began to make a list of the names.

As is the case with many homes in Palmerston North, she and her family had a "washhouse" behind the regular living quarters of the home. One day in the early 1970s, as she made her way to the washhouse, she carried with her the paper on which she had written the names of Jesus. According to her report to me, she placed the paper "on the windowsill against the window." The paper was in full view as she did the family washing.

Feeling in a very worshipful mood, she suddenly found herself singing. She expressed it to me as follows:

"While I was doing the washing, the Lord just gave me the first line, 'Jesus, name above all names,' to sing. I just started it and carried on singing. I sang the whole song just as you sing it today. I just opened my mouth and all of the words came out, the pitch and everything. I just sang.

"I thought, *Well, I'll write it down.* The Lord said Yes, so I left the washing and went down into the sitting room, found a key that was just right, and worked it out on manuscript paper. I said, 'Lord, is that okay? Is it all right like that?' Yes,

164

it was all right. That was all I wrote, and then I went back to the washing. It was just that simple. It was a straight-out lead from the Holy Spirit, absolutely. I can't say I thought about this or I thought about that; I just started on 'Jesus, name above all names,' and it carried on all by itself."

Soon thereafter the song was sung in Naida's church, New Life Church in Palmerston North. She didn't remember who sang it, but I can guess that it was she who presented it to her congregation. (She had a beautiful singing voice. She sang her song for me on the phone, and I prize the tape on which I recorded it. It is surprisingly clear and good, even long distance from New Zealand.) Visitors from other parts of her country who attended the church service took the song to their churches. Missionaries began to carry it overseas, where it quickly became a favorite. Soon it was being sung in several nations.

Naida reported to me: "I've had all sorts of people write to me asking that I add three more verses. I thought, *If the Lord had wanted three more verses, he would have given them to me.* All that needed to be said was said. The Spirit impressed on me that it was to be sung as a love song. It's all about Jesus. You are supposed to sing it softly, slowly, and reverently, as if he were our lover. This is what he wanted."

Naida was very active in her church, living a happy life with her Lord. She was a cheery soul and an interesting conversationalist, even on the phone from such a distance. She had a most infectious laugh.

Naida told me her story in 1999. I had another visit by phone with her in April 2001. In that same month, as I interviewed another songwriter from New Zealand, I was surprised to hear his report that she had passed away just one week earlier. She had gone to be with the one whose name is above all names and who had been her glorious Lord through so many of her seventy years.

As you consider the names given to our Savior, you, too,
will be drawn closer to him. As Naida suggested, sing "Jesus, Name Above
All Names" very softly. Sing it right now as a love song to him.

LORD, BE GLORIFIED

VERSE

In my life, Lord,
Be glorified, be glorified.
In my life, Lord,
Be glorified today.

VERSE

In my song, Lord,
Be glorified, be glorified.
In my song, Lord,
Be glorified today.

VERSE

In our home, Lord,
Be glorified, be glorified.
In our home, Lord,
Be glorified today.

The Lord First, Then Cindy

*I will praise thee, O Lord my God, with all my heart:
and I will glorify thy name for evermore.*

PSALM 86:12

Bob Kilpatrick is the middle of five children born to Southern Baptist air force chaplain August Kilpatrick and his wife, Delores, in 1952. His mom declared that he was singing by age two and could harmonize with others on such songs as "Ain't Gonna Study War No More." Bob remembers happy times in the car when the family would pick out things to sing about as they drove along. His music interest continued into high school where he played in the orchestra.

Bob related: "Once, in my early life, while living in Georgia, a friend took me on a retreat where I really was drawn to Jesus. I felt strongly that I needed him. I stood up in a meeting and committed myself to Christ. Then when I was eighteen years of age, our family moved to California, where I had an overwhelming experience of total commitment of my heart to the Lord."

Concerning the writing of his songs, Bob said, "When I became committed to Jesus, we went to the streets trying to tell people about Christ, all up and down California. I seemed to continually have an acoustic guitar in my hands, so it came naturally to make up songs to sing for the people who would listen. After a while I realized, *Maybe I have a talent for this. Maybe I should give the rest of my life to it.*"

Bob has written approximately 400 songs, with about 175 of them being recorded or published by most of the major Christian music companies in America. He confessed, "After the Lord gives me a song, I play it for my wife, Cindy. I want to please the Lord first, then Cindy."

As Bob zeroed in on the writing of "Lord, Be Glorified," my interview with him took on a wonderful atmosphere.

"In 1977, at age twenty-four, I was alone in my mother-in-law's living room in Atwater, California. Others of the family were in another part of the house watching television. I had my Bible open on my knees and my guitar in my hands. I paused and prayed, 'Lord, I'd like to write a song, and I don't want others to sing it. I want it to be a private prayer of dedication for Cindy and me to sing before our concerts.' At that time Cindy was traveling and singing with me. I then said, 'Lord, I'd like the song to be for the three of us.'

"I then began to put the song together. Presently Cindy came into the room and asked, 'What are you up to?' I said, 'I'm writing this song, but I'm having a little trouble with a certain part of it.' I sang it for her, and she made a suggestion that I thought sounded great. She then said, 'You know what, you should sing that tomorrow morning at church.' I had been invited to sing for the chapel service of the Castle Air Force Base. We were to visit there with Cindy's family, who were military people, as were mine. The next day I sang it for the small congregation.

"A week later I met up with Karen Lafferty, who was leaving almost immediately for a tour in Europe, and I shared the song with her and her keyboard player. She took the song to Europe, and the keyboard player, who didn't make that trip, took it to Calvary Chapel in Costa Mesa, California, where Chuck Smith was pastor. They sang 'Lord, Be Glorified' every Saturday night for the next two years."

The times the song has been recorded are too numerous to calculate. Maranatha recorded the song fifty times in a two-year period. Other major companies began to record and publish it. It has been placed in chorus books, hymnals, and choral arrangements with an inestimable number of copies being printed. It truly is a song that has been sung in many parts of the world.

Christ should "be glorified" in our very lives—mere words are not enough.
Someone many years ago said, "I'd rather see a sermon than hear one any day."

LORD, I LIFT YOUR NAME ON HIGH

VERSE

Lord, I lift Your name on high,
Lord, I love to sing Your praises,
I'm so glad You're in my life,
I'm so glad You came to save us.

CHORUS

You came from heaven to earth
To show the way,
From the earth to the cross,
My debt to pay,
From the cross to the grave,
From the grave to the sky
Lord, I lift Your name on high.

A Cyber Bible and My Guitar

Let them praise the name of the LORD: for his name alone is excellent;
his glory is above the earth and heaven.

PSALM 148:13

According to the CCLI Top 25 Songs list, "Lord, I Lift Your Name on High" has the distinction of being the number one praise and worship song sung in America's churches from 1997 to 2002. Rick Founds wrote this inspired piece of music. And although it is only one of more than five hundred songs he has written in his lifetime, it is by far his most popular.

Rick was born in 1954 to Doyle and Lorraine Founds of Idaho Falls, Idaho. His musical interest began early in life, and by age ten he already had a few songs under his belt, penning his first tunes for Sunday school. As a youth he developed a love for the guitar. Years later, in college, Rick took a number of music courses preparing him for his future ministry.

"Lord, I Lift Your Name on High" was born during Rick's daily devotional time, which he usually has in the morning. At the time the song was written, Rick was musical director of a large church. In order to sing and worship freely during his morning devotions, Rick chose an office in the back of the building, far away from the others who worked there. "Sometimes I made a lot of noise when I sang," Rick admitted, "but I felt comfortable in that office to sit and play my guitar while studying."

Using a small Macintosh computer along with a disc, which contained the entire Bible, Rick would worship while viewing passages of Scripture. "I developed a habit," he said, "of playing my guitar along with the reading of the Bible on my computer screen. I would read a portion of the New Testament followed by a portion of the Old Testament.

"One particular day, as I was having my devotional period, the Lord impressed on my heart that his work on our behalf was a cycle of events—Christ came from heaven to earth, gave his life on the cross for us, was buried, and three days later rose from the dead. He then went back to his heavenly Father, making the cycle and our salvation complete. That, essentially, is the lyric of the song. I picked up my guitar and began to sing, 'Lord, I lift Your name on high.'

"It's really just a simple song," Rick said, "but it's what the Lord dropped into my heart. The whole song came quickly—I didn't struggle with it at all. I did, however, continue to work on the latter part of the song for another four or five days before I felt it was complete. Then I sang it for an evening Bible study. They seemed to love the song. At the time I had no idea that it would be so popular—I had simply written another song, much as I had done so many times before."

Hearing his song sung by thousands of men during a Promise Keepers rally has been just one of the wonderful thrills Rick has experienced with "Lord, I Lift Your Name on High." The letters he receives on a regular basis touch his heart. Translated into multiple languages, this easy-to-remember song has quickly made its way into distant lands, encouraging all who sing it to worship more freely. It shows us just how powerful our God is and how he can use one person for his glory. This gives us reason, indeed, to lift his name on high.

There are times when we should worship the heavenly Father simply for who he is. There are times when we should worship God simply because of his holiness. And there are times when we should worship God for all that he has done to bring us to himself.

MAJESTY

Majesty, worship His majesty,
Unto Jesus be all glory,
Honor, and praise.
Majesty, kingdom authority,
Flow from His throne
Unto His own His anthem raise.
So exalt, lift up on high
The name of Jesus.
Magnify, come glorify
Christ Jesus the King.
Majesty, worship His majesty,
Jesus who died, now glorified,
King of all kings.

© 1981 Rocksmith Music
  Jack Hayford

At Churchill's Birthplace

*Who being the brightness of his glory, and the express image of his person, and upholding all
things by the word of his power; when he had by himself purged our sins, sat down on the
right hand of the Majesty on high.*

HEBREWS 1:3

Dr. Jack Hayford, for many years pastor of the famed Church on the Way in Van Nuys, California, is not only an outstanding preacher and Bible teacher but also a talented songwriter. His most famous song, the composition that has brought him the most acclaim, has a rather unusual history.

Years ago, Dr. and Mrs. Hayford traveled for ten days in Denmark, where he had speaking engagements. Following their stay in Denmark, they took advantage of two weeks of free time before another scheduled series of meetings, a seminar in Oxford, England. It was to be a study of "spiritual awakenings" under the direction of Dr. Edwin Orr.

The year was the silver anniversary of the coronation of Elizabeth II as queen of England. The celebrating, the countryside, and the spirit of enthusiasm of the English people, combined with the great historical significance of that kingdom, made those two weeks a very special time for the Hayfords.

Dr. Hayford reports that he was completely caught up in the emotion of the occasion. As he walked among the people and saw them move about amid signs of history on every hand, he sensed a feeling of grandeur and nobility. While touring the countryside, stopping here and there to examine a significant bit of history, the couple made a short visit to Blenheim, the palace where Winston Churchill was born and raised and where he would occasionally go for a short rest during the horrors of World War II.

Although that was a monumental chapter of history and a generation past, memories of those days and what had gone before came rushing back to Pastor Hayford. As he looked about, he sensed, too, that even though individuals are greatly used in the course of humankind's existence on this earth, there is a greater power, the one who is the Author of our destiny.

As he felt the courage and motivation of the English people, Dr. Hayford realized that there was also a deep feeling in their hearts for the royalty who stood with them in dark hours. Even now they were excited about sharing in the celebration of their monarch. Suddenly there came to his mind a feeling that Christ wants his church to have such a sense of loyalty and fellowship because he must be our leader in good times and bad.

As Dr. Hayford stood on the magnificent, well-groomed landscape surrounding Blenheim Palace, he said to his wife, "Honey, I can hardly describe to you all the things this setting evokes in me. There is something of majesty in all this, and I believe it has a great deal to do with why people who lived here have been of such consequence in the shaping of history. I don't mean that building and beauty can beget greatness, but I do feel that some people fail to perceive their possibilities because of their dismal surroundings."

As he talked to her of how Christ wants to exercise his kingdom authority in our lives and our being, one word seemed to charge to the forefront: *majesty!* The word seemed at the moment to represent the glory, excellence, grace, and power of Christ. By comparison, Queen Elizabeth seemed but a small reminder of the royal heritage we enjoy as we worship the majesty of our risen Lord.

As the Hayfords pulled themselves from that regal place and drove away, Dr. Hayford said, "Take the notebook and write down some words, will you, babe?" He then began to dictate the key, the notes, the timing, and the lyrics to one of the most popular songs now being used by Christians worldwide.

The song was edited and completed sometime later at the piano in the living room of their home. Never in their wildest dreams could the Hayfords have imagined the impact that this song would have on the singing of Christians in so many lands.

When we see the great King and are face-to-face with his glory, it will be wonderful to forever adore his majesty and his power. While we wait, we bow to his authority as we "lift up on high the name of Jesus."

The Majesty and Glory of Your Name

Verse

When I gaze into the night skies
And see the work of Your fingers,
The moon and stars suspended in space,
What is man that You are mindful of him?
You have given man a crown of glory and honor,
And have made him a little lower than the angels.
You have put him in charge of all creation,
The beasts of the field,
The birds of the air,
The fish of the sea.
But what is man?
Oh what is man that You are mindful of him?

Chorus

Alleluia, alleluia,
The majesty and glory of Your name.
Alleluia, alleluia,
The majesty and glory of Your name.
Alleluia, alleluia,
Alleluia, alleluia,
Alleluia, alleluia, alleluia.

(Bridge)

O Lord our God, the majesty and glory of Your name
Transcends the earth and fills the heavens.
O Lord our God, little children praise You perfectly,
And so would we, and so would we.

"I Was Crushed!"

O Lord our Lord, how excellent is thy name in all the earth!
who hast set thy glory above the heavens.

PSALM 8:1

Occasionally a worship song comes along that rises to a level that transcends the ordinary, that directs our focus, very sharply, on our wonderful heavenly Father. Such is this song taken from the Scriptures that soars upward on the wings of a beautiful melody that only God can give.

Tom Fettke, whom you met in the story behind "Adoration," also in this volume, has been used as a servant to the Lord in helping multiplied thousands of people focus on the majesty and glory of God.

Tom spoke of the writing of "The Majesty and Glory of Your Name."

"This work is not mine. The text is Psalm 8—I wasn't the author of Psalm 8. The lyric setting is by Linda Lee Johnson, and this was her first attempt at lyric writing. She was a choir member in Redwood Chapel in Castro Valley, California, where I was minister of music. Linda had written a children's Sunday school program that revealed some of her creative abilities. When I asked her to try writing a text based on my favorite psalm, Psalm 8, her response was less than confident, but she was willing to give it a try. A few days later she presented to me a lyric that I felt was nearly perfect and ready for my attempt at a musical setting.

> *I will declare thy name unto my brethren, in the midst of the church will I sing praise unto thee.*
>
> HEB. 2:12

"The original piece ended with 'Little children praise You perfectly, and so would we, and so would we. . . .' However, it never felt quite right and remained in a drawer in its old form for several months. Then, during a concert in which my choir performed the Ken Medema anthem 'Moses,' I saw something in that song that made me realize what was needed in 'The Majesty and Glory of Your Name.' It needed a warm, emotional, more fully developed personal response to God's majesty and glory expressed in the verses that Linda Johnson had written.

"The next day I wrote the 'Alleluia' section. Playing through the completed work was an incredibly moving experience, and I just knew that God had chosen to touch this musical and textual creation.

"I took it to my adult choir at church the next week. They didn't respond in a positive manner. I was crushed. I realized later that I had made the mistake of starting on the first section and tried to perfect it before moving on to the praise and worship section. I'm sure if I had started with the 'Alleluias,' the simplicity and emotional qualities of this experience would have immediately won them over. It took several weeks, but my choir finally fell in love with 'The Majesty and Glory of Your Name.'

"That's the story. This song is not mine; it's God's. It is one of those things in life that you know, beyond a shadow of a doubt, you had nothing to do with; you were only a tool in the hands of God to display his handiwork."

Choirs and congregations in many places have been lifted toward God with the singing of this masterful song of worship. I will repeat for this story what Tom said of the writing of another song. I'm sure he would again say, "God gave me the ability to write songs, but this specific one was God-given and anointed by him."

I love the songs that are taken from the Scriptures and that soar on the melodies that only God can give. They lift our spirits and give us strength.

How quickly we forget what it's all about.
We can get so strategic that we worship so our
church will grow, not because He is worthy.
But we're doing all this because God is worthy
and we want to worship Him.

TOMMY WALKER

MIGHTY IS OUR GOD

CHORUS

Mighty is our God,
Mighty is our King,
Mighty is our Lord,
Ruler of everything.
Glory to our God,
Glory to our King,
Glory to our Lord,
Ruler of everything.

VERSE

His name is higher,
Higher than any other name.
His power is greater,
For He has created everything.

© 1989 Integrity's Hosanna! Music
Don Moen | Eugene Greco | Gerrit Gustafson

Some Good Lyrics Just in Time

Thou art worthy, O Lord, to receive glory and honour and power: for thou hast created all things, and for thy pleasure they are and were created.

REVELATION 4:11

Three of the most talented and dedicated pioneers of the contemporary worship music genre put their hearts and hands together, and with the Lord leading them, gave to the world one of our most widely known worship songs. The men were Eugene Greco, Gerrit Gustafson, and Don Moen.

The writing of this song was begun by Greco, who was born in Rome, New York, in 1960. His dad, Eugene, and his mother, Nancy, recognized that Greco had a real bent toward music when he was five. He would try to duplicate on the piano what he heard his older sister play. He began taking piano lessons at age seven. His music study was a prelude to receiving a degree in piano from the Crane School of Music, a branch of State University of New York.

I asked Eugene to tell me of his songwriting and particularly the writing of his famous song "Mighty Is Our God." He said, "In 1987, I was offered a position at Christ for the Nations Institute in Stony Brook, New York, on Long Island. My wife, Joy, and I moved there, and I became head of the music department in a school of about 150 students. I followed Marty Nystrom in that position—the person who wrote 'As the Deer.'

"Every morning I met with the students and led them in worship. They had a tremendous desire for the presence of God. We sang the songs we knew again and again, and started looking for new expressions—worship songs that we might sing. That is when I focused in on writing songs suitable for congregational singing.

"As I continued to meet with the students, a sense of the need for new worship songs became even greater with me. I wanted something that those young people could catch on to very easily and enjoy singing.

"One morning, directly after one of our chapel services, the Lord gave me an idea for a song. I went to my office and began thinking of the greatness and might of the God we serve. I then wrote a simple, short chorus that I called 'Mighty Is Our God.' The students caught on to it quickly and sang it heartily.

"We decided to make a low-budget recording of several songs and put them on a tape for distribution. Little did I know that the other branch of Christ for the Nations in Dallas, Texas, was also making a tape for distribution. They put my song on their tape also. I really don't know where they obtained it. They sent the tape out across the United States, and soon 'Mighty Is Our God' was being sung in many churches and Christian concerts.

"The people at Integrity Music in Mobile, Alabama, somehow heard my song and wanted to put it on an album they were planning, although they thought it needed 'something else,' perhaps some verses."

Gerrit Gustafson, author, teacher, and songwriter with fifty recorded songs to his credit, was at that time part of the original creative team at Integrity Music. He and Don Moen, whom you've meet in this volume, and who also worked at Integrity, were gathering songs for the planned album. They went to Gerrit's home and down into his basement, where the piano was kept, to try to write a melody for "part B" of Eugene's song. They wrote a melody that they thought would be a nice addition to the song, but they had no lyrics.

They needed the song by the next day in order to record it. Gerrit told me, "I was to drive from Mobile, Alabama, to Pensacola, Florida, that day, so I took a note pad along, and as I drove I thought of some of the reasons for the greatness and the might of God. By the time I returned, the B part of the song was finished."

This song lifts the Savior as we sing it, reminding us once again of his might and power, even in the things he has created. It truly helps us in our worship of the King of kings.

MORE PRECIOUS THAN SILVER

A Fast Broken with Stolen French Fries

Receive my instruction, and not silver; and knowledge rather than choice gold. For wisdom is better than rubies; and all the things that may be desired are not to be compared to it.

PROVERBS 8:10–11

During Lynn DeShazo's first year at Auburn University in Auburn, Alabama, she developed a desire to write Christian songs—songs that would be expressions of her heart to the Lord and that would be meaningful to people who heard them. Those first efforts at songwriting were seemingly quite meager, yet people responded very positively. She was greatly encouraged by their attitudes toward her first unpublished songs.

After graduation, in 1978, with a degree in recreation administration, Lynn took a job at McDonald's—not the most likely place for an Auburn alumnus to work—yet it provided for her livelihood during the first months following graduation. She also learned very valuable spiritual lessons as she continued her involvement with a campus church at Auburn called Maranatha Ministries.

Lynn was learning that Christians should occasionally fast, and that fasting was a scriptural method of spiritual growth and accomplishment. She found herself one Wednesday in a precarious situation. Her boss at McDonald's had assigned her to "fry duty," the task of cooking the french fries. It just happened to be a day of fasting for her. Well, needless to say, the battle was on!

The fries smelled oh, so good! As the day wore on, her hunger made the breaking of her fast, by eating only a couple of those french fries, pale into insignificance. After looking around to make sure that no one would see her, she slipped a few fries into her mouth. At that moment she was almost overcome with guilt—guilt that she declared to me was "twofold." She knew that she had broken her fast and that she had done it with stolen french fries.

After work that day, and as soon as she could get alone with the Lord, Lynn earnestly asked his forgiveness for breaking her fast and for taking something that did not belong to her. She was led to Colossians chapter 2, and particularly to verse 7, where she found that in Christ are the hidden "treasures of wisdom and knowledge." She also went to Proverbs chapter 8, which reveals that there are spiritual things that are of more value than silver and gold or precious jewels, and that the earthly things we often desire are "not to be compared with it."

She had her guitar with her, and as she began to play, the Lord dropped a song into her heart. All of a sudden, there it was—"More Precious Than Silver." She felt so blessed. As the guilt had been twofold, so too was the blessing.

Lynn shared "More Precious Than Silver" with the worship leader of her campus church, Mark Vosel. He rejoiced in it and used it in subsequent worship services. She related how Mark had been a great encouragement and had urged her to continue in her songwriting.

Her song soon began to be sung in other places, places such as Christ for the Nations Institute, a Christian college in Dallas, Texas. The students loved it and began sharing it in services where they had an opportunity to minister. It soon was being sung far and wide. It was published by Integrity Music in 1982 and was presented on their fifth recording, *Glory to the King*, in 1986. Lynn has been a staff writer for Integrity Music since 1989.

"More Precious Than Silver" has since been translated into several languages and continues to be sung in other counties as well as in the United States. It ranks very high on the list of popular praise choruses.

When Lynn is not on the road ministering in other cities, she is very active on the worship team in her present home church, Liberty Church in Hoover, Alabama, a suburb of Birmingham.

When things seem to be going a bit sideways, examine yourself to see if the greatest longing of your heart compares with the one who is more precious than silver, more costly than gold, and more beautiful than diamonds. You might also check your heart to see if there is anything you desire that, in your estimation, compares with him.

MORE THAN WONDERFUL

"You Can Write a Better Song"

For unto us a child is born, unto us a son is given: and the government shall be upon his shoulder: and his name shall be called Wonderful, Counsellor, The mighty God, The everlasting Father, The Prince of Peace.

ISAIAH 9:6

Larnelle Harris and Sandi Patty won a Grammy Award for their duet performance of 'More Than Wonderful'; the song was voted Song of the Year in 1984 by the Gospel Music Association, and I was honored as GMA's Songwriter of the Year. Although my songs had been nominated seven previous times, it was the first time that a song from a musical, rather than from an artist's project, had ever been chosen as Song of the Year." That was Lanny Wolfe's brief history of his song.

Although highly educated and vastly experienced as a music professor, Wolfe is best known for his songwriting. Following is Lanny's account of just how difficult it was for him to bring into being one of his most honored and blessed songs. He told me the following story:

"During the 1970s, in addition to songs I wrote for the many albums recorded by the Lanny Wolfe Trio, I also wrote my first two musicals, *Greater Is He That Is in Me* and *Noel, Jesus Is Born*. Because of the impact of the latter, my publisher at that time, the Benson Company, wanted me to do another Christmas cantata.

"In the process of the meetings, Bob McKenzie, the president of the company, suggested that I write a song for the musical based on Isaiah 9:6. I responded to the assignment, and the song came easily.

"The song was written on the Lanny Wolfe Trio bus. As was my custom, I shut out all of the activities on the bus and got right down to the task. First I became thoroughly familiar with Isaiah 9:6. Then I began to write lyrics, parts of which came very easily. All of the lyrics flowed from the scripture. The song is built around the entire idea of 'How do you describe someone who is indescribable?' He's beyond description. Preachers and songwriters try, but in vain, to pull words together that will paint pictures of his likeness. I tried to use words like *amazing*—he's more. I tried *marvelous*—he's more. After I wrote about his promises in the first stanza and found them all to be true, the rest of the song came rather quickly."

Lanny added, "The trio was as excited about this new 'child' as I was. We all sensed the destiny of it. As a trio, we were able to tell when a song had spirit and excitement in its lyrics and music, which were all very apparent with this new song.

"After we had sung 'More Than Wonderful' in concerts for four or five months, I presented it to Bob McKenzie, who was given to quick decisions. His first reaction was that the song should not go into the new Christmas musical. 'Lanny, you can write a better song' was his response. It was difficult for Bob to assess the response that we were getting in the concerts. He wasn't there to feel what we had felt so many times. After much persistence on my part, Bob gave in and allowed the song to go into the cantata.

"Don Marsh arranged the song for his choir, but it just didn't click. He then went back to the drawing board and came up with the now famous duet/choir arrangement. I suggested that Sandi Patty and Larnelle Harris sing the duet on the demo tape, and it was agreed upon. Because of their concert schedules, Larnelle and Sandi were not present in the studio at the same time. Larnelle recorded his part, and later Sandi was brought in to add her part, under Don's direction.

"I learned so much about God from this chapter in my life. Occasionally, what we call bad times are really blessings in disguise. God is always working for our good, even when we might not have a clue as to what he is doing."

Not even a small fraction of God's glory and his majesty
can be imagined by people who are finite.

My Jesus, I Love Thee

VERSE

My Jesus, I love thee, I know thou art mine.
For thee all the follies of sin I resign.
My gracious Redeemer, my Saviour art Thou.
If ever I loved Thee, my Jesus 'tis now.

VERSE

I love Thee because Thou hast first loved me
And purchased my pardon on Calvary's tree.
I love Thee for wearing the thorns on Thy brow.
If ever I loved Thee, my Jesus 'tis now.

VERSE

In mansions of glory and endless delight,
I'll ever adore Thee in heaven so bright.
I'll sing with a glittering crown on my brow.
If ever I loved Thee, my Jesus 'tis now.

The Influence of a Sixteen-Year-Old

*If a man love me, he will keep my words: and my Father will love him,
and we will come unto him, and make our abode with him.*

JOHN 14:23

Occasionally, in the search for information concerning the story behind a particular hymn, great barriers are encountered. Such is the case with one of our best-loved hymns, "My Jesus, I Love Thee." It was not until recent years that the identity of the songwriter, William Ralph Featherstone (1846–1873), became known.

It is reported that he probably grew up in Canada, since it was in Toronto in 1862 that he became a Christian. His conversion must have been very special, because just afterward and in connection with this glorious event, this sixteen-year-old wrote the hymn that is still meaningful to so many people.

Some historians have said that William mailed the poem to a relative in Los Angeles, who must have sent it to England, because it appeared there in *The London Hymnal*, published in 1864, just two years following his conversion.

Sometime later, in Boston, Massachusetts, A. J. Gordon was busy putting together a hymnal for Baptist worshipers. During the process he was going through other hymnals, getting ideas and perhaps some songs for his hymnbook. In *The London Hymnbook* he saw "My Jesus, I Love Thee" but was not at all impressed with the musical setting. He thought he could make great improvements for the beautiful, meaningful lyrics by composing better music for the song. The melody that he wrote has carried Featherstone's lyrics to every corner of our world.

A. J. Gordon was born in New Hampshire on April 19, 1836. He was educated at Brown University and Newton Theological Seminary. He was ordained at age twenty-seven, and he became the pastor of a Baptist church in Jamaica Plains, Massachusetts. He later pastored the Clarendon Street Baptist Church in Boston and died there in 1895, at the height of his wonderful ministry. And yet the height of his ministry might actually have been in 1864, when he gave to the world the musical setting that has carried "My Jesus, I Love Thee" around the world.

The life of every Christian is changed after conversion. The Bible says that the "old things are passed away; behold, all things are become new" (2 Cor. 5:17). Perhaps this young man had keenly realized his guilt before the Lord Jesus became particularly near and dear to him. He must have sensed a tremendous need for forgiveness. And we know that those who are forgiven more love more.

As you look back on your life and see the things from which you have been forgiven, there should be a strong tendency to draw closer to and increase your love for the Savior.

If we will love him, then we must love others. If we pray according to his will, our prayer must be for others. We cannot love him without loving others.

My Life Is in You, Lord

CHORUS

My life is in You, Lord; my strength is in You Lord;
My hope is in You, Lord, in You, it's in You.
My life is in You, Lord; my strength is in You, Lord;
My hope is in You, Lord, in You, it's in You.

VERSE

I will praise You with all of my life.
I will praise You with all of my strength.
With all of my life, with all of my strength,
All of my hope is in You.

© 1986 Integrity's Hosanna! Music
    Daniel Gardner

A Gift He Couldn't Keep

Your life is hid with Christ in God. When Christ,
who is our life, shall appear, then shall ye also appear with him in glory.

COLOSSIANS 3:3–4

One Sunday afternoon in the mid-1980s, Dan Gardner knew he needed something, but little did he realize what God was about to give him. He gave him something he couldn't keep. And he truly didn't keep it, because it was a popular Christian song that has traveled around the world.

Dan Gardner was born in 1956 into the home of Leonard and Anna Rose Gardner, founders of the church where he is presently the worship leader—Zion Christian Church, in Troy, Michigan. He is one of four children, all of whom are musical.

In a preacher's home, Dan was face-to-face with the issue of knowing Christ, almost on a daily basis. Therefore it was natural for him to become a Christian at an early age. He was led to the Lord at age seven or eight; he doesn't remember the exact year.

Gardner graduated from Oakland University in Rochester, Michigan, in 1988 with a major in music. He said, "I crammed four years into ten while working full-time."

I asked Dan to tell me exactly how he wrote "My Life Is in You, Lord," and he shared the following story:

"In the mid-1980s, my wife, Joanne, my two daughters, and I were living at my wife's parents' home while our house was being built. I was raising a family, going to college full-time, and was the full-time worship leader at Zion Church. It was amazing to me that my wife could endure that kind of schedule. God bless her!

"On Sunday afternoon, after leading the worship for two Sunday morning services, I sat down to do some homework for my college music composition class. I barely had time enough to complete the assignment and still have time to prepare to lead the worship in the evening service.

"I felt so pressed by the hands of the clock, and I felt a real need for added energy. I knew it would help me if I would relax and wait on God. I sat down at the piano and began to play and sing spontaneously to the Lord, as I often had done during just such a time. As I was playing and singing, suddenly from my heart came, 'My life is in You, Lord.' The words and a melody kept coming until the whole of a song was given to me. It took a very short time. I was blessed! I don't recall if I sang it at the service that night, but if not, I'm sure I sang it shortly thereafter.

"As one of the Lord's worship leaders, I have sought to find that place of abandoning the control of my life to him. I am still learning to trust him completely. I know that when I do, he graces me with the strength of his presence in my life. I know that I cannot glorify him with my life apart from the power of his Spirit to do so."

Zion Church published "My Life Is in You, Lord," in 1985, and sometime later Integrity recorded it on a project featuring Joseph Garlington. Dan told me, "It really began to have a wide audience after that."

Dan continues to write songs occasionally. He feels blessed to see such a proliferation of writers with songs coming out of the praise and worship movement. He said, "It is difficult to keep up with all of the great material coming our way—a wonderful outpouring!" A couple of other songs that Dan has written that have been widely sung are "Exalt the Lord Our God" and "Blessed Be the Rock."

Thanks, Dan, for "My Life Is in You, Lord"; it is one of my favorites. I love the repeated listing of the words *life*, *strength*, and *hope* that we have in our Lord. And in return we praise him with all of our lives.

Can you think of anything more comforting than to come to the full realization that our very beings are engulfed in the heavenly Father through his precious Son? "In him we live, and move, and have our being . . . For we are also his offspring" (Acts 17:28).

MY TRIBUTE

VERSE

How can I say thanks for the things
You have done for me?
Things so undeserved,
Yet You give to prove Your love for me.
The voices of a million angels
Could not express my gratitude.
All that I am and ever hope to be,
I owe it all to Thee.

CHORUS

To God be the glory,
To God be the glory,
To God be the glory,
For the things He has done.
With His blood He has saved me,
With His pow'r He has raised me,
To God be the glory,
For the things He has done.

The Prediction of a Totally Radical Guy

*And now, O Father, glorify thou me with thine own self
with the glory which I had with thee before the world was.*

JOHN 17:5

This is the story behind a song that I consider to be Andrae Crouch's greatest. In an interview in 2001, he told me the following story. I'll let him tell it to you now.

"When I became eighteen years of age, God called me to work in the Los Angeles center of Teen Challenge, a recovery ministry for young people. The founder was David Wilkerson, author of the best-selling book *The Cross and the Switchblade*.

"Teen Challenge was housed in a large building, much like a huge mansion. During my first day at the center, I saw this guy, Larry Reed, half white and half Hispanic, who had been released from San Quentin Prison—an atheist who didn't want anything to do with the Lord. But he began to really love my music. He often would threaten to leave the center, and I would take him into the chapel and play music for him. I would tell him, 'Man, don't leave. You've been paroled to this place. It will really mess things up for you if you leave.' I would persuade him to stay another night.

"Larry finally got saved and turned his life around. He turned out to be a radical guy—totally radical. If he walked into a room where everyone was talking quietly, he would yell, 'Praise the Lord! Hallelujah!' Everyone would always say, 'Well, here comes Larry.'

> *And at midnight Paul and Silas prayed, and sang praises unto God: and the prisoners heard them.*
>
> ACTS 16:25

"Larry was at the center for two of the three and a half to four years that I was there. At the end of my stay at Teen Challenge, I went back to my home church to continue my music ministry there.

"One day I received a phone call. The person on the line said, 'Hey Andy!' I asked, 'Who is this?' And he said, 'This is Larry, *praise God!*' I kinda chuckled. He said, 'I had a dream about you the other night.' I said, 'What is it now, Larry?' He said, 'I dreamed that you were going to write a song that is going to go around the world. It will be the biggest song you ever wrote to this day.' I asked, 'Well, what do I have to read?' And he said, 'Read John chapter 17, a passage about Jesus before he went back to heaven and his glory.' In that passage Jesus said, 'Father, I have glorified thee, now glorify me.' I read the passage and didn't feel anything—no inspiration to write.

"The following morning I got up singing, 'To God be the glory.' I asked myself, *Where did that come from?* I quickly got my tape recorder and taped the line I had just sung. I then went to the piano—I had a small apartment in the rear of my parents' home—and wrote 'My Tribute' in about ten minutes. I played it for my mother, and she said, 'Praise the Lord.' I had forgotten that Larry had called, so I didn't connect my song with the scriptures he had suggested I read.

"That evening I was to visit in the home of my godchild, where I was scheduled to have dinner. I played the song for them, and we were all singing and weeping around the piano. We sang 'My Tribute' for about an hour.

"We went to the table and began to eat, and I said, 'Hey! Guess who called me yesterday.' They asked, 'Who?' I said, 'Larry Reed!' They chuckled—they knew Larry—and then I told them about Larry's prediction that I would write a song that would go all over the world. My friend Carrie Gonzalo said, 'You just wrote a song this morning!' I said, 'Yes, but it can't be that song!' She suggested that we read the scripture that Larry had told me to read. We read the passage as we sat there. 'I have glorified thee on the earth: I have finished the work which thou gavest me to do. And now, O Father, glorify thou me with thine own self with the glory which I had with thee before the world was' (John 17:4–5). I gasped and said, 'It's all about *glory!*'"

> *The greatest spiritual goal that you and I can ever set is to glorify our heavenly Father with our very lives. Let's make Jesus' life our example, and if there be any praise, "to God be the glory!"*

As worship begins in holy expectancy, it ends in holy obedience. Holy obedience saves worship from becoming an opiate, an escape from the pressing needs of modern life.

RICHARD FOSTER

No One Ever Cared for Me Like Jesus

VERSE

I would love to tell you what I think of Jesus,
Since I found in Him a friend so strong and true.
I would tell you how He changed my life completely,
He did something that no other friend could do.

CHORUS

No one ever cared for me like Jesus;
There's no other friend so kind as He.
No one else could take the sin and darkness from me;
O how much He cared for me.

VERSE

All my life was full of sin when Jesus found me,
All my heart was full of misery and woe.
Jesus placed His strong and loving arms around me,
And He led me in the way I ought to go.

Charles Frederick Weigle © 1932 Singspiration Music (ASCAP)
(Administered by Brentwood-Benson Music Publishing, Inc.)

Let 'er Rip!

Casting all your care upon him; for he careth for you.

1 PETER 5:7

Dr. Charles Weigle lived for nearly a century. He died in his ninety-fifth year in Chattanooga, Tennessee. He was probably the godliest person I have ever known. I had the privilege of directing the music for him in one of his evangelistic crusades when he was in his mideighties. He preached with such power from God that I saw grown men weep their way down to the platform area, wanting to get right with God.

Dr. Weigle lived on the campus of Tennessee Temple University in Chattanooga during the latter years of his life. As a student I was honored to chat with him from time to time, often sharing meals with him in the dining commons.

Charles Frederick Weigle was born in Lafayette, Indiana, on November 20,

1871. He was converted at the age of twelve. With the help of Christian friends and an unswerving faith in God, he became a true and faithful laborer for Jesus Christ. Later he felt the call of God and surrendered to preach the gospel. His life of service to God has been enhanced greatly by his ability to write gospel songs.

Troublesome times came to this giant of the faith, as they do to many of us. But out of these grievous sorrows flowed forth one of the most beautiful and widely known of his songs. It has been sung around the world and has been translated into many languages.

One day Dr. Weigle came home to find a note from his wife declaring that she was leaving. She was going to the "world" to get the things that she felt were owed to her. She didn't want to be the wife of an evangelist any longer.

She left him and became a woman of the world. He happened upon her five years later on the streets of Los Angeles, California. Soon after that chance meeting, when back home in Sebring, Florida, one night he walked to a nearby lake and out onto the end of the dock. He was in such a dark mental state that as he looked into the foreboding waters, the devil seemed to say, "You could end it all right here." He quickly drew back, for he knew that was not the answer. He walked slowly back to his home and into the living room and sat down at the piano. God did a wonderful thing for him that night. During the following twenty minutes, he poured into Dr. Weigle's heart "No One Ever Cared for Me Like Jesus." He later said that the lyric came "as fast as I could put it down." It was the first song he had written since his world fell apart.

At that moment he heard a small voice within saying, "Charlie, I haven't forgotten you. I still care for you." He fell to his knees, asking God to forgive him for not trusting him completely. He determined never again to let such a thought cross his mind.

He later became famous for the little saying "Let 'er rip!" He had learned not to worry about things over which he had no control. He left them in God's hands. He wrote a book titled *Quit Worrying*, which has been helpful to many Christians.

Myriad stories could be written about the songs of Charles Weigle. In all, he has written between four and five hundred, many of which have become very popular among Christians everywhere.

How often have you wondered, Does anyone really care? *Well, there is one who loves you and cares more for you than you care for yourself. Turn every problem over to him . . . right now!*

OH, HOW HE LOVES YOU AND ME

VERSE

Oh how He loves you and me,
Oh how He loves you and me.
He gave His life,
What more could He give?
Oh how He loves you,
Oh how He loves me,
Oh how He loves you and me.

VERSE

Jesus to Calv'ry did go,
His love for sinners to show.
What He did there
Brought hope from despair.
Oh how He loves you,
Oh how He loves me,
Oh how He loves you and me.

They Wanted More Lyric

*Herein is love, not that we loved God, but that he loved us,
and sent his Son to be the propitiation for our sins.*

1 JOHN 4:10

For more than forty years, the name Kurt Kaiser has been synonymous with Christian keyboard artistry, songwriting, conducting, and arranging.

The "windy city," Chicago, Illinois, is Kurt's hometown. He was born there in 1934. He said, "I was seven years old when one Sunday evening we were all gathered around the piano in the living room of our home singing, as was our custom each week. I began having a real urge from the Spirit of God to know him and to give my heart and life to Christ. My mother went with me to my bedroom, and we knelt down by the bed and I accepted Christ into my life."

After high school Kurt studied at the American Conservatory of Music in

Chicago. He then enrolled in Northwestern University, where he earned two degrees.

In 1959, Kurt joined Word, Incorporated, as director of artists and repertoire and later became vice president and director of music. It was not until 1969 that he got the opportunity to try his hand at serious writing. He and Ralph Carmichael cowrote a musical, *Tell It Like It Is*, out of which came Kurt's very popular "Pass It On." After that he continued to write very seriously, and since that time he has written more than four hundred songs.

Following is Kurt's account of the writing of his most popular song:

"Through the years I have been in the habit of keeping my ears tuned to things that people say, a phrase that may give me an idea for a song. I'll write it down quickly. I may come across a musical motive or a lyrical idea that I can file away in a special place in my office. Occasionally I will pull these things out and look at them. One day I came across this line, 'Oh, how He loves you and me,' and I wrote it down. I remember very well writing it across the top of a piece of manuscript paper, and that's all I had.

"I then sat down to think about that phrase, and the whole song quickly came to me. I could not have spent more than ten or fifteen minutes writing the whole of it. That's how rapidly it all came, the lyrics and the melody together. I sent it off to secure a copyright. I could not believe what came back in the mail.

"The Copyright Office in Washington said that there was not enough original lyric to warrant the granting of a copyright. I was extremely disappointed, because I knew the song was very singable. A couple of days went by, and I decided to write a companion verse, or a second set of lyrics. I sent it back to Washington, and this time I got the copyright."

"Oh, How He Loves You and Me" has traveled far and wide and into the hearts of millions of people. Many hymnals and chorus books have included it, as well as numerous choral collections. There is no telling how many times it has been recorded since it was written in 1975. In the opinion of this writer, the second "set of lyrics," or the second verse gives marvelous support to the original song. The message of Christ's journey to Calvary, showing just how much he loves you and me, is truly soul-stirring.

The strongest drive that manifests itself within the breast of every human being is the need to be loved by someone. Only when we get to heaven will we be able to understand God's love for us—the real meaning of the cross of Jesus Christ. "Oh, how He loves you; oh, how He loves me."

OH THE GLORY OF YOUR PRESENCE

CHORUS

Oh the glory of Your presence,
We Your temple, give You rev'rence.
Come and rise from Your rest,
And be blessed by our praise.
As we glory in Your embrace,
As Your presence now fills this place.

© 1983 Birdwing Music | BMG Songs, Inc.
Steve Fry

Winging Its Way Around the World

Now unto him that is able to keep you from falling, and to present you faultless before the presence of his glory with exceeding joy, to the only wise God our Saviour, be glory and majesty, dominion and power, both now and ever. Amen.

JUDE 24–25

Imagine singing to crowds of up to two thousand when only four years of age. Well, that's what Steve Fry did, in his dad's revival services. Steve's love for music grew so intense that by the time he was in the ninth grade, he had written a full piano concerto.

The son of Assembly of God pastors Gerry and Peggy Fry, Steven was born in Orange County, California, in 1954. He started his formal music training in elementary school. In the young adult phase of his life, he had the privilege of working with his parents in a large church that experienced the presence and the blessings of God.

I have a profound admiration for Steve Fry and his philosophy that Christians should have an active role in praising and glorifying God, as opposed to sitting in church services or various Christian gatherings as spectators, observing the worship of others who just happen to be the ones on the platform.

Following is a part of an interview with Steve in late 2001:

"In order to comprehend the story behind 'Oh, the Glory of Your Presence,' you have to understand a little of the spiritual environment that birthed it. My dad became the pastor of the Calvary Community Church, a small congregation of 125 people, in the San Jose, California, area. When he took the church, he was told that it was a pastor's graveyard. But my dad had been completely captivated by two precepts: the glory of the Lord and what it really means to glorify God, and the concept of worship as our first and most important ministry.

"With those two overriding guidelines in place, the church grew to four thousand in attendance in a matter of a few years. It was built on the presence of God and not on a 'program.' I was profoundly affected by the philosophy of my dad, who said, 'Success doesn't matter anymore. I want the presence of God, no matter how large or small the church, no matter how wide or how limited my ministry may be.'

"I became the youth pastor of the church, and with a great emphasis on worship, I saw a handful of kids grow to seven hundred students. I was able to build a teen choir of 120 voices that had a marvelous opportunity to minister. Today I lament over the loss of many of the choral activities in our churches.

"At age twenty-three, while still the youth pastor, I was in my parents' living room sitting at the small spinet piano worshiping the Lord. I had an overwhelming sense that the glory of God is all we need as Christians. With his presence comes the fullness of everything else. In Psalm 16:11, God says, 'Thou wilt shew me the path of life: in thy presence is fulness of joy; at thy right hand there are pleasures for evermore.' I was overcome by that truth, and I began to write, 'Oh, the glory of your presence . . .'"

The lyrics of Steve's song are thought provoking indeed. He not only recognizes Christians as the "temple" of God, which we are, but he goes back to Solomon's prayer in 2 Chronicles 6 for another line of the song, "So come and rise from Your rest and be blessed . . ." Solomon said to the Lord, "Now therefore arise, O LORD God, into thy resting place . . . and let thy saints rejoice in goodness" (v. 41). On the wings of the beautiful melody that the Lord gave to Steve, this worship song has made its way around the world.

As we dwell in the presence of God, we become acutely aware that each person near us is a life for which Christ died. We must also lead them into his presence.

OPEN OUR EYES, LORD

Open our eyes, Lord;
We want to see Jesus,
To reach out and touch Him
And say that we love Him.
Open our ears, Lord;
And help us to listen.
Open our eyes, Lord;
We want to see Jesus.

My Song Beat Me Back Home

*The eyes of your understanding being enlightened; that ye may know what is the hope of his
calling, and what the riches of the glory of his inheritance in the saints.*

EPHESIANS 1:18

Occasionally a song comes along that is not planned or expected or even hoped for, yet it is there. It flourishes and is spread around the world with the songwriter doing not one single thing to promote it.

First, let me acquaint you with Bob Cull. He was born in Los Angeles, California, in 1949. His parents, Robert and Mary Cull, arranged for his piano lessons starting at age six. A little later, while still in grade school, he began playing in the church band and then went on to learn more than a dozen instruments.

When it was time for Bob to go to college, Reverend Bill Stephens, pastor of the Medford Assembly of God, drove fifteen hundred miles to Southern California College just to talk face-to-face with the school's officials concerning Bob. He told them of the dedication and resolve of one of his young members and how he should be given a chance to further his education. Bob was accepted into the school and has since that time been extremely grateful to his pastor for the kind efforts on his behalf.

I'm glad I called Bob to get this story. You'll understand why as you continue to read.

"The circumstances were really simple as to the writing of the song. I was touring in Hawaii as a soloist and had been invited to a parochial school to give a concert. I just assumed that I would find a lot of Christians there since it was run by a religious organization. I arrived early for the concert, which was to be held for one hour in the middle of the day. I wanted to walk around and get acquainted with some of the people and talk about Jesus with them. I talked with every faculty member I could find, and none of them wanted to talk about Jesus. They just gave me a strange look.

"I then realized that the concert was basically for entertainment. I had made several trips to Hawaii as a concert singer, and they were playing my songs on their radio stations. So these people at the school only wanted to hear music. The message of the songs was of little concern to them.

"About thirty minutes prior to the concert, I was sitting at the piano thinking, *If nobody wants to hear about Jesus, then I will just bore them to death, because that is all I am going to sing about. I'm going to sing love songs to him.*

"I remember praying, 'Lord, what we need to see is the real Jesus. This is a religious school, but nobody wants to talk about you, and nobody seems to know you.' Then suddenly a simple little song fell into my head. I quickly put it on paper. It took about ten minutes to write it. I then sang for that school gathering and for the very first time, 'Open Our Eyes, Lord.'

"When I came back home to California, I remember going to a Thursday night Bible study at the Calvary Chapel in Costa Mesa, where I attended regularly. To my surprise they sang 'Open Our Eyes, Lord.' I found out that a number of people from that church had been in Hawaii and attended some of my concerts. Apparently someone, and I still do not know who, brought it back to the church.

"Maranatha Music asked me to write the orchestrations for their next album, *Praise II.* They gave me a list of songs to do, and to my surprise 'Open Our Eyes, Lord' was on the list. They had chosen it out of a list of about one hundred songs. I don't know how they got it. I didn't give it to them."

Bob said, "I have never done one thing to promote the song, and it has gone around the world and has been recorded in twenty languages. It was out of my control. It was a God thing."

May we continually "see" through God's Word what the will of the Lord is for our lives. And may we "hear" him daily as he speaks to us through his Word.

Open the Eyes of My Heart

VERSE

To see You high and lifted up,
Shining in the light of Your glory,
Pour out Your power and love
As we sing holy, holy, holy.

CHORUS

Open the eyes of my heart, Lord,
Open the eyes of my heart,
I want to see You,
I want to see You.

(BRIDGE)

Holy, holy, holy,
Holy, holy, holy,
Holy, holy, holy,
I want to see You.

"Hey! I'm Gonna Get Rich!"

They rest not day and night, saying Holy, holy, holy, Lord God Almighty, which was, and is, and is to come.

REVELATION 4:8

The response of Paul Baloche as he was sponsored into the Amway organization was, "Hey, I'm gonna get rich!" He received something more wonderful instead. A little further in this story Paul will give you the details of his unique experience.

Paul was born in Maple Shade, New Jersey, in 1962. His parents, Roger and Angele Baloche, were proud of young Paul, an altar boy who often expressed his desire to become a priest. But in his teen years, his life began to turn in the wrong direction. He began to play in bands that performed in unsavory places—in the clubs of Philadelphia and Atlantic City. He became caught up in the rock music scene. What happened next is unusual.

"At eighteen years of age, I went to one of the weekend Amway conferences where they tell you how to grow your business. Sunday morning was an optional part of the weekend, so I decided to attend a nondenominational service, expecting to pick up some pointers on how to become successful in this business. The same guys were up giving testimonies who had been speaking in the meeting the day before. They told us, 'It's not about money; it's about Jesus.' They told about how their lives had been changed. I was like—*Wow!* I was really affected by it all.

"When they gave an altar call for any who wanted to receive Christ, I went forward and asked the Lord to come into my life, and he totally changed me."

Later, Paul moved to California and began to play guitar for singers who were leaning toward the worship part of ministry. He usually attended First Evangelical Free Church in Fullerton, California, where Chuck Swindoll pastored or Church on the Way, in Van Nuys, pastored by Dr. Jack Hayford.

Paul had always kept a journal in which he put word ideas or prayers that were meaningful to him. He didn't consider himself a songwriter, but he began to put some of the prayers in his journal to music. That leads us to his very meaningful explanation of how he came to write his famous song.

"'Open the Eyes of My Heart' is a prayer that comes straight from Ephesians 1:18. The essence of the song is our petition, asking God to open the eyes of our hearts. There were some contributing factors that had a bearing on my thinking. I have led a great number of worship schools with organizations such as Youth With A Mission, Integrity Music, and Maranatha Music. It hit me one day that the conferences are good and valuable, but I was not teaching in exactly the way I should have been.

"I began to realize it is not more teaching we need, but a revelation of God and a crying out to him, saying, 'God, open the eyes of my heart. Reveal to me how I might taste and see who you really are, so that I might be changed from the inside out. Help me to have a response of gratitude and admiration, and a sense of awe and worship toward Jesus.'

"During a service when people were being prayed for in our church, I had already sung several songs we knew. Then I began to sing some of the prayers of

> *Praise ye the* LORD. *Blessed is the man that feareth the* LORD, *that delighteth greatly in his commandments.*
>
> PS. 100:4

my heart, such as 'Open the eyes of our hearts, Lord,' a prayer that I had taken from the scripture. I sang it through a few times and suddenly thought, *Hey, that almost feels like a song.*

"I recorded the song on a project but did not feel any different about it than any of the other songs on the CD. I remember that I was surprised when I later heard that it was being used at great youth rallies."

In addition to Paul's travel schedule and his recordings, he is the worship leader of Community Christian Fellowship in Lindale, Texas, and has been there in that capacity for more than two decades. He and his wife, Rita, author of "I Will Celebrate" and other popular worship songs, have three children.

May God grant you the ability to see clearly today—from the eyes of your heart—that our heavenly Father invites us to worship and fellowship with him.

*Whenever His people gather and worship
Him, God promises He will make His presence
known in their midst. On the other hand,
where God's people consistently neglect true
spiritual worship, His manifest presence
is rarely experienced.*

RALPH MAHONEY

OUR GOD REIGNS

VERSE

How lovely on the mountains
Are the feet of Him
Who brings good news, good news,
Announcing peace,
Proclaiming news of happiness:
Our God reigns! Our God reigns!

CHORUS

Our God reigns! Our God reigns!
Our God reigns! Our God reigns!

VERSE

Out of the tomb
He came with grace and majesty
He is alive, He is alive
God loves us so: see here
His hands, His feet, His side.
Yes, we know, He is alive.

Total Triumph Out of Dark Despair

The LORD hath made bare his holy arm in the eyes of all the nations;
and all the ends of the earth shall see the salvation of our God.

ISAIAH 52:10

I was fired from every high school I taught in. I would have kids finish their assignments in four days, and on Fridays I asked them to bring their Bibles. All day long we studied God's Word. I brought my guitar, and we sang songs together. I had a great time, but it was too much for the school authorities to handle. So they all fired me—from four different high schools." That was Leonard Smith's assessment of his career after nine years of college training and five years as a high school teacher.

Lenny continued, "By 1973, for reasons already discussed, I had rendered myself very near unemployable in the education world, on the high school level. By then my wife, Marian, and I had two children. She was a former Catholic nun, whom I met two weeks after she left a six-year stay in a convent. I sought employment wherever I could find work—painting houses and carpentry, and often I couldn't find those jobs. I saw myself as a highly educated man being forced to do menial, blue-collar work. The total of my circumstances reduced me to an extremely depressed state.

"I came home one day in this grim, dejected state and sat down to read the Bible. During those days I was reading the Bible two to three hours every day. I had been reading through the book of Isaiah, and that particular evening my attention was drawn to Isaiah 52:6–7, 'Therefore my people shall know my name: therefore they shall know in that day that I am he that doth speak: behold, it is I. How beautiful upon the mountains are the feet of him that bringeth good tidings, that publisheth peace; that bringeth good tidings of good, that publisheth salvation; that saith unto Zion, Thy God reigneth!'

"I immediately thought of Jesus' feet. I realize that most people think of missionaries when they read verse 7, but that never entered my mind. As I read the passage and came to the words 'Thy God reigneth!' it seemed as if the Lord definitely spoke to my heart. His message to me was, 'I know you are out of work, I know you are depressed, and I know you feel like a failure, but these are my doings. I will bring you through this and you will shine as the sun. Everything is fine!'

> *Then they that were in the ship came and worshipped him, saying, Of a truth thou art the Son of God.*
>
> MATT. 14:33

"I was so comforted I began to weep. Although I was in the room alone, I had heard from the Lord. And though I had already written about fifty songs and had no thought of writing a song at this time, I picked up my guitar, and in about ten minutes I had written 'Our God Reigns.' The whole of it was a total and complete gift from heaven. In the days that followed, the song was so encouraging to me that often I would sing it, and then sing it again and again, sometimes for two hours straight.

"Several weeks later I presented it to our church. As I finished the song, Pastor John Poole literally sprang from his chair and said, 'Let's sing that again!' We sang it several times.

"A little more than a year after its writing, Bob Mumford took 'Our God Reigns' to a Shepherd's Conference in Kansas City, Missouri, where he was to speak. He taught it to the multitude of pastors gathered there, who in turn took it back to their churches.

"It was then published by Dave and Bill Garrett in Australia in one of their Scripture in Song publications. Shortly thereafter a very popular singer, Evie Tornquist, recorded it, greatly accelerating its flight around the world."

Often we as Christians find ourselves enduring tough times, only to find out later that God was preparing us in a special, unusual, and sometimes severe manner for a great task to be performed for his glory. "He knoweth the way that I take: when he hath tried me, I shall come forth as gold" (Job 23:10).

*Surely that which occupies the total time
and energies of heaven must be a
fitting pattern for earth.*

PAUL E. BILLHEIMER

PEOPLE NEED THE LORD

VERSE

Ev'ry day they pass me by;
I can see it in their eyes—
Empty people filled with care,
Headed who knows where.
On they go through private pain,
Living fear to fear.
Laughter hides the silent cries
Only Jesus hears.

CHORUS

People need the Lord.
People need the Lord.
At the end of broken dreams
He's the open door.
People need the Lord.
People need the Lord.
When will we realize,
People need the Lord?

VERSE

We are called to take His light
To a world where wrong seems right.
What could be too great a cost
For sharing life with one who's lost?
Through His love our hearts can feel
All the grief they bear.
They must hear the words of life
Only we can share.

He Looks Out of a Different Window

For God sent not his Son into the world to condemn the world;
but that the world through him might be saved.

JOHN 3:17

B oth Greg Nelson and Phill McHugh grew up in the Midwest: Greg is from Bismarck, North Dakota, and Phill from Aberdeen, South Dakota. As a team they have written scores of songs, some of which have already become standards and will be sung by Christians around the world until the Lord returns.

Greg said of Phill, his cowriter, the master poet, "He is a songwriter who has that certain something that you can't put your hand on—a gift from God. Wishing and hoping for his ability is fruitless. You can hone it, but you can't own it completely, apart from God's endowment. He looks out of a different window."

Greg was born in 1948 into the home of musical parents, Corliss and Irene Nelson. Greg learned piano and theory from his mother. By age twenty-one Greg was conductor of the Bismarck Civic Orchestra, a position he maintained for several years.

Phill, born in 1951, to Frank and Beatrice McHugh, had very little formal music training outside of a few piano lessons. As a college-age young man, he became involved with the culture of the late 1960s, traveling and performing in clubs of various kinds. Phill said, "All of this affected me a great deal and drove me to look for answers. I began to read the Bible on my own, which started a process that led to my conversion."

> *I will sing of mercy and judgment: unto thee, O LORD, will I sing.*
>
> PS. 101:1

In an interview in 1989, Greg told me that he and Phill, at that point, had written more than fifty songs together. Greg and Phill gave me the story behind what is unquestionably their most popular song to date.

"We were trying to write a song one day and spent most of the morning talking about ideas. We decided, about lunchtime, to go to a restaurant near my office in Nashville. After we were seated, a waitress came to our table, and as she approached us she smiled. Yet it seemed that her eyes were so empty. She was trying to convey a cheery attitude, but her face seemed to say something else. She took our order and walked away.

"We looked at each other, and one of us said, 'She needs the Lord.' We then began looking around the restaurant at all of the people. They, too, seemed to have an emptiness in their faces. We sensed a real heaviness in our hearts as we watched them.

"Suddenly we realized that all of those people needed the Lord. Just as quickly, we both thought, *We need to write that—people need the Lord.* We finished our meal and went back to my office and sat down to write what was in our hearts. The pictures from the restaurant that remained in our minds, coupled with the realization that millions of people around the world are also groping for some ray of light, gave rise to 'People Need the Lord.'

"God has his own timing, and he orchestrates all things under his control. Consequently, it was three years before the song was recorded. We had tried to interest several people in the song, but they just didn't 'get it.' Finally, the song was presented to Steve Green—he 'got it.'"

Phill agrees that it is the most often used of all of their songs. I remember that I heard it sung by two teenagers on New Providence Island, about 150 miles off the Florida coast, in a small church made up mostly of Haitians. As Amy and Tina stood to sing the song that often seems to missionaries to be the most meaningful song ever written, I remember that I had never "really" heard that song until that occasion—as I looked into the faces of those poor, needy people.

The element that makes the song meaningful to almost every Christian who hears it is the infectious melody that carries its lyrics, driving the heart cry of lost humanity right into our very souls.

I hope you "get it"! You and I don't have to go to a foreign land,
such as Africa, Asia, South America, or China, to find people who are
without Christ. We need only to go across the aisle at work, at school,
at the office, or across the driveway to the house next door.

When we worship together as a community of living Christians, we do not worship alone, we worship "with all the company of heaven."

MARIANNE H. MICKS

A Perfect Heart

Verse

Morning sun, light of creation,
Grassy fields, a velvet floor,
Silver clouds a shimmering curtain;
He's designed a perfect world.
I'm amazed at His talents,
Stand in awe of One so great.
Now my soul begins to sing out
To the source from which it came.

Chorus

Bless the Lord who reigns in beauty.
Bless the Lord
Who reigns with wisdom and with power.
Bless the Lord
Who fills my life with so much love.
He can make a perfect heart.

The Little Lake Song

*And I will give them an heart to know me, that I am the LORD: and they shall be my people,
and I will be their God, for they shall return unto me with their whole heart.*

JEREMIAH 24:7

The Bible has a great deal to say about our hearts—that part of us that causes us to think the thoughts we think, say the words we say, and do the things we find ourselves doing. This is the reason David says to us in Psalm 119:11, "Thy word have I hid in mine heart, that I might not sin against thee." God wants you and me to have a perfect heart, and that can only happen when we let Christ take over the "control center."

Dony and Reba (Rambo) McGuire have written many wonderful songs, one of which deals with this complex subject. Crossing the lines of musical categories, it has become a favorite of thousands of people in the United States and other nations of the world.

The McGuires remember well what a thrill it was to arrive at a large gathering in Zimbabwe, Africa, and hear thousands of Christians singing their song "A Perfect Heart." Reba said, "I was so moved that I was reduced to an emotional basket case for a few moments." Indeed, for a songwriter there is no higher honor than hearing his or her song being sung in distant lands. Here is the story of how God brought this beautiful song to the world.

It began with a vacation trip on a houseboat. The McGuires had determined to make this a working vacation, giving special attention to their songwriting. They prayed earnestly that the Lord would do something special through them during that week. By week's end they had completed a number of songs and had also done work on a musical.

On the last morning of the trip, Dony got up very early to try to catch a catfish for breakfast. "I was so full of faith in his fishing ability," Reba said, "that I proceeded to the kitchen and started to cook bacon and eggs.

"The sun was peeking over the hills and a mist was rising from the water," Reba continued. "It was a glorious morning. I looked out the small porthole and caught a glimpse of Dony with a strange look on his face. Some people come down with a cold, but Dony comes down with a song! I couldn't explain it, but I knew something good was about to happen. I turned off the burners on the stove and removed the food. I gathered our songwriting materials and sat down to wait for him to come in.

"When he came in a few minutes later, he sat down before a small electric piano and began to play. As he played what the Lord was giving to him, I began to write lyrics as they were being given to me. That kind of inspiration had only occurred a few times in our short songwriting career together. It was as if God was saying, 'You've been faithful in your praying and studying for a week; now I'm going to give you something just because I have the power to do so.' I wrote as fast as I could write while Dony continued to play. We both completed the whole composition and have never changed a word or the musical setting."

The McGuires dubbed it their "little lake song" and used it as a devotional song at their office and a few small churches. "One day," Reba recalled, "Bill Gaither came by our office and heard us singing it during our devotional period. He asked where we got it, and we told him it was our 'lake song.' He expressed such a keen interest in it that Dony made a tape of it for him. That started it on its way."

And so, several years later, halfway around the world in Zimbabwe, the McGuires heard their "little lake song" being sung by the great host of Africans gathered there.

How wonderful to have a perfect heart, made by a perfect Lord, in order that we might have fellowship with him in a more perfect manner.

THE POTTER'S HAND

VERSE

I'm captured by Your holy calling.
Set me apart;
I know You're drawing me to Yourself.
Lead me, Lord, I pray.

VERSE

Beautiful Lord, Wonderful Savior,
I know for sure
All of my days are held in Your hand,
Crafted into Your perfect plan.

CHORUS

Take me, mold me,
Use me, fill me,
I give my life to the Potter's hand.
Call me, guide me,
Lead me, walk beside me,
I give my life to the Potter's hand.

© 1997 Hillsong Publishing, Integrity's Hosanna! Music
Darlene Zschech

A Heart's Cry, Put to Music

O LORD, thou art our father; we are the clay, and thou our potter;
and we all are the work of thy hand.

ISAIAH 64:8

Darlene Zschech, born in Brisbane, Queensland, Australia, in 1965, said, "I can't remember a time in my life when music wasn't a critical part of the atmosphere in which I existed.

"The first song I ever wrote was at age fifteen, following my salvation experience. Our church sang it one night, and to be honest, rather than being elated, I was totally blown away by the spiritual responsibility of putting a praise and worship song in someone else's heart for them to sing. I then put writing worship songs on the shelf for the next five years until I understood a little more about the power of 'in spirit and in truth' worship."

Today this mother of three works alongside her husband, Mark, at the Hillsong Church in Sydney, Australia. Darlene is the author of scores of songs, several of which are well on their way to becoming "standards" in the worship ministry of churches around the world, while others have already reached that plateau—songs such as "Shout to the Lord" and "The Potter's Hand," the subject of this story.

Darlene declares, "Worship is the very first commandment: to love the Lord your God with all your heart and all your soul and all your mind and all your strength. Worship should be a priority in your life—to love Jesus, to put him first in your life and to serve him, whatever he calls you to do. Live to delight the heart of God! He loves your praise of him; so much so that he says he inhabits [dwells in] the praises of his people. The whole Bible is punctuated with outbursts of praise."

On a notable day in 1997, in prayer and communion with her heavenly Father, Darlene, at age thirty-two, made what she has described as "a totally honest and pure cry from my heart that God would do all that he needed to do in me—break me and change me." During those moments, because she is a dedicated worship leader and songwriter, she sensed a desire to set the thoughts of her heart to music. She added, "The result was a song. It was not really crafted; it was just a heart's cry put to a melody given to me from the Lord. I never expected it to have an impact outside of my own experience and journey in God."

In this gift to Darlene, God has given to his church a song of complete surrender and yieldedness to himself. Not since "Have Thine Own Way, Lord," written by Adelaide Pollard in 1902, has the church experienced a greater song of dedication to the Savior. Darlene prayed in her song that God would "take me, mold me, and use me," and as she did so, she somehow must have sensed the biblical message of Isaiah 64:8: "We are the clay, and thou our potter."

"The Potter's Hand" has made its way around the world and has been used in countless churches and Christian gatherings. It has been recorded by Darlene and myriad other worship leaders and Christian recording artists.

Darlene and Mark continue their great work for Christ in Sydney. The Hillsong television program *Life Is for Living* is now seen in eighty different countries. Darlene leads the worship every week on this program. She also is the associate director of Hillsong Conference, which is the annual music and leadership conference of Hillsong Church, and it enjoys an attendance of more than twenty thousand full-time delegates.

The crowning moment in the life of all Christians is when
they are yielded to the Potter's hand, allowing God to mold and
shape them into vessels that please, praise, and honor him.

Rise Again

VERSE

Go ahead, drive the nails in My hands.
Laugh at Me, where you stand.
Go ahead, and say it isn't Me.
The day will come when you will see.

CHORUS

'Cause I'll rise again;
There's no pow'r on earth can tie Me down.
Yes, I'll rise again;
Death can't keep Me in the ground.

VERSE

Go ahead, and mock My name.
My love for you is still the same.
Go ahead, and bury Me;
But very soon I will be free.

© 1977 Going Holm Music
Dallas Holm

Placed in the Graveyard of Songs

He is not here: for he is risen, as he said. Come, see the place where the Lord lay.
And go quickly, and tell his disciples that he is risen from the dead.

MATTHEW 28:6–7

Information about the early life of Dallas Holm can be found in the story behind "Here We Are" in this volume.

Dallas's notoriety and fame as a contemporary Christian musician was augmented by the fact that he traveled with David Wilkerson, made famous by his best-selling book *The Cross and the Switchblade*. It was while with Wilkerson that Dallas formed the band he called Dallas Holm and Praise. Shortly after forming the band, he began to write songs for them to sing, and his first effort is the subject of this story. "Rise Again" still holds music charting records. When Dallas wrote this song, contemporary Christian music was not yet clearly on the horizon. The following is his story:

"After we had decided to form the band, I realized that I would need to write some new material. I knew that the music should be different from the things I was used to writing. So I got out my pen and paper and thought, *I need to get busy and write some songs.* I often had a disciplined approach to songwriting and have written some of my better songs in that frame of mind. But this particular day I couldn't come up with a single idea. I drew an absolute zero.

"I began to pray, which I should have done in the first place, and in the course of my praying, I remember saying, 'Lord, if you were singing, what would you sing?' That thought really stuck in my mind. I didn't know if I had ever heard a song from a first-person point of view. As hokey as it may sound, I had this mental image of the Lord, dressed as we often picture him in our minds, standing on a street corner with a guitar, singing. It was as if you could translate Jesus into modern times, with singing as his form of communication. What would he sing?

"As soon as I focused in on that approach to my task, I began to write as if I were taking dictation. I wrote the music and the words in about ten minutes—no changes. I titled it 'Rise Again.'

"As I finished I looked at the song and realized that this didn't come out of my head. I have often said that God wrote the song, and I just delivered the message. That describes the way I feel about that experience.

"Dallas Holm and Praise had only been together six weeks when we recorded a 'live' album in the Lindale High School auditorium in Lindale, Texas [the home of Paul Baloche, author of "Open the Eyes of My Heart" and "Above All"]. It seated about 350 people. We had a mobile unit come in from Nashville to do the recording, and we spent a whopping five thousand dollars.

"'Rise Again' ended up as cut four on side two, the worst place, and generally referred to as the graveyard of songs. We basically did everything wrong: live albums were not selling, we put the song in the wrong place, and we rushed into the project. We had only been together for a few short weeks. Nevertheless, somewhere someone on the radio played 'Rise Again,' and word spread. *Dallas Holm and Praise . . . Live!* went on to be one of the first three albums to receive a Recording Industry Association of America gold-certified record.

"To me it was a great lesson. If God puts his finger on something, and if he anoints it, it doesn't make any difference if all of the right marketing plans and promotional schemes are used. We didn't know anything about that stuff. Having Christ say, 'Go ahead and drive the nails in my hands,' impacted the listener. It stayed on the *Singing News Magazine* charts for four years. As far as we know that has never happened before or since."

It is Christ's triumph over the tomb that allowed him to keep his divine promise to those around him when he declared, "I will rise again!"

SEEK YE FIRST

VERSE

Seek ye first the kingdom of God
And His righteousness,
And all these things
Shall be added unto you.
Allelu, alleluia.

VERSE

Ask and it shall be given unto you,
Seek and ye shall find,
Knock and the door shall be
Opened unto you.
Allelu, alleluia.

"I Thought I Missed the Call of God"

*But seek ye first the kingdom of God, and his righteousness;
and all these things shall be added unto you.*

MATTHEW 6:33

With her music and the spoken Word, Karen Lafferty shares her Christian faith to the farthest places on our planet. She has an extremely varied background, and the Lord uses her experiences in her ministry.

This talented woman was born in Alamogordo, New Mexico, February 29, 1948. During her early childhood, her parents, Walter and Ollie Lafferty, began to carry her to the local Southern Baptist church. She later attended Eastern New Mexico University, graduating with a degree in choral music and oboe.

Karen told me, "I made a commitment to Christ at age eleven, but in college began to drift from the Lord. I had a wonderful friend, Rhonda Ray, with whom I had grown up, who became involved with Campus Crusade for Christ. She was a dedicated, vibrant Christian, and I became hungry to have what she had. I realized that Christ was not on the throne in my life. I had ego and ambitions on the throne, and not Jesus. I was faced with a strong decision, I said, 'Okay, I'm not going to be a hypocrite about this. I'm going to live for Christ or I'm not.'" Karen found that she had learned to put on three faces, one for her family, one for the church, and another for the clubs in which she performed. She said, "I truly felt like a hypocrite."

Karen learned about a Christian music conference in California with Campus Crusade for Christ and jumped at the chance to attend, since she was seeking to know how she could best use her music for God. There she saw people using contemporary Christian music in ministry and knew that was for her.

I asked Karen to tell me about the circumstances surrounding the writing of "Seek Ye First." She said, "Starting to learn about ministry and being part of the Maranatha Music fellowship was very exciting, and I knew I was in the right place. In those days we had very few models of what being in contemporary Christian music really meant. Many of us had to work other jobs. Yet I remember the night that God called me to stop singing in the restaurants so that I could have my nights free for ministry. I quit my five-hundred-dollar-per-week job and began teaching guitar lessons. At five dollars per lesson, I found that I just couldn't pay my bills. The rent was due, the car payment was behind . . . and I was discouraged. I thought that I had missed the call of God.

"I knew God wanted me in full-time music ministry, but what was I going to do about my bills? Even though I had a college degree in music, I couldn't even get a job at a music store teaching guitar lessons. I was starting to sing at churches and coffeehouses where I'd get honorariums, but it just wasn't enough.

"In my unhappiness, I still knew that I needed what the church had to offer. I attended a Monday night youth Bible study where the subject for that evening was Matthew 6. During the lesson I heard that God's people should seek first the kingdom of God and his righteousness and all of these other things, will be added unto us. Somehow I was able to believe God's Word, and I went home happy. The bills still weren't paid, but I had my joy back.

"I began to pluck around on the guitar and came up with a melody. It would closely fit with the scriptural passage in Matthew 6:33, which we had studied that night, 'Seek ye first the kingdom of God, and his righteousness; and all these things shall be added unto you.' *I had written a song!* And I went to bed happy about it.

"The following Monday evening I taught 'Seek Ye First' to everyone at the Bible study. It was so singable it quickly spread to other Bible study classes."

Karen's song has literally gone around the world, being sung in many languages.

We must learn that we cannot outgive God. He is more eager to give us the things we need than we can ever imagine. God's plan is so simple. First we seek his kingdom and his cause, and then he adds to us all of these "things."

SHINE, JESUS, SHINE

VERSE

Lord, the light of Your love is shining,
In the midst of the darkness shining,
Jesus, Light of the world, shine upon us,
Set us free by the truth You now bring us,
Shine on me, shine on me.

CHORUS

Shine, Jesus, shine!
Fill this land with the Father's glory.
Blaze, Spirit, blaze! Set our hearts on fire.
Flow river flow—
Flood the nations with grace and mercy.
Send forth Your Word, Lord,
And let there be light.

VERSE

As we gaze on Your kingly brightness,
So our faces display Your likeness.
Ever changing from glory to glory,
Mirrored here may our lives tell Your story,
Shine on me, shine on me!

Rescued from the File Cabinet

I am come a light into the world, that whosoever believeth on me should not abide in darkness.

JOHN 12:46

B arely a day goes by without a [Graham] Kendrick song being sung by a group of Christians somewhere on the planet." Cole Moreton wrote this in London's *The Independent* on a Sunday. Few songwriters from the United Kingdom, or any nation on earth, have touched the lives of God's people as has Graham Kendrick.

He was born in 1950, in Northhamptonshire, England, the son of a Baptist preacher. Although he had prepared himself to be a teacher, as a young man of twenty-two years, he began his singing and songwriting career. Although his first efforts in Christian music were of the contemporary folk music style, he has moved his skills of storytelling and memorable tunes into a worship vein. As a result, his songs have penetrated deeply into almost every area of Christendom.

Graham is the cofounder of the March for Jesus movement, which had its beginning in the mid-1980s and has involved more than 55 million people over the years. They are prayer, praise, and proclamation events. Graham received a Dove Award in 1995 for his international work. In 2000, Brunei University conferred upon him an honorary doctor of divinity degree in recognition of his contributions to the worship life of the church. At least two major hymnals have included Kendrick songs.

Graham said of his success as a songwriter, "I don't have any formal musical training and often envy people who do. I've learned mainly by trial and error. I take the 'hit and miss, try it this way, try it that way, hope for happy accidents' approach."

Graham's song has become the most popular modern hymn of the last decade in the United Kingdom. Graham said, "This song is a prayer for revival. A songwriter can give people words to voice something that is already in their hearts but that they don't have the words or the tune to express, and I think 'Shine, Jesus, Shine' caught a moment when people were beginning to believe once again that an impact could be made on a whole nation."

> *And they ministered before the dwelling place of the tabernacle of the congregation with singing . . .*
>
> I CHRON. 6:32

Graham pointed me to his Web site for the story behind his famous song.

"Bearing in mind the worldwide popularity of this song, perhaps the most surprising thing about the writing of it is the ordinariness of the circumstances. I had been thinking for some time about the holiness of God, and how that as a community of believers and as individuals, his desire is for us to live continually in his presence.

"My longing for revival in the churches and spiritual awakening in the nation was growing, but also a recognition that we cannot stand in God's presence without 'clean hands and a pure heart.' So I wrote the three verses and 'tested' it in my home church. Though there was clearly merit to the song, it seemed incomplete, so as I was unable at the time to take it any further, I put it back in the file. Several months later I was asked to submit new songs for a conference songbook, and as I reviewed this three-verse song, I realized that it needed a chorus. I remember standing in my music room with my guitar slung around my neck trying different approaches. The line 'Shine, Jesus, shine' came to mind, and within about half an hour I had finished the chorus, all but some 'polishing.'

"Though I felt an excitement in my spirit at the time, I had no inkling at all that it would become so widely used. There were other songs I rated more highly at the time that most people have never heard of!" Graham's story behind his song appears on his Web site and is used here by his permission.

Graham and his wife, Jill, have four daughters. The Kendricks attend Ichthus Christian Fellowship, an independent free church, where Graham serves as a member of the leadership team. They make their home in London.

The overriding message of "Shine, Jesus, Shine" is that those who follow Christ, the Light of the World, should ask him to "set our hearts on fire," in order that our "lives tell the story." In that way we point men, women, boys, and girls to the Savior, "the true Light, which lighteth every man that cometh into the world" (John 1:9).

It is in the process of being worshipped that
God communicates His presence to men.

C. S. LEWIS

SHOUT TO THE LORD

VERSE

My Jesus, my Savior,
Lord there is none like You.
All of my days I want to praise
The wonders of Your mighty love.
My comfort, my shelter
Tower of refuge and strength,
Let every breath, all that I am,
Never cease to worship You.

CHORUS

Shout to the Lord
All the earth; let us sing!
Power and majesty,
Praise to the King!
Mountains bow down
And the seas will roar
At the sound of Your name.
I sing for joy
At the work of Your hands.
Forever I'll love You,
Forever I'll stand.
Nothing compares to the promise
I have in You.

© 1993 Hillsong Publishing
   Darlene Zschech

Face the Wall While I Sing

Honour and majesty are before him: strength and beauty are in his sanctuary. Give unto the
LORD, O ye kindreds of the people, give unto the LORD glory and strength.

PSALM 96:6–7

For more than a decade, Darlene Zschech and her husband, Mark, have been
leaders at Hillsong Church in Sydney, Australia. Among other duties, Darlene

is the worship director and is responsible for vocals on all church projects, and Mark is the director of the television ministry, now seen in eighty countries.

Darlene said, "When I was fifteen, my dad, my beloved hero, who had been attending church and recommitted his broken life to Christ, took his just-as-broken eldest child to a youth group called 'Royal Rangers.' I attended for a few weeks, making friends, tying knots, learning about camping, teamwork, and the code of life, and most importantly, the giver of life, Jesus Christ.

"My memories of a particular evening are so clear, the irresistible invitation to receive Jesus into my life. My longing to be made *whole* overtook my limited understanding, and I got out of my seat and walked toward the leader, with a couple of others, who then led us into the most beautiful prayer I have ever prayed."

Darlene insists that it was no big occasion when she wrote "Shout to the Lord," the song that is the focus of this story. She said, "I really didn't sit down one day and decide to write an incredible song that would touch nations." She has been surprised and humbled by all of the attention the song has received, because she realizes that the song came as a gift from God. She didn't think of herself as a songwriter, although she has written songs since age fifteen.

> *I will sing a new song unto thee, O God.*
>
> Ps. 144:9

During a time when Darlene was going through some "dark days" in her life, she sat down at an old piano and began to improvise, not really playing anything particular. A song began to flow from her heart, and from Psalm 96, the scriptures that she had just read. She continued to sing it again and again. Through the singing of her song, she realized that her depression had lifted and that her faith and joy in the Lord returned. During the reading of the psalm, her mind had been completely centered on the heavenly Father.

During the following days she continually thought about the song. She began to say to herself, "I think the Lord has given me a worship song." She reluctantly mentioned it to Geoff Bullock, at that time the music pastor at the church, and Russell Fragar, telling them that she had written what she thought to be a worship song. They insisted that she play and sing it for them. Between apologies for the song, and in spite of a fit of nervousness, she agreed to do so.

She later confessed that her hands were so sweaty and shaky that it was difficult for her to play the piano. Fearful and shy about the whole situation, she asked Bullock and Fragar to turn and face the wall, looking away from her. As she finished the song, they turned around and expressed that the song was magnificent. Darlene was convinced that they were only being polite.

Sometime later, Darlene's pastor, Brian Houston, heard the song and predicted that it would be sung around the world. How accurate his prediction has become! The song quickly made its way to many other nations. Darlene said, "We hadn't even recorded it, and I began to receive letters from people all over the world who had sung the song in their churches." It was later put on an album titled *Shout to the Lord*.

Darlene continues to be an integral part of the music ministry of Hillsong Church, all the while writing songs and recording them. She has many albums to her credit and has performed throughout her native Australia, as well as Great Britain and other European countries. She has approximately fifty songs published. Darlene and her husband, Mark, have three children.

When you and I come before the Lord, realizing through his Word that he not only made everything, but has everything under his control, then we, as Darlene Zschech, will see that the Lord will bring happiness, comfort, and blessings— perhaps not with a song, but with the sweet assurance that he loves us greatly.

*Worship is first and foremost for His benefit,
not ours, though it is marvelous to discover that
in giving Him pleasure, we ourselves enter into
what can become our richest and most
wholesome experience in life.*

GRAHAM KENDRICK

Surely the Presence of the Lord

VERSE

In the midst of His children
The Lord said He would be.
It doesn't take very many;
It can be just two or three
And I feel that same sweet Spirit
That I've felt oft times before.
Surely I can say
I've been with the Lord.

CHORUS

Surely the presence of the Lord is in this place.
I can feel His mighty power and His grace.
I can hear the brush of angel's wings;
I see glory on each face.
Surely the presence of the Lord is in this place.

The Song Came Just in Time

Thou wilt shew me the path of life: in thy presence is fulness of joy;
at thy right hand there are pleasures for evermore.

PSALM 16:11

Born in Columbus, Ohio, to Pearl and Precious Wolfe, Lanny Wolfe was exposed to music early on because his mother sang and played guitar. Lanny, his brother, Larry, and his sister, Sharon, rode the city bus to church as children. Lanny said of his salvation experience at age eleven, "I gave my heart to the Lord, was baptized, and received his Spirit."

Lanny gives others credit for his early music training and experience. "Two people helped nurture my love for music in general, and gospel music in particular—Ruth Morgan, my junior high school teacher, and Lois Newsstand, a pastor's wife who played piano and organ, and directed choirs, and who allowed a teenager to play piano for the camp choir."

In interviewing songwriters for more than four decades, I have had many songwriters relate to me that the Lord suddenly dropped a song into their hearts. Some even said that they were not expecting to write a song, that the experience came as a complete surprise. But what happened to Lanny one day in Columbus, Mississippi, is different from all the rest. In 1977, he had gone there with the Lanny Wolfe Trio to participate in a very important church function. Wolfe relates his experience:

"We were there to be a part of the festivities for the dedication of a new church auditorium. The mayor of the city was there, along with a number of other dignitaries and officials. The newness of the building was apparent, and everyone was dressed properly and in his place. It was everything you might expect at a church dedication.

"While other festivities were taking place, and our trio was waiting to sing, the Lord suddenly dropped a tune and a lyric right into my head. What was unusual about this incident was that the music went in a certain progression that I would not ordinarily go to, especially not being at a keyboard. But as I sat there, the Lord gave me the whole chorus.

"When it was time for us to sing, I stepped to the piano and began singing the new song, just as the Lord had given it to me. When I finished singing it through one time, I taught it to the audience. The other members of our group were learning it along with the congregation."

In the foyer of that Columbus church hangs a framed scrap of paper on which Lanny scribbled the words to his song, while still seated, and as the Lord was giving it. It is a reminder to the congregation of what happened in their midst on that special day—a memento that they witnessed the birth of a famous song. "Surely the Presence of the Lord Is in This Place" has never been changed and has gone around the world.

Lanny now resides in Houston, Texas, where he oversees the ministry of his company, Paragon Music Productions. He also travels to many places in our nation conducting his successful choir clinics. He is highly educated with two bachelor's degrees, two master's degrees, and one honorary degree. Let me have Lanny close this story for you:

"What does God have in store for Lanny Wolfe? I don't really know, but I've learned that whatever God wants to do, he will do it in spite of anything or anybody—and that includes Lanny Wolfe. As for now, I'm gonna trust him, I'm gonna trust him, I'm gonna trust him all my life."

When you and I feel the presence of the Lord in our lives, it is
his goodness that allows such a thing, and it is wonderful! Remember,
the Bible says, "In thy presence is fulness of joy" (Ps. 16:11).

SWEET, SWEET SPIRIT

VERSE

There's a sweet sweet Spirit in this place,
And I know that it's the Spirit of the Lord.
There are sweet expressions on each face,
And I know they feel the presence of the Lord.

CHORUS

Sweet Holy Spirit,
Sweet heavenly Dove,
Stay right here with us
Filling us with Your love.
And for these blessings
We lift our hearts in praise.
Without a doubt we'll know
That we have been revived
When we shall leave this place.

VERSE

There are blessings you cannot receive
Till you know Him in His fullness and believe.
You're the one to profit when you say,
"I am going to walk with Jesus all the way."

© 1962. Renewed 1990 Manna Music, Inc.
    Doris Akers

"I Hate to Leave This Room!"

The effectual fervent prayer of a righteous man availeth much.

JAMES 5:16

Doris Akers, born in Brookfield, Missouri, in 1923, was one of ten children. She started writing songs at age ten and has written more than three hundred. She was a recording artist, music arranger, and director. Her songs are found in many songbooks and hymnals and have been sung by millions of worshipers. She founded and directed the Skypilot Choir of Skypilot Church in Los Angeles, California.

"You are not ready to go in," Doris Akers said to the Skypilot Choir one Sunday morning. She didn't believe they had prayed enough! They were accustomed to spending time with her in prayer before the service, asking God to bless their songs. She had once said, "I feel that prayer is more important than great voices." They had already prayed, but this particular morning she asked them to pray again, and they did so with renewed fervor.

As they continued to pray, Doris began to wonder how she could stop this wonderful prayer meeting. She even sent word to the pastor about what was happening. Finally, she was compelled to say to the choir, "We have to go. I hate to leave this room, and I know you hate to leave, but you know we do have to go to the service. But there is such a sweet, sweet Spirit in this place."

Doris said to me, "We songwriters always have our ears open to the possibilities of a song. The song started 'singing' to me. I wanted to write it down, but couldn't. I thought the song would be gone after the service. Following the dismissal I went home, and the next morning, to my surprise, I heard the song again, so I went to the piano and began to write, 'There's a sweet, sweet spirit in this place.'"

In Doris's song she recognized the "Spirit" in the room as the "Spirit of the Lord." She could see in the "sweet expressions" of the choir members that they also recognized the "presence of the Lord." In the chorus of the song she calls us back to the New Testament where the Spirit of God descended like a dove, lighting upon Jesus at his baptism (Matt. 3:16). She calls him "sweet heavenly Dove," asking him to stay right there with them, filling them with his love.

Doris Akers not only wrote songs individually but as a cowriter, having joined her close friend Mahalia Jackson in one songwriting venture. In her lifetime she received many awards, one of which was an honor bestowed upon her by the Smithsonian Institute, which labeled her songs and records as national treasures.

Doris Akers passed away in 1995, but her songs will live on in the hearts of those of us who have sung them and have learned to love the God she wrote about. Until her last day on earth, she believed that God wants his children to pray.

Not very much worthwhile was ever accomplished apart from prayer.
How long has it been since you really, really prayed about some
need in your life or in the life of a friend or loved one?

There Is None Like You

"So Overwhelmed I Began to Weep"

O LORD, there is none like thee, neither is there any God beside thee,
according to all that we have heard with our ears.

1 CHRONICLES 17:20

Lenny LeBlanc became involved in music quite by accident. He related to me, "One day I was visiting in a friend's home and several of the young people there were playing instruments. They asked me if I would sing with them. I agreed to do so, and after a few songs, they said, 'You sound pretty good.' I responded, 'I do?'

"They then asked me to get a bass guitar. I asked, 'What's a bass guitar?' They said, 'It's the one with the four big strings on it.' I said, 'Okay.' So I went to work at Eckerds to earn enough money to buy a bass guitar. I taught myself to play it. By the time I was seventeen years of age, I was supporting myself with my music."

Lenny went on to a very successful career in pop music, at first as a studio musician on recordings for singers such as Crystal Gayle, Joan Baez, Roy Orbison, Hank Williams Jr., and The Supremes, just to name a few.

Lenny confessed, "My career was my god, and I began to worship the gift God had given me. I was not at a low point in life, nor was I looking or searching for God, but a good friend, a drug smuggler, called me late one night and said, 'Lenny,

I got saved, and I'm going to heaven.' He then said, 'Lenny, I want you to be there with me. Are you saved?' Without thinking, I said yes, not even knowing what being saved meant. I had, however, had some contact with Christian musicians.

"My friend sent me a Bible, and for the next few weeks God began to reveal his love to me. I began to realize how shallow and selfish my life was, and there in my home I cried out to Jesus for mercy and forgiveness. I could have continued in the field of pop music, but I sensed that God had something different for me."

In 1991, Lenny was asked by Integrity Music to be the worship leader on a CD project, *Pure Heart,* so he tried to carve out time from his schedule to write some songs for the endeavor.

He related this story: "One morning, while at home alone, I was playing the keyboard, and suddenly a tune and some lyrics began coming to me. Before I had finished, I had written the major part of a song, which I titled 'There Is None Like You.' I was so overwhelmed by the Spirit of God that I began to weep. I found it hard to believe that God would give me such a wonderful song. Because it was so meaningful to me, I soon had it committed to memory."

A few months later, Lenny's song was launched and would find its way around the world by way of the Integrity project *Pure Heart.* The album was recorded live at Faith Tabernacle in Florence, Alabama, where Lenny coordinates the total worship ministry.

Several years ago Lenny accompanied Don Moen on a trip to Korea, where they were engaged in some extraordinary meetings in an outdoor square with sixty thousand young people present. During one of the sessions they sang "There Is None Like You" in English. Don then had them sing it in their own language. Much to Lenny's surprise, they already knew it; it had been translated into Korean some time before. People would come up to him and say, "Didn't you know that your song is one of the most popular Christian songs, if not the most popular, throughout all of Asia?" He was completely overwhelmed. He said to me, "It blew me away." The song has been translated into at least a half-dozen languages in the Orient.

Lenny, blessings on you for your wonderful crossover, from pop songs into the Lord's music that ministers to so many hearts.

As we read through the Scriptures and consider all of our Lord's
wonderful deeds, his loving-kindness, and the works of his hands,
we remember that the psalmist said, "O LORD our Lord, how excellent
is thy name in all the earth! who hast set thy glory above the heavens"
(Ps. 8:1). O Lord, there is none like you!

There's Something About That Name

Jesus, Jesus, Jesus,
There's just something about that name.
Master, Savior, Jesus,
Like a fragrance after the rain.
Jesus, Jesus, Jesus,
Let all heaven and earth proclaim;
Kings and kingdoms may all pass away,
But there's something about that name.

Forty Years Before I Arrived

Wherefore God also hath highly exalted him, and given him a name which is above every name.

PHILIPPIANS 2:9

Gloria Gaither told me of an experience in South Africa, where the Gaithers had gone in December 2005. "We were in Johannesburg, producing a homecoming video, and while there a young lady came up to me and said, 'I want to tell you something.' I said, 'Sure, go right ahead.' She said, 'I watched that video where Mark Lowry makes fun of you, telling you that nobody knows that song you wrote. You tell Mark Lowry that I know that song. We know all of your songs in Africa. They have been here for forty years.'

"I myself, who had thought in earlier years that God might be calling me to go to Africa as a missionary, had never gotten there. Did I hear God wrong? It seems as if I heard, 'You might not have gotten there, but your songs did.' I did what I knew to do in the best way I knew to do it.

"As Bill and I write songs, the idea comes first. Often after breakfast Bill will take his coffee and go in and begin to fiddle around at the piano. We have a book where we write down ideas for songs. He will have a melody in his mind and then think, *This will be a good melody for that idea.* He shows me how the melody goes with the idea, and then it is my job to put the words around it. Usually the lyrics come very quickly.

"After 'There's Something About That Name' was written, I wrote a reading that goes with the song. Before writing it in 1970, a couple of notable events transpired in our lives.

"Prior to the writing of it, our daughter Suzanne had chronic tonsillitis for a long time. We were very frustrated with that problem. Her fever would peak, and I often thought, *She is going to go into convulsions with this fever.* I would sit there and watch her and breathe the name of Jesus, and then see the fever break.

"We were sitting beside Bill's grandmother Hartwell when she was in the dying process. Out of her delirium when she reached down into her subconsciousness, she kept saying, 'Jesus, Jesus, oh, he is so precious to me! He is so precious!'

"We thought, *What a gift!* When she reached down into the depths of her consciousness, there was *Jesus.* He went clear to her core. What a comfort!

"The images that are in the reading that goes with the song came from our experiences. The images of the tyrants came from history—horrible men who tried to persecute Christians until they were gone—to wipe them from the face of the earth. We are heading in that direction again."

Following is the reading that goes with "There's Something About That Name":

Jesus. The mere mention of His name can calm the storm, heal the broken, raise the dead. At the name of Jesus, I've seen sin-hardened men melt, derelicts transformed, the light of hope put back in the eyes of a hopeless child.

At the name of Jesus, hatred and bitterness turn to love and forgiveness; arguments cease.

I've heard a mother softly breathe His name at the bedside of a child delirious from fever, and I've watched as that little body grew quiet and the fevered brow became cool.

I've sat beside a dying saint, her body racked with pain, who in those final fleeting seconds summoned her last ounce of ebbing strength to whisper earth's sweetest name—"Jesus, Jesus . . ."

Emperors have tried to destroy it; philosophers have tried to stamp it out. Tyrants have tried to wash it from the face of the earth with the very blood of those who claimed it. Yet still it stands.

And there shall be the final day when every voice that has ever uttered a sound—every voice of Adam's race—shall rise in one mighty chorus to proclaim the name of Jesus, for in that day "every knee shall bow and every tongue shall confess that Jesus Christ is Lord!"

So, you see, it was not mere chance that caused the angel, one night long ago, to say to a virgin maiden, "His name shall be called Jesus." Jesus, Jesus, Jesus. There is something—something about that name.

CHORUS

Think about His love,
Think about His goodness;
Think about His grace that's brought us through.
For as high as the heaven's above
So great is the measure of our Father's love.
Great is the measure of our Father's love.

VERSE

How could I forget His love?
How could I forget His mercy?
He satisfies, He satisfies,
He satisfies my desires.

© 1987 Integrity's Hosanna! Music
   Walt Harrah

No Way to Describe My Feelings

Oh that men would praise the LORD for his goodness, and for his wonderful works to the children of men! For he satisfieth the longing soul, and filleth the hungry soul with goodness.

PSALM 107:8–9

Although our songwriter for this story has lived in California for most of his life, he was born in St. Louis, Missouri, in 1948. He was one of eight children born to Pastor Calvin Harrah and his wife, Allegra, and they saw to it that little Walt was singing in church with the family by age four. He played in a school band as early as the fifth grade. As Walt grew older, he entered the University of Southern California, where he graduated with a degree in church music, and then earned a master of divinity degree from Fuller Theological Seminary.

Now for the writing of "Think About His Love." The year was 1987, and as was his custom, Walt was at home enjoying his daily quiet time with the Lord. As a composer he was going through a period when songs were being born quite regularly.

Walt told me, "I was trying to be obedient to Psalm 107:43, 'Whoso is wise, and will observe these things, even they shall understand the lovingkindness of the

Lord.' As was my custom, I was reading the Bible, thinking and praying before I put anything on paper. I then wrote down some rough lyrical ideas that essentially suggest that we forget about ourselves and our own circumstances and think about God's loving-kindness, his mercy, and his goodness.

"I don't remember a single song that I have written that came to me instantaneously. So, true to my customs, I took my ideas and then began my usual process of writing and rewriting, tweaking and changing bit and parts of the song here and there. It is a process of refining and improving my work. With this particular project I must have gone through fifteen to twenty rewrites—often coming back to it and looking it over very carefully. The whole process took several days."

Harrah related that the first church service in which "Think About His Love" was used was at the Newport Mesa Christian Center in Costa Mesa, California. However, the most meaningful time for Walt to hear his song was on a Sunday morning at the Brooklyn Tabernacle in New York City. Haven, the group in which Walt sang, was invited to minister at that church for both the morning and evening services. He said, "As we were ushered into the morning service, the congregation was singing at the top of their lungs, with the most exquisite fervor imaginable. And they were singing 'Think About His Love.' It was overwhelming. There is no way to describe what I was feeling at the time."

Walt and his wife, Sherry, have three children, Mindy, Beth Anne, and Drew. At the time of this writing Walt had just resigned his position with Haven Ministries after twenty-four years. He is now a worship leader at Grace Evangelical Free Church in La Mirada, California. He also assists the Bible Institute of Los Angeles in a new department designed to train worship leaders and to teach the true essence of worship and praise. He continues to contribute his wonderful songs to the Christian music world.

Our imaginations are not stretched in the slightest when we are asked to "think about His love." Every good and right and holy thing that we are allowed to experience and participate in, throughout every waking hour, is a reminder of "His love" and "His goodness."

This Is the Day

This is the day,
This is the day,
That the Lord hath made,
That the Lord hath made.
We will rejoice,
We will rejoice,
And be glad in it,
And be glad in it!
This is the day
That the Lord hath made.
We will rejoice and be glad in it!
This is the day,
This is the day,
That the Lord hath made.

Les Garrett © 1967, 1980 Scripture in Song/Maranatha Music/ASCAP
(All rights administered by Music Services)

My Only Song

The LORD is my strength and song, and is become my salvation.

PSALM 118:14

Here is an interesting thought from Les Garrett, who lives in Australia and is the author of one of the most popular Christian songs in the world today. "Often during a service the only hymnbook we would have was the Bible. So we sang out of the Bible. I know approximately three hundred songs that we could sing right out of the King James Version of God's Word."

As you will see, Garrett's love for God and his thirst for the Bible were the greatest contributing factors in the birth of his song. Les remembers the events that led up to the writing of "This Is the Day," and he related them as follows:

"In 1967, at age twenty-four, I moved with my family to Brisbane, Queensland, in Australia. We were going through a difficult time in our lives. I was starting to minister as a traveling evangelist and was going through a bit of a valley. We had very few finances. Actually, we couldn't even buy petrol for the car.

"I was reading my Bible through on my knees, and on this particular day I was reading in Psalm 118. When I came to verse 24, I paused and read that verse a second time, and as I did a tune came to me—all of sudden. I simply was reading my Bible and worshiping the Lord, and had no thought of writing a song. I have very little musical ability and do not play an instrument; therefore I can only believe that it was a gift from God.

"I didn't teach the song to anyone for two years. The song was given to me near the end of 1967, and all through 1968 and '69 no one was singing it but me. The more I sang it, the more I thought, *Well, it is just a little thing that God has given to bless me with.*

"Near the end of 1969, I was asked to return to New Zealand to speak at a camp being held in a tent pitched by a river. One night during a meeting, the pastor of the church sponsoring the camp said, 'Does anyone have anything that he or she would like to share before Pastor Garrett speaks?' An elderly lady stood and looked straight at me and said, 'There is someone here that has something that was given to you by the Lord, and you are not sharing it. God has given you something that you are supposed to share.'

"As she sat down I felt real conviction that I had never shared my song. I stood up and said, 'I think that message is for me. I have a song that the Lord gave to me, and I have been singing it for a couple of years. I want to teach it to you tonight.'"

From that one camp "This Is the Day" was spread over New Zealand to the extent that in six months it was being sung throughout the whole of that island nation. The following year it was published in the first edition of the famed Scripture in Song series of songbooks published in Australia by David Garrett. That publication launched it on its orbit around the world. Les has heard his song sung in many of the twenty-three nations where he has preached. He remembers, "The people in China were so excited to know that I had written the song they were singing. It is sung all over China."

Now for the most unusual part of this story. After interviewing scores upon scores of songwriters, many of whom have written several hundred songs, and some two and three thousand, I was astonished to hear Les say, "That is the only song I have ever written. I did get a quickening about another verse in the Psalms years ago, but I didn't write it down, so it left me."

Les now resides with his wife, Caroline, in Queensland on the east coast of Australia.

This is a Scripture song that is oh, so easy to sing, but oh, so difficult to live by. How I wish that each day I would gain the victory that can be mine with the singing and the believing of Les Garrett's Scripture song "This Is the Day."

Trading My Sorrows

VERSE

I'm trading my sorrows,
I'm trading my shame.
I'm laying them down
For the joy of the Lord.
I'm trading my sickness,
I'm trading my pain.
I'm laying them down
For the joy of the Lord.

CHORUS

Yes, Lord, yes, Lord, yes, yes, Lord.
Yes, Lord, yes, Lord, yes, yes, Lord.
Yes, Lord, yes, Lord, yes, yes, Lord, Amen.

(BRIDGE)

I am pressed but not crushed,
Persecuted not abandoned,
Struck down but not destroyed.
I am blessed beyond the curse
For His promise will endure
That His joy's gonna be my strength.
Though the sorrow may last for the night,
His joy comes with the morning.

"In Iraq They Sang My Song"

Surely he hath borne our griefs, and carried our sorrows.

ISAIAH 53:4

In Toronto, Canada, at the World Youth Day conference in 2002, over 250,000 young people from around the world joined in singing three favorite Christian songs. It was a testimonial of their love for the songs and the messages they contained.

The three songs, "Trading My Sorrows", "Let the River Flow", and "Forever", were all written by one young man, Darrell Evans.

Darrell was born to Darrell Sr. and Jan Evans in San Francisco, California, in 1968. The Evanses raised their son in the Roman Catholic Church. Darrell Jr. said, "I didn't know that I could have a personal relationship with Jesus and that I could walk with God." Then he told me of his salvation experience.

"My parents had recently come to know the Lord by kneeling in our living room and accepting Christ as Savior while watching Pat Robertson's *700 Club*. My dad then began taking me to several churches that had a lot of life in them. We had moved to Olympia, Washington, and in that city found a small Four Square Church that cared a lot for me. I felt that they really loved me, and as a twelve-year-old I was saved in that church.

"A few months later, in 1980, I attended a Leon Patillo concert that was praise oriented, and at that concert at the age of twelve, I decided not only to be a believer but to be a follower of Jesus. The presence of the Lord in their worship drew me in."

I asked Darrell about his songwriting, and he said, "I had taken about a half semester of guitar in the seventh grade. As soon as I learned three chords, I wanted to start writing songs. I remember attending a summer camp where they were singing a lot of great songs. I came home, pulled out my guitar, and started playing those songs. I then started writing songs myself. Since that time I have written approximately 150 songs with some 60 of them published or recorded."

I asked Darrell about the writing of "Trading My Sorrows."

"I was a lead worshiper at Open Bible Fellowship, a church in Tulsa, Oklahoma, which met in a storefront at the time. During an altar call I was up front with the worship team, and people came forward to pray. As the people were praying, we were trying to keep in an attitude of worship for them.

"It was a very tender moment. Our church was not a very celebrative church. Some were weeping. As we were singing quietly, I began to watch people at the

> *Sing unto him, sing psalms unto him: talk ye of all his wondrous works.*
>
> *Glory ye in his holy name: let the heart of them rejoice that seek the LORD.*
>
> PS. 105:2–3

altar, and I asked myself, 'If I were there at the altar, instead of up here singing, what would I be saying?'

"I had never heard of the term *trading* being used in this situation, but it came into my heart. While playing four chords on my guitar, I began singing what is today 'Trading My Sorrows.' The band began to follow. At this tender moment, I was singing, 'I'm trading my sorrows, I'm trading my shame." I put shame into the song because Jesus suffered our shame on the cross [Heb. 12:2]. It is a matter of our recognition of that fact.

"The phrases 'Yes, Lord' were agreements with what he was doing in our lives and the lives of the people kneeling at the altar. It was like saying 'Amen' to what God was doing. The next day I went back to my office and finished the song.

"I did nothing with the song immediately. The Lord spoke to me and said, 'Stop promoting your songs. (I had a couple of songs published already, one of which was "Let the River Flow.") I know who you are. I know where you live, and I know what I have given you for other people. You pursue me and don't promote yourself. The doors I open will be better for you.'

"I never imagined that the song would be sung by congregations as it has been. On at least one occasion, and it was shown on CNN, soldiers in Iraq during a service were singing 'Trading My Sorrows.'"

The Lord will never be outgiven. He will always give us more than we can ask or think if we simply turn ourselves over to his love and guidance.

The time has come for a revival of public worship as the finest of the fine arts. . . . While there is a call for strong preaching there is even a greater need for uplifting worship.

ANDREW W. BLACKWOOD

WE ARE SO BLESSED

VERSE 1

We are so blessed
By the gifts from Your hand.
I just can't understand
Why You've loved us so much.
We are so blessed,
We just can't find a way
Or the words that can say,
Thank You, Lord, for Your touch.

CHORUS

When we're empty,
You fill us 'til we overflow.
When we're hungry,
You feed us and cause us to know.
We are so blessed.
Take what we have to bring,
Take it all, ev'rything,
Lord, we love You so much.

Prompted by a Television Song

Blessed be the God and Father of our Lord Jesus Christ,
who hath blessed us with all spiritual blessings in heavenly places in Christ.

EPHESIANS 1:3

I have learned in my research of the stories behind songs that most compositions that are truly meaningful were written as a direct response to a prompting of the Lord. In fact, many times the whole song came as a wellspring, even without prior notice to the writer that a song was being born.

The writing of "We Are So Blessed" was a group effort. When two or three songwriters collaborate on a song, they can feed off of each other's ideas, and each can judge the quality of the other's writing. This usually makes for a much better song. The writing of this song was the result of a gathering of very talented musicians who had become concerned about the flippant way a particular song was being sung on a national TV broadcast. They had gathered in the home of one of the writers with no thought to writing a song, but the subject soon moved to songwriting. Greg Nelson was among those songwriters.

Greg was born in Bismarck, North Dakota, in 1948, into the home of musical parents, Corliss and Irene Nelson—a singer and a pianist. Greg's dad sang in the operas and operettas that he and his wife produced. They encouraged the participation of their children in the music of the community as well as in their church. Greg made a profession of his faith in Christ as a young child, but years later, at age twenty, under the preaching of the late Dr. Bill Bright, founder of Campus Crusade for Christ, made sure of his complete commitment to the Savior.

Greg, his brother, Corliss Jr., and his sister, Sigrit, a child prodigy who could play the classics at age five, all learned piano and theory from their mother. Greg said, "I basically grew up in an orchestra. I also played with my brother and sister as a trio—Sigrit played piano, Corliss played violin, and I played cello. By age twenty-one I was conductor of the Bismarck Civic Orchestra."

> *O God, my heart is fixed; I will sing and give praise, even with my glory.*
>
> Ps. 108:1

This musical background has greatly contributed to the quality of the songs that have come from Greg's heart and his pen. Having written or cowritten literally hundreds of songs, and with a large number of them recorded or published, he will no doubt go down in history as one of the great composers of Christian music. Among the favorites Greg has written or cowritten are "People Need the Lord," "There Is a Savior," "Calvary's Love," and "Lamb of Glory."

Following is Greg Nelson's account of how he and the Gaithers wrote "We Are So Blessed":

"In 1982, Bill and Gloria Gaither and I were visiting in the home of Bob MacKenzie, a music executive and long-term producer for the Bill Gaither Trio. As might be expected, music was the topic of our conversation. Bill began to express his concern about the treatment of a particular song that he had heard on television. It was a song that spoke of the blessings of the Lord in our lives. He thought the song was being sung too lightly and too flippantly.

"He then said, 'Why don't we write a song describing how Christians are *so* blessed.' I expressed a few ideas concerning the music, but nothing beyond that was actually done during our visit. I took the idea and went back to my home and shortly thereafter wrote a musical setting. I later came back with the music completed and showed it to Bill. He, in turn, shared the music and the idea with Gloria, who wrote the lyric. It was later recorded by the Bill Gaither Trio and many other groups."

From there "We Are So Blessed" has found its way into the hearts and hymnals of Christians everywhere. A better song of thanksgiving could not be found. Millions of people have engaged in corporate prayer as congregations and audiences have together sung "We Are So Blessed." It is the repeated phrase "we are so blessed" that makes the song unique. Gloria's lyric acknowledges the Lord's blessings—when we are empty he fills us to overflowing, and when we are hungry he feeds us. His goodness is more than we can understand, and we cannot find an adequate way to express our true gratitude to him other than to say, "We love you!"

As we try to enumerate the blessings of the Lord, we become overwhelmed with his kindness toward us. "He that spared not his own Son, but delivered him up for us all, how shall he not with him also freely give us all things?"
(Rom. 8:32).

As is true with many terms used among Christians, the word "worship" can become a cliché devoid of significant content if we don't stop to consider its meaning.

JERRY SOLOMON

WE ARE THE REASON

VERSE

As little children
We would dream of Christmas morn
And all the gifts and toys
We knew we'd find.
But we never realized
A Baby born one blessed night
Gave us the greatest gift of our lives.

CHORUS

We are the reason
That He gave His life.
We are the reason
That He suffered and died.
To a world that was lost
He gave all He could give,
To show us the reason to live.

Playing for Andrae Previn at Age Sixteen

*For Christ also hath once suffered for sins, the just for the unjust, that he might bring us
to God, being put to death in the flesh, but quickened by the Spirit.*

1 PETER 3:18

David Meece has been out front in the genre of worship music since the release of his first album in 1976. He has sung to large audiences for many years. His famous Christmas song, "One Small Child," which he wrote at age fourteen, along with "We Are the Reason," have become standards. Hymnals and choir music have helped carry their messages to millions of people.

David remembers being enthralled with the piano at a very early age. He says, "I can remember wanting so badly to press the keys down, and I couldn't get up there. Somebody had to come and help me, but once I was up there, I was happy."

He grew up in the small town of Humble, Texas, near Houston. David distinguished himself as a child prodigy and began touring as a concert pianist at the age of ten. By fourteen he performed the *Mozart Piano Concerto in F Major* with the Houston Chamber Orchestra. He won a nationwide talent show at the age of fifteen, which allowed him to tour England, Germany, France, Switzerland, and Holland. When he was only sixteen, David was the featured soloist with the Houston Symphony under the direction of renowned conductor Andrae Previn, performing the difficult *Khachaturian Piano Concerto*, which is forty-five minutes in length.

David received a scholarship to the prestigious Peabody Conservatory of Music in Baltimore, Maryland. While there he became a follower of Christ. His story follows.

"I grew up in church and was active in all the youth and choir programs, but it was not until my sophomore year in college that I made a real commitment to Christ. I was nineteen at the time and had been reading a book about basic Christianity. The author kept talking about a 'personal relationship with Christ' and 'surrendering your life to him.' I was alone in my dorm room, and I got down on my knees and asked Christ to come into my heart."

As the interview continued, David told me about the writing of "We Are the Reason."

"In the summer of 1980, I was in the studio recording my fourth album. I remember playing for the producer some music that I had written. He loved the composition, and we decided to go ahead and record the music for that song, although I had no lyrics.

> *Now we know that God heareth not sinners: but if any man be a worshipper of God, and doeth his will, him he heareth.*
>
> JOHN 9:31

"As the days went on, we worked on the album and had gotten almost finished, when one day he said, 'David, we've done everything else except the vocals for that one musical composition. We must put the words in tomorrow because we are running out of time and budget.' I said, 'I still don't have the words.' He said, 'Well, you had better go write some, because we must have this finished by tomorrow.'

"I had previously written four sets of lyrics for the music, but I was dissatisfied with all of them. So I went to my hotel room, got down on my knees, and began to pray. I prayed and prayed. I knew that God had something to say in the song, because I was assured of that in my heart. I just didn't know what.

"I finished praying and picked up my Bible and began to read in the book of John. All of a sudden the phrase 'We are the reason He gave His life' just popped into my head. 'We are the reason He suffered and died.' I began to write as fast as I could write. It was like having it dictated to me. I couldn't believe it. In about fifteen minutes I had the whole song. I knew those were the lyrics I needed. I then thanked the Lord for the song."

The next day the album was finished. The song has now gone to many places in our world and has been translated into a number of other languages. David is also very active in Teen Challenge, an organization that helps young people with addiction problems.

To borrow a thought from another famous song, when Christ was dying on the cross to pay for our sins, he was thinking about you—and me.

To worship is to quicken the conscience by the
   holiness of God
To feed the mind with the truth of God
To purge the imagination by the beauty of God
To open the heart to the love of God
To devote the will to the purpose of God

WILLIAM TEMPLE

We Bring the Sacrifice of Praise

We bring the sacrifice of praise
Into the house of the Lord.
We bring the sacrifice of praise
Into the house of the Lord.
And we offer up to You
The sacrifices of thanksgiving.
And we offer up to You
The sacrifices of joy.

© 1984 John T. Benson Publishing Company
Kirk Dearman

There Goes Kirk, Writing a Song

*Praise the LORD of hosts: for the LORD is good; for his mercy endureth for ever:
and of them that shall bring the sacrifice of praise into the house of the LORD.*

JEREMIAH 33:11

As twenty-eight-year-old Kirk Dearman was driving down a Metroplex freeway in Grand Prairie, Texas, he was writing the chorus to "We Bring the Sacrifice of Praise." That may sound reckless, but it was not really as perilous as it may seem. You see, he was writing it all in his very musical head—the melody and the lyrics. He could hardly wait to get home to play and sing it for his wife, Deby.

Beaumont, Texas, is Kirk's hometown. He was born there on July 10, 1952. His parents, Cecil and Dorothy Dearman, started his music training when he was only six. He studied classical piano for the next eight years. Piano playing seemed to come naturally for Kirk. He also became involved in the graded music ministry of the First Baptist Church of Beaumont, where he gave his heart to Christ at age nine.

At age twenty-eight, Kirk joined the staff of a church in Grand Prairie. It was there that he and Deby were to experience some great victories in their young lives. They told me their story.

Deby said, "We began to move from just being doers to being worshipers. We, for the first time in our lives, were being taught what it means to really worship the Lord. We entered into a period of our lives when songs began to pour into us.

Kirk wrote many of his most popular songs during that time. We were beginning to understand what it means to love Jesus and worship him.

"We had a guest teacher come to our church, Charlotte Baker, who taught us what it means to bring a sacrifice of praise into the house of the Lord. We had never heard of the concept of 'bringing a sacrifice of praise.'"

Then Kirk said, "I said to myself, 'This subject really needs to be in a song.' As we were driving along the freeway, going home from church on Sunday morning, I began to think how I might write such a song. Suddenly I began to hear this catchy tune in my mind, and within five minutes I had the chorus of a song written—in my head. As we arrived home, I said to Deby, 'Hey! I have this song,' and I played and sang it for her. We both liked it but had no idea it would ever amount to much as far as being used by other people.

"The following Sunday I taught it to the congregation. Sitting in the church were a number of students of Christ for the Nations Institute in Dallas. The school had recorded several cassette tapes of the students singing and had sent them out to churches and individuals across the nation and even to other countries. Apparently the students at the church the morning I first taught the song carried it to their school. Not long afterward the institute recorded another tape of songs and began to mail it out, this time with my song on it. It went around the world. We had no idea that the song had been recorded and distributed in this way. It took two or three years for news to get back to us that the song was being circulated. We were surprised at the sudden popularity of the chorus. We never dreamed that it would go anywhere."

The Dearmans have now written between two and three hundred songs, with approximately 75 percent of them being recorded or published. They presently make their home in Nashville, Tennessee, and have two grown daughters and several grandchildren.

If what we are offering to God costs us nothing, it is not worthy to present to him. He wants our very lives to be a sacrifice of praise to him.

WE FALL DOWN

VERSE

We fall down,
We lay our crowns
At the feet of Jesus.
The greatness of mercy and love,
At the feet of Jesus.

CHORUS

And we cry holy, holy, holy,
And we cry holy, holy, holy,
And we cry holy, holy, holy, is the Lamb.

"May I Play My Song for You?"

The four and twenty elders fall down before him that sat on the throne, and worship him that liveth for ever and ever, and cast their crowns before the throne, saying, Thou art worthy, O Lord, to receive glory and honour and power: for thou hast created all things, and for thy pleasure they are and were created.

REVELATION 4:10–11

C hris Tomlin has a distinction that no other songwriter has ever had. At the time of writing, four of his songs appear on the CCLI's Top 25 List in the United States. Millions of people in many lands are now singing his songs.

Chris was born to Connie and Donna Tomlin in Tyler, Texas, in 1972. He is the oldest of their three children. In an interview some years ago, Chris told me of his conversion experience.

"I was saved at age nine as a result of a Southern Gospel music concert that I attended with my dad. It was just down the road from our church. That night I understood what it means to give your life to Christ. Later that evening I talked with my pastor about my decision, and I was baptized the following Sunday at the Main Street Baptist Church in Grand Saline, Texas."

Tomlin began writing songs in his early teen years and became involved with the music of the church. To date he has written some two hundred songs with approximately thirty-five of them being recorded or published. Following is his account of how he wrote "We Fall Down":

"I was at a youth camp where Louie Giglio was speaking. I had only recently met Louie, who is the leader of Compassion, a student ministry that attracts thousands of young people to their conferences. He was teaching on Revelation chapter 4, which pictures the throne room of God with the angels and the living creatures around the throne. The twenty-four elders fall down before him and say, 'Thou art worthy, O Lord, to receive glory and honour and power . . .' I was really taken by it. Our worship should be a response to God when he has revealed something to us. I felt that I had just seen a bit of the picture of the throne room of God. As I wrote the song, I was responding to that scene.

"Later, in my hotel room, I took my guitar and my open Bible and began to sing, 'We fall down, we lay our crowns at the feet of Jesus.' As I sang I didn't know where the melody was coming from. I was blown away by the experience.

"I went to Louie's room and knocked on the door. As he answered the door, I said, 'Tonight you spoke on Revelation chapter 4, and I have just written a song based on that Scripture passage. May I sing it for you?' He politely listened as I sang. When I had finished the song, he just looked at me. That was not at all the response I was hoping far. Then as he spoke—and I'll never forget his words—he said, 'I think the whole world is going to sing that song.' I had never had anything like that said to me before. My response was, 'I don't know about the whole world singing it; I was just wondering if we could sing it tomorrow night.' Louie then said, 'Why don't you make a tape of it?'

"I made a tape of it and he passed it along to Sam Perry. About six months later, in 1997, as I was attending a Passion Conference in Austin, Texas, with about two thousand people present, I suddenly heard a familiar melody being played on the piano; it was 'We Fall Down.' Sam Perry began to sing the song and lead the congregation of young people as they sang it. I had never heard someone lead one of my songs. As I saw the response of the students, the Lord seemed to say to me, 'I've given you the gift of writing songs; now go do it!'

"Not long afterward I heard from BMI records, who informed me that they wanted to publish the song. The song has since been translated into many languages of the world."

Chris is very active in the worship ministry of the Austin Stone Community Church in Austin, Texas, a church he helped plant, along with Pastor Matt Carter.

When we see God in his holiness, we too will fall
prostrate before him in worship and adoration.

We Shall Behold Him

VERSE 1

The sky shall unfold, preparing His entrance;
The stars shall applaud Him with thunders of praise.
The sweet light in His eyes shall enhance those awaiting,
And we shall behold Him then face to face.

CHORUS

And we shall behold Him,
We shall behold Him,
Face to face
In all of His glory.
We shall behold Him,
We shall behold Him,
Face to face
Our Savior and Lord.

The Weeping Stopped the Car

*Behold, he cometh with clouds; and every eye shall see him, and they also which pierced him:
and all kindreds of the earth shall wail because of him.*

REVELATION 1:7

Dottie Rambo's ventures in poetry and songwriting started at age eight and continued until her death in 2008, with hundreds of songs emanating from a very creative mind. Unlike many other songwriters, numbers of her songs have unusual stories behind them. Such is the writing of the song that is the subject of this story. She has written songs in times of sadness and in times of celebration and joy—hundreds of them.

One evening in 1981, after seemingly reaching the top of her writing career, Dottie was once again to receive from the Lord a truly marvelous worship song. She was singing with her husband, Buck, and a young woman in a tent revival in Ohio. While she and the young woman were traveling to the large tent from their motel room—Buck had gone on ahead with the ministers—well, let's have Dottie tell the story.

"As we pulled out of the driveway of the motel, it was about time for the sun to set. I looked up and saw beautiful and unusual cloud formations. I have always loved unusual cloud formations and have often been fascinated when I saw in the clouds something that resembled a person or an object.

"I sensed as I watched that the Lord was about to give me something wonderful for the church. I saw colors that I had never seen in my lifetime. It seemed that the clouds almost took on the form of angels. The colors were so brilliant and unusual—blues, azures, and amber.

"Presently the clouds parted and there seemed to be a straight passageway through the formation. By this time I was weeping so much that I couldn't see to drive. It seemed, as the clouds parted, as if I could see, in my mind's eye, the Savior coming in the clouds, with trumpets sounding. I said to my young companion, 'Patty, you're going to have to drive. I can no longer see.' We changed places and continued toward the tent. Patty asked, 'What is wrong? Are you sick?' She didn't know that the Lord was giving me a song. It was being written in my heart because I had nothing on which to write.

"I then said, 'Patty, would you like to hear what the Lord just gave to me?' I began to sing my song. Soon she was weeping and had to pull the car to the side of the road. We were a little late to church that night, but before we reached the tent, the Lord had given me the whole song. When I got there I could play the entire piece on my guitar. Every phrase was exactly as it should be. Changes were not necessary. It just came like a dayspring."

Sandi Patty recorded "We Shall Behold Him" and helped make the song known in almost every nook and cranny of our nation. Because of this song, Sandi Patty was named Vocalist of the Year in 1981. In that same year, Dottie Rambo received a Dove Award as Songwriter of the Year, and the song itself was named Song of the Year. Thank you, Dottie Rambo, for giving to the world this marvelous Christian song.

The Lord's coming is the beginning of an eternity of joy
for every Christian. What a marvelous day when we behold
the Savior—"face to face, in all of His glory"!

YOU ARE MY ALL IN ALL

VERSE

You are my strength when I am weak,
You are the treasure that I seek,
You are my all in all.
Seeking You as a precious jewel,
Lord to give up I'd be a fool,
You are my all in all.

CHORUS

Jesus, Lamb of God,
Worthy is Your name.
Jesus Lamb of God,
Worthy is Your name.

VERSE

Taking my sin, my cross, my shame,
Rising again I bless Your name,
You are my all in all.
When I fall down, You pick me up,
When I am dry, You fill my cup,
You are my all in all.

Playing with One Hand, Writing with the Other

I can do all things through Christ which strengtheneth me.

PHILIPPIANS 4:13

Israel, Anne, Hannah, Glory, Judah, Galen, Raina, Ezra, and Asa are the nine children of Dennis and Melinda Jernigan, with whom they share their love. Sapulpa, Oklahoma, is Dennis's hometown. He was born there in 1959, into a family with some influence in music. Dennis's father, Samuel, led the singing in the First Baptist Church of Boynton, Oklahoma. Playing the piano came very easily for Dennis, and by age nine he was regularly playing for the worship services at the church. He learned to play by ear, and as a child, he spent hours practicing at his grandmother Jernigan's house. She taught him how to "chord" on the piano and was a great spiritual influence in his life.

He said of his conversion experience, "When I was nine years old, Jesus began calling me to himself. On September 8, 1968, I asked my mother how to be saved. She explained God's plan of salvation, and I was saved that Sunday afternoon and baptized that very evening."

Dennis enrolled in Oklahoma Baptist University and later said of the experience: "Because of my lack of musical studies growing up, my training at OBU was like learning a whole new language. To be able to actually read and write the music I could see and hear was the opening of a whole new world. That ability would be very valuable later in life as I started to express my heart and feelings in song."

During an interview I asked Dennis to explain how he came to write "You Are My All in All." Following is his description of the event:

"It all came about one morning several years ago. Each morning, Monday through Friday, I was leading a prayer group in Oklahoma City in early worship and prayer. I would sit at the piano and lead in certain aspects of worship as the people had particular needs brought to their minds. We always started with the Lord's Prayer as a guide.

> *Praise ye the LORD. I will praise the LORD with my whole heart, in the assembly of the upright, and in the congregation.*
>
> PS. III:I

"On the particular morning in question, September 12, 1989, I was focusing on interceding for other people in general and remembering what the Lord had done for me particularly. As I thought on those things a melody began to form in my mind, and I played it on the piano. Lyrics came at the same time, and I began to sing to myself, 'You are my strength when I am weak,' and so on. I continued playing with my left hand and put the song on manuscript paper with my right hand. I just happened to have some paper on the piano at that time. That's how fast it was coming. I continued until I had written the complete song, just as it exists today." Dennis was reminded of Psalm 45:1, "My tongue is the pen of a ready writer."

He added, "The next morning I sang it with the prayer group. They picked it up quickly and began to enthusiastically sing it with me. The whole of the song is a prayer set to music. We used it for about a year before I recorded it. By way of that recording and by word of mouth, it began to be known far and wide."

Word, Incorporated, picked up the song and recorded it about two years later. From there it has been carried to many other places in the world and has been placed in chorus books, choir arrangements, and hymnals, thus making it more accessible to the population in general.

Dennis and his family call Boynton home, but they actually live some sixteen miles away near Muskogee, Oklahoma. A sign at the Boynton city limits announces: "Home of Dennis Jernigan, Christian Songwriter and Author." The Jernigan family are founding members of the New Community Church where Dennis leads worship about twice each month. He also serves in the capacity of pastor to a small home community group, a part of the church.

As our own private worship should be, this song is a combination of yielding to Jesus as the Lamb of God in the midst of our failures and fears.

Worship is our first or foundational ministry. It is not our only ministry, but the one that all other spheres of ministry should be built upon. As one peruses Scripture the constant thread of worship runs through the lives of those who were intimate with their God and used mightily by Him.

CARL TUTTLE

YOU ARE MY KING

VERSE I

I'm forgiven
Because You were forsaken.
I'm accepted;
You were condemned.
I'm alive and well;
Your Spirit is within me
Because You died
And rose again.

CHORUS I

Amazing love! How can it be
That You, my King, would die for me?
Amazing love! I know it's true;
It's my joy to honor You.
In all I do I honor You.

A Song to Bridge a Gap

*All we like sheep have gone astray; we have turned every one to his own way;
and the LORD hath laid on him the iniquity of us all.*

ISAIAH 53:6

Billy Foote was born into a minister's home in Louisville, Kentucky, in 1966. His parents, Billy and Winky Foote, demonstrated their support of their son's musical aspirations by providing guitar lessons, starting at age nine. He quickly advanced to the point of playing in his dad's revival services.

It was in one of those services that young Billy gave his heart to Christ. He told me, "I would hear my dad preach about the need to have Christ in your life. I remember responding to an invitation. I had been under conviction about my need for about a month before I actually surrendered to Christ."

By age sixteen Billy knew that God had work for him to do. He said, "I had no idea what kind, but I had the assurance that God was going to use me somehow."

Foote enrolled in East Texas Baptist University, in Marshall, Texas, in 1985. In the summer of 1986, he met a person who was to be a friend and mentor—one who would influence him as a worship leader more than any other. That person was David Guion. He was leading worship at a camp in which Billy was a counselor. Billy was greatly affected by the way David led the students in worship. He said, "My eyes were opened to what it means to blend the old and new songs, and to call people to ascribe worth to the Lord."

Billy also said that his eyes were more opened during that camp to what worship can really be in a corporate setting. He told me, "I went back to college and helped start a night of worship each week. We had a time of worship through singing, and then a friend of mine, Neil McClendon, would speak to us. Students were able to make much of God and what he means to them."

Billy said of his early songwriting, "I had been out of college for about six years and had been leading worship full-time since my graduation. At that point in my life, I would not have considered myself a songwriter. In fact, I had only written a couple of songs before 'You Are My King.'"

Following is how he described the writing of his now famous third song: "I happened to be at a night of worship, and the phrases 'I'm forgiven because You were forsaken' and 'I'm accepted' kept running through my mind. I wrote those phrases down on a piece of paper, and the whole song came together.

"I believe the Spirit of God just reminded me of truths I had been taught at a young age. I knew I was forgiven because of what Christ did for us on the cross. I really don't have a grand story of how it came together. I just believe it was a gift from God. As with many of my songs, the melody came with the words. I was able to run the lyrics by a couple of men whom I trust with their understanding of the Bible. They believed the lyrics to be of sound theology, and so I started using the song wherever I was leading worship.

"I remember the first summer church camp that I sang the song. From the very first line, it seemed as if the students had known the song their entire lives. It was incredible to watch students respond to the Lord.

"It is so encouraging to know that this song is being used to help people bless the Lord around the world. We are forgiven and accepted because Christ was forsaken and condemned. We are alive and well because Christ arose from the grave. It really is amazing!"

Billy and his wife, Cindy, lead worship together as a team. Cindy, a graduate of Southwestern Baptist Theological Seminary, has become the lead vocalist for the worship band since Billy was diagnosed with a condition that affects his voice. Billy continues to write songs as he seeks to obey God's call on his life.

Carry the cross patiently and with perfect submission, and it shall carry you.
—THOMAS A. KEMPIS

261

YOU'RE WORTHY OF MY PRAISE

CHORUS

I will give You all my worship,
I will give You all my praise.
You alone I long to worship,
You alone are worthy of my praise.

VERSE

I will worship (I will worship)
With all of my heart (with all of my heart).
I will praise You (I will praise You)
With all of my strength (all my strength).
I will seek You (I will seek You)
All of my days (all of my days).
I will follow (I will follow)
All of Your ways (all Your ways).

Classical Music Was the "Grounding"

Let them praise the name of the LORD: for his name alone is excellent;
his glory is above the earth and heaven.

PSALM 148:13

Many thousands of Christians the world over join in singing David Ruis's "You're Worthy of My Praise" each Sunday in their churches. His contribution to the singing of Christians is no small matter. David says, "The way I'm wired, I value community. Whether it's my immediate family or my church family, worship just gives language to the heart of the journey we're on together. So much of worship is all about community."

David was born in Calgary, Alberta, Canada, in 1963. He was adopted as an infant by Jack and Alice Ruis. They were wonderful parents to him, and it was they who helped him find the peace of knowing Christ as Savior. In an interview David told me of his conversion experience.

"When I was seven years old, one morning in church our pastor gave a message that burned in my heart all day. In the middle of the night, I could not sleep. I knew the Lord was calling me. I went to my parents, quite broken, and they prayed with me and helped me to understand how to turn my life over to the Lord. I did so that night."

He continued, "I was involved with classical piano from the age of five. I was a charter member of the Calgary Boys Choir, singing and training with them from age eight through thirteen. I then became the pianist for one of the touring choirs. Classical training had a tremendous influence on my later music ministry—the grounding.

"I was involved with classical music until college. I listened to contemporary music, but it was not a part of my life. I was raised in a very conservative church where hymns and gospel songs were used almost exclusively."

About the writing of "You're Worthy of My Praise," David said, "It was in 1991, during the very early days of the first church that we planted—New Life Fellowship Baptist Church in a city in British Columbia, Canada. This type ministry was very new to us.

"I had visited the Anaheim Vineyard in 1987 and that also was a huge paradigm shift. Worship became central. While there I was in services where we would just stop singing because the whole of the congregation was in tears. I, along with them, experienced several encounters with God.

It came even to pass, as the trumpeters and singers were as one, to make one sound to be heard in praising and thanking the LORD.

2 CHRON. 5:13

"Back in Canada, worship was becoming a central part of the life of our church. So 'You're Worthy of My Praise' was one of the first worship songs that I wrote. I crafted it at home on our small piano. My oldest daughter, who was only about two at the time, would sing the echo part for me. The song developed over a period of time.

"During those days I was not traveling as I do now; therefore I had no way of exposing the song to others, nor did I have a way of publishing it. Slowly it began to make its way around to other churches. But I had nothing to do with that. We did a custom recording, and that helped somewhat in getting the song to other congregations.

"I later moved to Kansas City, Missouri, and was associate pastor of a church that was part of the Metro Vineyard Fellowship. I also helped with some of the worship services. As part of the music ministry of that church, we made a live recording, and on that album we put a song I had written entitled 'I Lift Your Name.' That caught the eye of the Maranatha people, and when they contacted me about that song, 'You're Worthy of My Praise' was also brought to their attention. They decided to publish it also, and that took it to another level of exposure.

"This song marked for me an emergence into the writing of songs that others will sing. Plus, I think the song in some ways says it all in regard to worship."

Once we recognize the love, the goodness, the omnipotence, the omniscience, and the omnipresence of our wonderful Lord, then we, too, can sincerely join in singing, "You're worthy of my praise."

The worship service features two sides of a sacred conversation. Those who lead in worship need to help people recognize themselves in the presence of God. But before such a sacred conversation happens in worship, it must happen for those who lead in worship in their own soul.

CRAIG BARNES

ACKNOWLEDGMENTS

I want to express my appreciation to the songwriters for allowing me to tell their stories. I find great delight in placing these stories into this volume of music history, not only for those who will read it now, but also for generations who will follow. Very little in this book is from "research." I have gotten the stories, in almost every case, directly from the authors. The tape recordings of the interviews are prized possessions.

I am grateful to my wife, Marilyn, who has been extremely supportive and very helpful in reading and rereading the manuscript and offering valuable suggestions.

Mark Whitlock, formerly with Thomas Nelson, believed in the project and carried the ball through all of the necessary areas of consideration by the publishers.

Matt Baugher, vice president and publisher of Spiritual Growth and Practical Living, and Jennifer McNeil, editor, Spiritual Growth and Practical Living at Thomas Nelson, have been most encouraging, offering wonderful suggestions that have enhanced the worth and uniqueness of this volume. The accompanying CD was Matt's idea. And such an excellent idea it was. I want to thank those songwriters who not only granted interviews in order that I might get their stories but who later stepped up to a microphone and recorded their stories specifically for the accompanying CD.

Darlene Zschech and Andrae Crouch, who wrote the introduction and the foreword in this book, also gave me the stories behind their wonderful songs which appear in these pages. To them I extend my heartfelt gratitude.

I want to thank Kregel Publications for allowing me to adapt four stories from two books I had earlier written for them, *Stories Behind 50 Southern Gospel Favorites, Volume One* and *Volume Two.*

Finally, I want to thank my good friend Garry Cohn for long hours spent in helping to develop the accompanying CD. I want to recognize his unique ability to take the recorded stories, sent to him from around the United States and several other countries, and balance and blend them into a one-of-a-kind album of recorded stories.

Companion CD for the book

I COULD SING OF YOUR LOVE FOREVER

Stories behind popular worship songs—told by the authors.
Mastering Engineer: Garry Cohn

1. Don Moen - God Will Make a Way
2. Babbie Mason - All Rise
3. Billy Foote - You Are My King
4. Bob Fitts - Blessed Be the Lord God Almighty
5. Brian Doerksen - Come, Now Is the Time to Worship
6. Chris Tomlin - Holy Is the Lord
7. Daniel Gardner - My Life Is in You, Lord
8. Darlene Zschech - Shout to the Lord
9. David Huntsinger - Holy Spirit, Thou Art Welcome
10. Dennis Jernigan - You Are My All in All
11. Eddie Espinosa - Change My Heart, O God
12. Kurt Kaiser - Oh, How He Loves You and Me
13. Jamie Harvill - Ancient of Days
14. Kelly Carpenter - Draw Me Close
15. Kirk Dearman - We Bring the Sacrifice of Praise
16. Laurie Klein - I Love You, Lord
17. Lenny LeBlanc - Above All
18. Lynn DeShazo - More Precious Than Silver
19. Marc Byrd & Steve Hindalong - God of Wonders
20. Mark Altrogge - I Stand in Awe
21. Marty Nystrom - As the Deer
22. Martin Smith - I Could Sing of Your Love Forever
23. Matt Redman - Blessed Be Your Name
24. Pam Thum - Hallelujah, Praise the Lamb
25. Paul Baloche - Open the Eyes of My Heart
26. Rick Founds - Lord, I Lift Your Name On High
27. Tim Hughes - Here I Am to Worship
28. Tom Fettke - The Majesty and Glory of Your Name